RELIGIOUS REVOLT IN THE XVIIth CENTURY: THE SCHISM OF THE RUSSIAN CHURCH

by **Nickolas Lupinin**

THE KINGSTON PRESS, INC.
P.O. Box 1456
Princeton, N.J. 08542

Cover illustrations:
Left — Patriarch Nikon
Right — Tsar Aleksei

© Copyright 1984 by the Kingston Press, Inc.
P.O. Box. 1456
Princeton, NJ 08542

ISBN No. 0-940670-12-7

Printed in the United States of America

TO

VERA ANTONINOVNA LUPININ, my mother
and to the memory of
BORIS IVANOVICH LUPININ, my father

Table of Contents

Prefatory Note

In terms of the technical aspects of the text the following may be said. In using proper names and places names I have generally maintained the Russian form (in transliteration). Thus, for example, Lavrentii, not Lawrence, Feodor not Theodore. The exceptions are standard names such as Moscow. These do not need transliteration or explication. Transliteration itself has been according to The Library of Congress and occasionally the system of George Vernadsky, Ralph Fischer, and Sergei Pushkarev, in their *Dictionary of Russian Historical Terms from the Eleventh Century to 1917* (New Haven and London: Yale University Press, 1969). There are just a few exceptions to this in the text. Dates are almost invariably in the Old (Julian) Style. All translations from Russian sources are my own. Comment on the sources is occasionally interspersed in the text or footnotes.

List of Abbreviations

(Note: I have generally refrained from using a great number of abbreviations. The list is limited to those cited below. Complete source reference for these will be found in the bibliography).

Borozdin	A.K. Borozdin, "Protopop Avvakum." Zapiski Istoriko-Filologicheskago Fakul'teta, Imperatorskago s. Peterburgskago Universiteta.
ChOIDR	Chtenie v Imperatorskom Obshchestve Istorii i Drevnostei Rossiiskikh.
Makarii, Istoriia	Istoriia Russkoi Tserkvi Makariia, Mitropolita Moskovskago i Kolomenskago.
Materialy	Materialy dlia Istorii Raskola za Pervoe Vremia ego Sushchestvovaniia.
PDPI	Pamiatniki Drevnei Pismennosti i Iskusstva.
PSZ	Polnoe Sobranie Zakonov Rossiiskoi Imperii. Sobranie Pervoe.
RIB	Russkaia Istoricheskaia Biblioteka.

Trans. Rus.-Amer.	Transactions of the Association of Russian-American Scholars in the U.S.A.
Zenkovsky, Epics	Serge Zenkovsky, Medieval Russia's Epics, Chronicles, and Tales.
Zenkovsky, Staroobriadchestvo	Serge Zenkovsky, Russkoe Staroobriadchestvo.
ZORSA	Zapiski Otdeleniia Russkoi i Slavianskoi Arkheologii Imperatorskago Russkago Arkheologicheskago Obshchestva.

Chapter 1

Introduction

The Russian Church in the middle and latter parts of the seventeenth century went through a crisis unmatched in its history. The statement is not really mitigated by two other major crises of the Russian Church which readily come to mind. One is the period of the Mongol dominance, but that, despite surface features to the contrary, has long been shown to be a misconception. It is now generally accepted that the Mongols degree of religious toleration was relatively high and that the leniency granted the Church was a not inconsiderable factor in helping it be one of the major steadying influences combating the centrifugal forces unleashed by the Mongol incursions.

The other is the crisis born of the Russian Revolution of 1917 and all its aftermaths. Here the attempt was no less than extirpation of religion and eradication of the Church as a viable institution. The task, which still demands the attention of the Soviet State, led to measures never previously perpetrated on any Christian Church and it is a testament to the resiliency of Russian Orthodoxy that it has still survived, muffled though its form may be.

The point is that in both cases the crises were initially (and in the main) external, though it cannot be denied that the Soviet period has also seen the Church gripped in an internal crisis. The strength of the anti-Church measures, the stridency of the anti-religious propaganda, and wholesale "re-education" are all partly responsible.

In the latter seventeenth century, in contrast, the crisis is internal. It is not the result of wars, of outside intervention, of attacks on the Church as a body. It will be seen, in many cases, that dissatisfaction arose from allegedly insufficient responses to the Church and to the religious experience. The Old Believers, for example, are frequently indignant at Nikonian measures for reform which they deem harmful to the spirit and practice of Orthodoxy. And Patriarch Nikon with his supporters argue in turn that too stringent an adherence to old rituals by the Old Believers really belies an ignorance of doctrine and dogma which thus, in effect, also is detrimental to Orthodoxy.

Being internal this crisis must also be viewed in terms of a power struggle. Three major elements were vying for control of the Church. First were the Nikonites, the reformers, whose innovations precipitated the struggle. Second was the party of Old Believers which, by virtue of its distinctively dogmatic response, prolonged the struggle beyond possible reconciliation. Third, and somewhat surprisingly, was the State. I say surprisingly because it is generally assumed that the Church-State relationship in Muscovite Russia was, if not purely diarchical, at least characterized by a high degree of mutuality. Yet we will see, for reasons made clear in the text, that the State wound up prosecuting both opponents and ultimately asserting its own hand in Church affairs. The Councils of 1666-1667 are paramount here, though many intermediate steps must be traced beforehand. This is an extremely important point and as such, it is a major precondition for Peter's inclusion of the Church into the State apparatus.

It is highly ironic that all this occurs under Tsar Aleksei who is one of the most pious of all Russian Tsars. Surely he realized the direction in which Church affairs were moving. Was he not able to at least forestall the rupture? The role of Tsar Aleksei in this struggle has rarely been treated at all in any detail.

The third major framework of the period was the paradoxical situation of Patriarch Nikon and the Old Believers.

12

Nikon, in earlier days (1640's) had been, along with most of the later leaders of Old Belief, a member of the Zealots of Piety. Their goals had been to increasingly elevate the role of the Church and priest, to rid Church practice of hindering accretions, and make the common man more appreciative and responsive to his Church. They had been relatively successful and prospects for the future were favorable. Yet with Nikon's accession to the Patriarchate in 1652, the processes of internal edification were seemingly subvented for it was not long till Nikon struck course on a path that shook the Church to its roots. The question must be asked why Nikon and the Zealots, with such convergent aims wind up with such divergent practices and such disruptive effects. It is not without reason that a parallel with the Western Reformation is sometimes drawn.

The latter parallel, I suspect, is more useful metaphorically than in a strict historical investigation. But it does suggest the seriousness and the scope of the problem involved. One of the prime considerations for any study of the Russian Church of this period is the necessity of recognizing the tremendous role of the Church in Russian life. It was a role that extended to the least minutiae of daily affairs. Being so, any problem that beset the Church as a whole would soon reverberate not only among the nobility but likewise the common man. We cannot otherwise explain the schism that occurred and the great numbers of people who felt compelled to break with the established Church. In the context of Russian piety of this period this phenomenon is simply astounding. It is a phenomenon that is historical, theological and religious, and psychological at once and which does not lend itself easily to normal formulation. Without an appreciation of this religious intensity and the realization of the Church's presence in all affairs such vital points as how could, for example, a few external changes in ritual be so wrought with emotionalism and reaction (here in its non-political sense) will not be understood.

Thus what we really have is not just a matter of ecclesiastical policy or a matter solely bearing on Church and State (in the institutional sense), but a matter of deep concern to all of society.

13

I find it most curious that at a time when the Russian State was finally approaching a stability sorely undermined by the disruptions of The Time of Troubles it was struck by an internal religious crisis that made unstable one of its primary institutions and society itself. Yet, it surely is one of the distinctive features of the whole seventeenth century in all of Europe that stability was not the rule, and Russia was no exception.

Chapter 2

The Church at Mid-Century

In 1645 Aleksei Mikhailovich was crowned Tsar, the second in the Romanov line. The boiars praised and were praised, the prelates prayed for the health and well being of the royal family, and the multitudes cheered. Scarce was it suspect anywhere in the realm of Muscovy that the years of Tsar Aleksei's reign were to be tumultous and wrought with the evil of religious discontent. No one could guess to what elevations discordance could rise, and all in the reign of a Tsar who was to earn the accolade of "the humblest". But the religious history of Russia of this period was to pivot on more than the humility or any personal characteristic of any one man even though that man be Tsar and overseer of the Third Rome.

The Church was undoubtedly the single largest and most important institution in Russia. By mid-century the shocks which had buffeted the Russian Church in the Time of Troubles had been long absorbed and disseminated, partly through the able guidance of Patriarch Filaret (d. 1633), and partly by time. Patriarch Filaret had been, in effect, co-ruler with his son, Tsar Mikhail. After assuming the Patriarchy (vacant from 1612-1619) he began the work of reconstruction. He had been granted jurisdiction over the spiritual and civil affairs of the subjects in his domain in 1625. Two years later, he involved himself in the land

15

allotment policy. He issued many decrees jointly with the Tsar, handled petitions, received foreign ambassadors and boiars, with all the attendant mix of problems. This secular involvement actually strengthened his role in Church policy where he truly dominated.

Some of the endeavors crossed over from the secular to the ecclesiastical and back. Usually, this was along organizational and administrative lines in which Filaret excelled. A cogent example is his work in the organization of those prikazy (government departments) which dealt with Church related concerns. Established were the Sudnoi Prikaz (or Patriarshii Razriad) which was entrusted with court matters. The Kazennyi Prikaz was charged with collections from the clergy and the votchinas. The Prikaz Tserkovnykh Del had jurisdiction over matters of piety and religion at the day to day administrative level. Other efforts in purely ecclesiastical terms were the attempts to restore Church discipline and administrative order, enlarge (successfully) the printing efforts of the Church to further spread religious books, and to continue corrections and collations of religious texts. Thanks to Filaret, the process of building was again normal and the Church was back in the groove of centuries.

Building must be taken literally and figuratively. It is attested, for example, that the XVII century saw over two hundred new monasteries built.[1] In Dobroliubov's work on the monasteries and churches of the Riazan diocese, there is solid evidence that considerable building took place.[2] And, a recent work contends that, in general, the formation of major monastic groupings ended in the XVII century.[3] Statistics are, of course,

---

1. V.V. Andreev, *Raskol i ego Znachenie v Narodnoi-Russkoi Istorii* (SPB, 1870), p. 104.

2. Ivan Dobroliubov, *Istoriko-Statisticheskoe Opisanie Tserkvei i Monastyrei Riazanskoi Eparkhii* (Zaraisk, 1884-85, 2 vol.). Examples abound throughout this work and are too numerous to be mentioned here.

3. Akademiia Khudozhestv SSSR, *Istoriia Russkago Iskusstva* (Moscow: Gosudarstvennoe Izdatel'stvo "Iskusstvo", vol. I, 1957), p. 136.

extremely tenuous for this period but even allowing for considerable error, we may concede substantial growth.

More important than this however, is the notion of stability in the land which allowed for further building. There is one notable exception, the southern frontier. Here the outposts, be they monastic, military, or agricultural, were still subject to attack not only from the Crim Tatar but from roving bands of marauders as well. The Voskresenskaia Church in the Riazan' area was destroyed in 1618 during a raid and not rebuilt until 1683 when it was rebuilt in stone.[4] An attack on the Sretenskii Karachunskii Monastery (founded in the early XVII century on the right bank of the Voronezh River) in 1659 by the Tatars led to the capture of many of the brethren and serfs and the monastery remained destroyed until the late 1660's.[5] Toward the end of the 1670's the hegumen[6] Aleksei of the Borskov Monastery (40 versts south of Voronezh) was killed in a raid, local in nature, deriving from land and boundary squabbles.[7] But the monastery evidently was the victim of various kinds of raids and to give itself some measure of protection, was built like a fortress. And in 1684, the Bogoslovskii Monastery, twenty five versts north of Riazan', close to a point where the Oka River splits, was raided by brigands. It netted them 1500 rubles, 100 pieces of gold, 11 silver ladles, 8 horses and other goods.[8] This shows how extensive and serious a raid could be and how much a monastery could lose. Yet, conversely, we are given an example of how much a monastery could have on hand; 1500 rubles was a considerable sum in the XVII century.

---

4. Dobroliubov, op. cit., I, pp, 30-31. He gives many more examples of this.

5. P.V. Nikol'skii, *Monashestvo na Donu* (Voronezh, 1909), p. 39.

6. The hegumen is an elected head of a monastery in Eastern Orthodoxy and thus corresponds to the abbot in Latin Christendom.

7. Nikol'skii, op. cit., p. 21.

8. "Sbornik Tserkovno-istoricheskikh i Statisticheskikh Svedenii o Riazanskoi Eparkhii", *Chtenie v Imperatorskom Obshchestve Istorii i Drevnostei Rossiiskikh*, Oct. - Dec. 1863, bk. 4, p. 241. Other volumes in this series will hereafter be cited as *ChOIDR*...

Being the country's major institution the Church possessed considerable wealth. It is almost impossible to gauge it accurately, especially when Church vessels and ornaments are considered among the assets. Somewhat more valid are estimates based on land holdings which were not insubstantial. "As before, cultivation of and by the Church was substantial. The Holy Trinity Monastery possessed some 17,000 peasant households (dvors) in 40 districts (uezds). 9,000 peasant households were within the Patriarchal patrimonial estate (votchina) while the Church as a whole ruled some 120,000 dvors".[9] The households ruled by the Patriarchy were themselves scattered over 23 districts though essentially they were concentrated in the central regions.[10]

The Church was not averse to obtaining additional holdings when opportunities arose. A pertinent example is the lands wasted during the Time of Troubles. As the years went on and a measure of stability returned to Russia, the claiming of these waste lands ever increased. The Patriarchy was chief and most successful claimant.[11] And if the Church was not able to put the lands into immediate use itself, it frequently rented them to those who could.[12] An interesting speculation would be the degree to

---

9. A.M. Sakharov, *Obrazovanie i Razvitie Rossiiskogo Gosudarstva v XIV-XVII vv.* (Moscow: Vyshaia Shkola, 1969), p. 137. Hereafter cited Sakharov, *Obrazovanie i Razvitie...* The figure 120,000 also approximates the figure given in the classic work by Gorchakov. Gorchakov, referring to Kotoshikhin, gives 118,000 as the number of households administered by the Church. M. Gorchakov, *Monastyrskii Prikaz, 1649-1725* (SPB, 1868), p. 21. Hereafter cited as Gorchakov, *Monastyrskii Prikaz.*

10. A.M. Sakharov, *Russkaia Derevnia XVII v.* (Moscow: Nauka, 1966), p. 39. Hereafter cited Sakharov and full title. The difficulty of dealing with these land questions is somewhat exemplified by Sakharov himself (see footnote 9) for he finds frequent need to refer to a still seminal work written in 1871. See M. Gorchakov, *O Zemel'nykh Vladeniiakh Vserossiiskikh Mitropolitov, Patriarkhov, i Sv. Synoda 988-1738 gg.* (SPB: 1871). Hereafter cited as Gorchakov, *O Zemel'nykh Vladeniiakh...*

11. Sakharov, *Russkaia Derevnia XVII v.*, pp. 42-6. Many of these waste lands were still so called even years after they were resettled and cultivated.

12. V.I. Kholmogorov, "Istoricheskie Materialy o Tserkvakh i Selakh XVI-XVII St." *ChOIDR*, 1896, bk. 4, sect. I, p. iv.

18

which the Church facilitated the increase in grain productivity (and crop capacity) in the XVII century for grain productivity was somewhat higher in the monastic holdings (as also in those of the major landowners). The Kirillo-Beloozerskii Monastery earned some 8,000 rubles yearly from the sale of salt and used portions of this capital to increase tillage.[13]

The fact that the Patriarchy was party to more privilege (in this regard as in many others)[14] should not be surprising. It was the supreme office of the Church and less subject to normally constrictive rulings. In the person of the Patriarch many were disposed to see one half of the dyarchy of Russian rule. Thus Reutenfels in his description of Muscovy saw the Patriarch and Tsar as almost equally sharing the important function of defending the faith.[15] Baron Meierberg was even more emphatic, though wrong, in stating (1661) that in Russia the Patriarchs rule with unlimited power "and never does the Tsar deny them in their request for confirmation of their verdicts".[16]

Such an evaluation is seriously overstated. Yet, we cannot react too strongly in the opposite direction and unnecessarily minimize the Patriarch's influence and power. The bishops and bishoprics, as many monastery establishments, likewise generally had a number of privileges from the government, be they administrative or judicial, though these were less than those granted to the Patriarch.[17] The question of Patriarchal power vis a vis the State came to a head with Nikon (see chapt. 5).

---

13. Sakharov, *Obrazovanie i Razvitie...* p. 136.

14. We shall see later that Nikon was to obtain more than the normal share.

15. Iakov Reitenfels (Iacobus Reutenfels), "Skazaniia Svetleishomu Gerzogu Toskanskomu Koz'me Tret'emu o Moskovii", *ChOIDR*, 1906, bk. 3, sect. III, p. 1666.

16. "Puteshestviia v Moskoviiu Barona Avgustina Meierberga", *ChOIDR*, 1873, bk. 3, sect. IV, pp. 47-8. This exemplifies again how frequently even well placed foreign observers were wrong about the essentials of Russian life. (The author therefore laments the too frequent reliance on, and popularity of, books and manuscripts on Russia of "outsiders" who never came to fully learn the nation's culture. Original sources should be consulted more).

17. Ecclesiastically, vis a vis the Church, the Patriarch, metropolitans, and bishops were all equal, all bishops.

Despite occasional governmental attempts to limit Church and Patriarchal authority and influence, there is still evidence of certain accretions in the power of the Patriarch. Of major significance here are the two key Patriarchs of Russian history, Filaret and Nikon though, after the perturbations occasioned by Nikon's demise at the Council of 1666, we have another, somewhat lesser manifestation in Patriarch Ioakim who took the Patriarchal seat in 1674. The whole question is erased when Patriarch Adrian dies in 1700 and Peter fails to name a successor, ultimately creating the Holy Synod.

In terms of land holdings there is an interesting point made by Gorchakov. He states that with the establishment of the Patriarchate in Russia there gradually evolved a change in the judicial aspect of the Church's land holdings. Previously, the land owned by the highest ecclesiastical office (the Moscow Metropolitanate) was seen in an institutional sense whereas with the Patriarchy, it gradually came to have the nature of a personal holding.[18] A source of discontent has sometimes been adduced in the contention that whatever wealth the Church and Patriarchy possessed centrally did not often enough finds its way vertically ((a charge also leveled against the Latin Church of the Middle Ages). There is, of course, merit in this though it must also be observed that one of the most accurate guides to determining the well being of any eparchy (diocese), let alone individual parishes in distant locales, is the relative wealth or poverty of the surrounding area itself. It is particularly apt in view of the overwhelmingly agricultural nature of Russian society.

It has been suggested above that there was a tendency for monastic and Church lands to be somewhat better off due to greater agricultural productivity. Thus a correlative tendency may be evidenced. This is the not infrequent attempt of poor monasteries to be registered under the holdings of the Patriarch. Very few monasteries could approach the level of privileges

---

18. Gorchakov, *O Zemel'nykh Vladeniiakh*, pp. 314-15.

granted the Patriarchy. Since the general level of taxes of various forms was rather heavy on monastic houses in the XVII century, it is not without a measure of reason that the poorer ones attempted to place themselves under the protective aegis of the Patriarchy. An added advantage was that a large number of these (more so in the second half of the century) were given autonomy in handling matters relative to the management of the land under their control.[19] This also occurs, though it is difficult to say with what frequency, on the personal level. In 1661, for example, two serfs, Eliseiko Ul'ianov and Vasilii Aleksandrov, belonging to Prince Mikhail L'vov, were (along with their families) given their freedom. They then submitted a petition requesting that they be accepted into the patriarchal village of Pushkino. After having submitted their papars of manumission, they were accepted.[20] There is the converse example also. One peasant, Lukashka Ivanov of the village of Tritskoe, turns in another peasant, Ivashka Minin, who with his family had run away from the patriarchal votchina.[21]

The relationship of the people to the Church (and the reverse) is not, as may at first appear, that difficult to establish. The initial clue must, however, always be the sheer fact of the enormous interplay between the two. One may invoke the image of the intricate weave. This is especially important in view of contemporary disabilities in viewing the relationships of people to religious institutions. Historical hindsight does allow us to see the inordinate degree to which Church and people were intertwined.

A substantial portion of this was observed in discussing the land holdings of the Church and, derivatively, the peasants under its direct economic control. While this did not include even a majority of the peasant population of Russia, practically all the

---

19. Ibid., pp. 338-39.
20. Gorchakov, *O Zemel'nykh Vladeniiakh*, Appendix, p. 89.
21. Ibid., p. 94.

people were directly involved with the Church in other ways. People came to the Church (I leave the religious aspect aside until the next chapter) to have a petition written, an item read, advice given. Assuming that the priest was literate (and too often he was not)[22] the parishioner received the required help. He also went to him on questions of marriage, christening, deaths, prayers for crops and good health and various other problems. The relationships of the lower clergy to their flocks were intensely personal for fate had bound them together in the frequently arduous task of eking out a living from a Russian soil not always responsive to the demands of man. The village priest was also a peasant, a brother under the cassock, and he too was as subject to the hand of nature as was the villager who came to him to confess his many transgressions. Their language was the same.

It is thus hard to accept Miliukov's judgement that people and priests were disassociated early in Russian history, the process, according to him, constantly widening through the ages.[23] At best, this was only partially true with regard to the hierarchy, the bishops, but certainly not in respect to the common priest who was still inherently connected to the village and the local populace. Sometimes the relationships became too personal as when Avvakum was severely beaten by his parishioners, or, less damagingly, when a peasant brought to court a priest who had cursed him in a vile manner.[24] Or, in 1663,

---

22. An age old problem. Miliukov pointed out, for example, that Gennadii, Archbishop of Novgorod in the late XV c. and the Stoglav Sobor, 1551, had stated that the Church would be devoid of priests unless illiterates were ordained. Patriarch Nikon was very reluctant to ordain illiterates and even banned the practice (without notable success).

23. Paul Miliukov, *Religion and the Church* (New York: A.S. Barnes & Co., 1960. Outlines of Russian Culture, part I), pp. 9-10. No leading Church historian makes such a claim, so Miliukov's dictum can probably be attributed to his intellectual and political leanings. Even if partly true, the claim could not apply prior to the 19th. c.

24. *Russkaia Istoricheskaia Biblioteka.* (Russia. Arkheograficheskaia Kommissiia. Akty Kholmogorskoi i Ustiuzhskoi Eparkhii, 1500-1699. vol. XII, XIV, XXV). vol. XIV, col. 993-96. Hereafter cited *RIB*.

an archpriest filed a complaint to the Tsar against the elder of his church for not willing to give 400 rubles for the completion of a new church. The money, it seems, had already been allotted for this purpose.[25] These examples, if anything, show that the people were inclined to accept the priest as one of them, perhaps too much so, even to the point of occasionally abusing his calling.

Points of friction were not limited to the priest-parishioner relationship. They were as prevalent in the structural hierarchy of the Church itself. The archpriest Vladimir of the Uspenskii Cathedral in the Ustiug area complains to Metropolitan Iona of Rostov that the lower clergy subordinate to him do not listen to his admonitions. Furthermore, they are lax in carrying out his strictures on the proper observance of the liturgy for they celebrate it at the wrong time, read the hours after the service, talk openly in church, and, in general, do not heed him.[26] This is to be expected for, aside from natural inclinations to disagreement with superiors, the lower clergy was not overly ready to submit to standard discipline. And, in a nation with a relatively high degree of a church-related population, many could be found who were content to be undisciplined. M.I. Slukhovskii, in an excellent work, gives a figure of 10% as the church-related population of Moscow in the XVII century.[27] He includes in this figure the clergy, deacons, choristers and the like.

The nature of the complaint offered by the archpriest Vladimir above was doubtlessly the most common, and the most difficult to enforce due to the endemic aspect of the problem it cites. The simple matter of talking unnecessarily in church during a service, for example, could be disruptive to its proper celebration. The people themselves were constantly guilty of this and frequent edicts forbidding the practice were quickly forgotten.

---

25. *RIB*, XII, col. 382-83.

26. *RIB*, XII, col. 300-01.

27. M.I. Slukhovskii, *Bibliotechnoe Delo v Rossii do XVIII veka*, (M: Kniga, 1968), Appendix of Materials, #94, p. 163. Incidentally, an idea of the clergy's dress in this period may be gleaned from A. von Meierberg, *Al'bom Meierberga — Vidy i Bytovyia Kartiny Rossii XVII veka* (SPB: 1903), p. 23.

Then, too, it was the habit of the poor to wander about during the service and ask the people for alms to help relieve them of their indigence. Presumably, it would be a greater strain on the conscience to deny them in the House of God itself. The Council of 1667 found the practice sufficiently impertinent and widespread enough to warrant specific condemnation. It stated: "Also, let it be ordered that all priests firmly see to it that during holy liturgy a guard or some person be placed by the doors of the church and keep the poor from wandering about the church begging for alms; that they, the poor, stand quietly as the others..."[28]

In view of the major problems which the Russian Church had to face in the second half of the XVII century, it could almost be thankful for problems whose scope was as limited as these. An interesting sidelight here is the fact that be a particular ecclesiastical problem of major or minor proportion, it was rarely, in pre-Petrine Russia, compounded by dogmatic argumentation.[29] The practical side was paramount. It is not meant, thereby, to deny the very substantial spirituality in Russian religon but we are here primarily discussing the daily aspects of Church life as they applied to the average man. Elements of ascesis will be brought out later.

And, as was pointed out above, the daily contact was formidable. It could proceed from the formal relationship of a person to the Church, change to one along business lines as exemplified by an account list of 1669 which treats the business of one church in the Kholmogorsk region (touching on such things as the sale of barley, the buying of wax, the church bell, money from obrok, etc.),[30] and end in judicial affairs between parishioners and the Church. These latter are far greater in scope than a modern society would allow. Thus, in the following cases,

---

28. N.I. Subbotin (ed), *Materialy dlia Istorii Raskola za Pervoe Vremia ego Sushchestvovaniia* (Moscow: 1874-90, 9 vol.), II, p. 137. Hereafter cited *Materialy*.

29. M.V. Zyzikin, *Patriarkh Nikon. Ego Gosudarstvennye i Kanonicheskie Idei* (Warsaw: 1931-39, 3 vol.) I, p. 181.

30. *RIB*, XII, col. 71-81.

among others, every Christian was subject to ecclesiastical jurisdiction: a) in matters touching upon superstition and idolatry, b) sorcery, c) the changing of one's faith, d)heresy, e) dissent in religious matters, f) insubordination to the dictates of the Church, g) immorality, h) blasphemy, the robbing of dead bodies, etc.[31] These, as may be seen, refer essentially to spiritual questions. There were, in addition, many civil matters which were also subject to ecclesiastical jurisdiction. Among these were a) family matters such as marriage, the establishment of consanguinity, and divorce, b) disputations between spouses concerning property, c) violations of conjugal rights and duties, d) illegitimate birth, e) inheritance, f) crimes of children against their parents.[32] The listing here given does not exhaust the powers of ecclesiastical courts. They also had jurisdiction in a number of criminal cases, questions of Church discipline, alcoholism, and others. In certain cases they shared jurisdiction with the civil courts as, e.g., in cases where the litigants were, respectively, from the lay and from the clerical world. And they handled most matters pertaining to the clergy and the monasteries.

The Church was very prominent in the distribution of various forms of aid, thereby fulfilling an ancient and honored duty. Much of this aid was purely along financial lines and a poor parish could, and frequently did petition the Church for aid in rebuilding, new service books, vestments, or just for money to be used constructively for daily religious needs. Aid was often forthcoming for the building of new churches and chapels. As an example, a priet and deacon of a church in Moscow petition (1651) for aid in obtaining money from the parishioners so as to be able to put up a stone church.[33] Interestingly enough, peti-

---

31. The list is based on Ivan Perov, *Eparkhial'nyia Uchrezhdeniia v Russkoi Tserkvi v XVI i XVII Vekakh* (Riazan': 1882) pp. 134-141. Also, I.S., "*O Tserkovnom Sudoustroistve v Drevnei Rossii*", *ChOIDR*, 1865, bk. i, pt. 1, pp. 5-8.

32. Perov, Ibid. pp. 148-58.

33. See the text of the petition in *ChOIDR*, 1906, bk. 3, sect. V, pp. 7-8.

tions for aid to local churches and clergy were frequently addressed to the Tsar himself (a pattern constantly appearing in Muscovy where even the minutest affairs were thought to be worthy of the Tsar's attention. With the rise of court ceremonial under Ivan III, contact with the Tsar and his inner circles became more difficult compared to Medieval times. It was, nevertheless, quite expected and assumed in the XVII c. that the Tsar and his aides were directly accessible and would respond. The documents of this century certainly indicate this). Thus, in mid-century, the Don Cossacks ask the Tsar to help them in the construction of a church in their "capital". Along with a request for money (which is later to be repeated) they ask for books, vestments, church wine, frankincense, a censer, and a priest.[34] Even when the Tsar decided to personally involve himself in such a matter, and the degree to which he did so was high, he would still go through the Church to facilitate the manifestation of the request.

Not all petitions sought material aid in and of itself. Requests were multitudinous and could be made concerning questions of ritual, on points of discipline, on matters relevant to ecclesiastical policy. The proclivities of the lower clergy, as of the minor governmental officials, to petition their superiors on any conceivable subject are astounding. Sometimes the action is reversed and it is done so primarily in two instances: when a new directive is being sent, and when the Church or one of the prikazy's (government departments) finds a parish or a monastery delinquent in its dues. An instance is the notice sent from the Prikaz Bol'shogo Dvortsa to the customs (or tax) official in Ostashkova. It is claimed that the Nilova pustyn' (hermitage) has not paid the necessary tax on its sale of fish.[35]

---

34. S.G. Pushkarev, *"Donskoe Kazachestvo i Moskovskoe Gosudarstvo v XVII veke"*, Transactions of the Association of Russian-American Scholars in U.S.A., 1968, v. II, pp. 20-21. Hereafter source cited as *Trans. Rus-Amer. Scholars, & Volume No.*

35. Gorchakov, *O Zemel'nykh Vladeniiakh*, Appendix, p. 92. Generally aside from the Church itself, money from Church related affairs or lands might be obtained by two prikazy; the Prikaz Bol'shogo Dvortsa (or Bol'shoi Dvorets), and

With the attendant fact that the Church occupied a central position in Russian life, it is only in keeping with this tenet that the Church did not necessarily wait for petitions or for the constant quests of the indigent to lend aid. Much was done simply as a matter of course and of normal function. If there were prisoners in jail, the clergy, as representatives of the Church, would often give them extra food on Sundays. (This is a practice which continued in Russia right up to the cataclysms of 1917). Every Sunday in Riazan' five rubles supplied by the bishopric were distributed to the prisoners in jail.[36] Money was allotted also The Metropolitan Ilarion of Riazan (1657-69) contributed money for this purpose. He also is known to have sent money to aid in the payment of troops, once in the sum of 100 rubles, another time — 1600 rubles, and a third contribution was of 1500 rubles.[37]

Nikon, when still Metropolitan of Novgorod in 1649 gave out grain and money to the needy to relieve the terror of famine which had again struck; 400 extra people daily were fed. This particular form of aid is especially peculiar to the monasteries which throughout Russian history play a role replete not only with the richness of the spiritual, but also with the rewards of the social endeavor. Without leaving the confines of the XVII century, we have a number of examples, especially telling in times of serious unrest and grief. The monasteries of the land opened up their grai supplies in the famine year of 1601 and aided many who so desperately needed food. And just a few years later, in the gruesome upheavals of the period 1605-1613, they did so again, though many were in a state as hopeless as that of the

---

the Prikaz Bol'shogo Prikhoda (or Bol'shoi Prikhod). The first was the department responsible for the buildings, lands, peasants, etc., which made up the Tsar's household, the latter was the central financial organ of the State. See G. Vernadsky and R.T. Fisher, Jr. (ed's) and S.G. Pushkarev (compiler), *Dictionary of Russian Historical Terms from the Eleventh Century to 1917* (New Haven and London: Yale University Press, 1970), p. 104. My usage of historical terms (and many of their definitions) throughout this work is generally based on this source.

36. Perov, op. cit., pp. 97-98.
37. Ibid., p. 99.

populace. The role of the Troitsa Sergievskaia Lavra (Holy Trinity Monastery) is particularly noteworthy here, as is, in a different setting, the political role it played in helping to preserve and then reorganize the Russian State. Timothy Ware states emphatically that prior to Peter the monasteries were "the chief centres of social work".[38] This reaffirms the level of interaction between the clerical and the lay spheres of Russian life.

Monasteries and hermitages, irrespective of their organization, strove to be self-sufficient. Some of them could not attain this goal for a number of reasons. The land, especially if the location of a particular monastery was formidable climatically, was too often inhospitable and bread had to be bought on the outside. A business, if engaged in, could be unremunerative and subject to periodic fluctuations. Or, the monks or nuns could be too old and infirm to properly see to the well being of their house. In such cases the monasteries became not the dispensers but the seekers of aid. The Agrafenina Nunnery in the Riazan' area received a yearly supplement of ten rubles (meted out, incidentally, from the taxes on taverns). In 1677, Dominica, the Mother Superior, complains to Tsar Feodor that the money had not been received. In replying, the Tsar ordered that instead of ten, twenty five rubles be given the nunnery[39] and the sisters could remain at peace for the remainder of the year. Suggestive here is the implication that even the loss of a relatively small source of income like ten rubles could impose umpleasant economic burdens. The Semilutskii Preobrazhenskii Monastery in the Voronezh area) was founded in 1620 and gradually came to be settled by wounded and crippled cossacks. It came to be known as a house of the disabled. In the 1650's, "wordly contributions" declined to the point where the brethren had to seek the good offices of the Tsar. During the 1650's and 1660's the monastery was constantly helped by the government. Increments

38. Timothy Ware, *The Orthodox Church* Baltimore: Penguin Books, 1963), p. 127.
39. Dobroliubov, op. cit., I, p. 118.

in lands were given, financial aid distributed, certain fishing rights granted and the like.[40]

Another type of difficulty is illustrated in the following. The brethren of the Pechensk Hermitage in the Kholmogorsk region petition Tsar Aleksei. They state that it is now already five years that the young men from their lands have been serving consecutively in the army. Their fathers have already aged to the point where they cannot work and the land stands unworked. This means no money can be collected and the hermitage finds itself in difficult straits. The brothers ask to be relieved of the payments of duties and of obrok (payment in kind).[41]

Other monasteries, though experiencing occasional tribulations, continue in a mode which insures their relative well being. Such a house is the Ferapontov Monastery in the Mozhaisk area. Founded toward the end of the 14th century by St. Ferapont, a man of boiar lineage, at the request of Andrei Dimitrievich Mozhaiskii (a son of Dimitrii Donskoi) the monastery was able through the years to accumulate a large number of lands and privileges. Coupled with prudent management it is at the beginning of the XVII century in no particular danger of demise in fortune. By the middle years of the century its material position had declined. A possible reason is the alleged change for the worse in the position of the peasants of the region. Another very concrete manifestation was a fire in 1664 which destroyed half of the monastic cells.[42] Fire as arch destroyer is nothing new in Russian history but each succeeding outbreak in no way lessened its power to damage. The Ferapontov Monastery does not, however, suffer ultimate catastrophe. It is strong enough to accept exiles from the outside world. The proud Patriarch Nikon, after his formal deposition at the Council of 1666, is banished here and stays until

---

40. Nikol'skii, op. cit., pp. 39-40.

41. "Chelobitnaia Tsariu Alekseiu Mikhailovichu Pechenskoi Pustyni Stroitelia Sergiia s Bratieiu ob Osvobozhdenii ikh Votchinoi Derevni Durnevskoi ot Obroka i Podatei", *RIB*, XIV; col. 417-20.

42. This paragraph is essentially based on V.T. Georgievskii, *Freski Ferapontova Monastyria* (SPB: 1911), pp. 2-6.

1676 when he is transferred to the **Kirillo-Beloozerskii** Monastery.

A successful monastery was the Solotchinskii and it is instructive to observe it in some detail. Dating like the Ferapontov to the late XIV century, the Solotchinskii Monastery is, at the beginning of the XVII, rather affluent. It possessed a good number of votchinas and dvors, its archimandrite occupied a high place among monastic heads, and its correspondence with civilians, clerics, and government officials was wide.[43] In 1678 the monastery possessed 12,369 desiatiny of land (1 desiatina usually equals 2.7 acres), 35,00 desiatiny of forested land, and some 1,187 desiatiny of swamp land. Its holdings were scattered in many regions and it even owned dvors in Riazan' and Moscow. Its income was primarily derived from its lands, though contributions cannot be discounted. They derived in from visitors, from lay dwellers, from the government, and from church officials. They were both monetary and in the form of goods. Thus, in March of 1673, it receives 3 rubles and 16 altyn (1 altyn equals roughly three kopeks) in commemoration of the Tsar's namesday with the proviso that it be divided among the brethren and the beggars. The sum is not huge, but obviously not all were. Some, however, were very substantial and usually came from the coffers of the bishopric of Riazan'. The bishops of Riazan' in the XVIIth century contributed heavily. For example, **Archbishop** Iosif once gave 46 rubles and 31 altyn, the **Metropolitan** Paul — 200 rubles, and **Metropolitan** Iosif gave over 1000 rubles. Other gifts were more quaint. When a priest named Ivan took monastic vows in 1692, he presented the monastery with eight beehives.[44]

In the latter part of the XVIIth century the number of monks in the Solotchinskii Monastery usually varied from 40 - 65 and

---

43. The material given here on the Solotchinskii Monastery is based on the lengthy, descriptive, and invaluable work, based exclusively on archives by A.P. Dobroklonskii, 'Solotchinskii Monastyr' — Ego Slugi i Krest'iane v XVII veke'', *ChOIDR*, 1888, bk. i, sect. III, part 3, pp. 1-132. The citation here is from pp. 4-5.

44. Ibid, pp. 13-18, 22, 40.

was supplemented by monastic workers (sluzhki monstyrskie or slugi) who were from the lay world but who were monastic dwellers. Their number went as high as forty and their work for the monastery was invaluable. Most had specific duties assigned to them. Among their tasks were those of treasurer, cellarer, judicial elder, keeper of books, choir master, cook, miller, brew master, not to mention such obvious undertakings as vegetable gardening, maintenance, and carpentry.[45] In terms of the work assigned to them they differed little from the monks themselves who did similar labor. Naturally, this did not exhaust the number of hands who worked either for the monastery or under monastic supervision. The census book of 1678 lists 787 dvors belonging to the votchina of the Solotchinskii Monastery. The total number of peasants and monastic workers (slugi) was 4,066 males. Of this figure the percentage of monastic workers to the number of peasants was 5½ - 6%.[46]

Monastic workers were under direct monastic control. The peasants were not if only by virtue of living outside the monastery. Many of their dealines with the monastery were via intermediaries of their own elected officials, both of whom were responsible for defending their interests.

These men could hold minor police or protective functions, be appointed as an okladchik (one who distributed money and materials in the dvors) or a collector of duties, be a measurer of land (an important position in that the person was elected by the mir, the peasants thereupon swearing to uphold his rulings on distribution of land, gardens, etc.), or be an elder. The latter was also elected by the mir with the confirmation of the monastery. He was the main peasant official and in petitions from the peasantry to the monastery his name was usually at the head of the list. He went to Moscow or other cities with various payments, was partly responsible for the actual collection of taxes from the peasants, kept his own books, and among many other

45. Ibid, p. 11.
46. Ibid, p. 17.

31

functions, not least was that of the mediator.[47] The fact of the peasant's greater degreeof independence from the monastery as opposed to the monastic worker was somewhat offset by the more substantial duties and payments to which he was subject. These may be most generally categorized under the heading of extras or occasional duties and could entail guard duty in a forest, obligations connected with transportation of passing militia, supplying needed materials such as oak planks and bricks, and a whole series of others.[48] They were particularly onerous in that they were so varied, so demanding of precious time, and so constant in their imposition. This dislike for this type of duty was shared by all the peasants of Russia.

The Solotchinskii Monastery's position vis a vis the State was quite enviable. From its foundation to this juncture it had accrued a whole series of privileges. The monastery was well known to the princes and the nobility of Moscow and Riazan and many gramoty (deeds, letters, documents) attest to their generosity. Ivan III, Ivan IV, the first False Dimitrii, Vasilii Shuiskii, Tsars Mikhail and Aleksei and others had all granted privileges or gifts. These were titles to new lands, exemptions from certain duties, privileges in the judicial sphere, and many others. One by Tsar Aleksei in 1675 gave it certain forest privileges.

Needless to say, it was to the monastery's own best interest to maintain and keep active as many of these as possible. Why ache under unnecesary burdens? Was not the monastic calling demanding enough? This did not mean that help was not needed as time went along. Violations against the monastery by peasants and noble landowners were contested and sometimes needed outside help. Thus, in 1660, in reply to a petition from the monastery, Tsar Aleksei instructed Archbishop Ilarion of Riazan' to take care of the unpleasant matter. In 1662 he had written similarly to Ilarion's predecessor, Misail.[49] A further positive

---

47. Ibid., pp. 29-31.
48. Ibid., pp. 62, 65, 77, 78, et. al.
49. Ibid., pp. 21-22.

element in the good relationships with the State was the fact that some of the privileges granted to the monastery likewise extended to the peasantry in its keeping. Thus, on the lands of the Solotchinskii, monastic officials collected government taxes for central governmental officials were not allowed to do this. A minor thing, perhaps, on the surface, but quite significant when added to two or three other points just as minor.

In thus describing the position of the Solotchinskii **Monastery** vis a vis the State we must not assume a one sided relationship. It is important to realize that the state maintained a number of its own rights and in so doing the monastery's independence was invariably (to whatever degree) limited. The same may be said in regard to the rights of the Church office (between 1649-1677 it was the Monastyrskii Prikaz) as well as of the local bishop and his diocese. Both, like the State, maintained certain rights over the monastery.

Perhaps the farthest reaching of these was the right of financial review. Both the local bishop's office and the Church checked the monastery's books and, if necessary, could make adjustments. If the adjustment turned out to be one designating an increase in payments then the right was surely a powerful one. Less troublesome were the bishop's rights in adjudicating cases where monastic peasants put in a claim or a complaint against the monastery. The bishop could also demand extras such as the fixing of roads. But neither of these had the far reaching implicatios of financial assessment. The State, in addition to the financial assessment, thrust certain obligations and duties at the monastery. Among these may be cited obligations in maintaining recruits, allowing some of the monastery's lands to be used for grazing purposes, and (usually from the Church) taking care of individuals who were sometimes sent to the monastery for purposes of education and/or rehabilitation.[50]

There is one point in all this which must be given cardinal significance. Despite a large number of privileges inherent to the

---

50. Ibid., pp. 23-24.

Solotchinskii Monastery, the State, nevertheless, had not abrogated certain of its basic rights. A balance of sorts existed between the two and it is a balance which during the period under discussion was gradually, and sometimes abruptly, being tipped toward the State. It culminates in the XVIII century with Peter and then Catherine, but the trend is already there. Without understanding this it is most difficult to understand the history of the Church in this period.

It is apparent that growing Westernization was a fact in Russian life in this period. More and more Westerners found their way to Russia in one capacity or another and Moscow had a fairly sizeable foreign colony. It may be asked: to what extent was religious toleration prevalent? The question does not have a ready answer for xenophobia, though not by any means rampant, still held considerable sway. Aside from more traditional antipathy to things European there are some explanations of closer memory. Borozdin, in his fine work on Avvakum, suggests (correctly, I believe) that religious toleration among the people was greater than generally thought. And, he goes on to say, in reference to the foreigners, "The people had the right to expect from them the same treatment of their faith and their mores. The foreigners, however, did not distinguish themselves by a particular delicacy in these matters and mocked Orthodoxy, its rituals..." etc.,.[51] The point is judicious in that it would be quite difficult to establish whose ignorance of each other was greater. A debate at the University of Uppsala in 1621 even considered whether the Russians were Christians.

One source of close memory which, by close contact, served to heighten xenophobia and religious intolerance rather than the reverse, was the Time of Troubles. Here the Russians were appalled at the behavior of foreign armies on their soil and were not

---

51. A.K. Borozdin, "Protopop Avvakum", *Zapiski Istoriko-Filologicheskago Fakul'teta Imperatorskago S. Peterburgskago Universiteta*, XLVII (47), 1898, p. 44. Hereafter cited Borozdin.

apt to soon forget the treatment accorded not only the people but the churches as well. Excesses against the latter were severe and served only to dishonor. This, as Professor Zenkovsky notes, "... undoubtedly helped the development of a national religious reaction among the clergy, the government, and the cultural elite."[52] And it may be added, the people. By the time of Tsar Aleksei's reign this was likely diminishing.

George Florovsky's brilliant analysis noted that the Time of Troubles had left Russia shaken. Politically and socially a catastrophe, the period also was one that could be labeled a moral turning point. The psychosis of the people had changed. They had become troubled, more suspicious and impressionable, and more unsure of themselves. Traditional forms of life had been shaken and the people had emerged shaken. "This was an age of lost balance, an age of unexpected and the inconstant, an age of unprecedented and unheard of events."[53] It truly was an age of encounter and clash with the West and the East. People had become spiritually unsure.

There was a problem connected with lands that Sweden acquired from Russia during the Time of Troubles. The population in these areas was principally Orthodox and Sweden, knowing full well that it would invariably turn its eyes to Mother Russia, initiated a campaign of conversion. Gustavus Adolphus even established a Russian press in 1625 which would aid in the process of conversion by making available to the Orthodox the Lutheran catechism and various religious tracts. Many Russians simply ran away, back to the bosom of their own land. It is interesting to observe that Nikon, when still Metropolitan of Novgorod, was very concerned for the fate of these Russians.

---

52. Serge A. Zenkovsky, *Russkoe Staroobriadchestvo* (München: Wilhelm Fink Verlag. Forum Slavicum, Band 21). 1970, p. 73. Hereafter cited Zenkovsky, *Starobriadchestvo.*

53. George Florovsky. *Puti Russkago Bogosloviia.* Paris, 1937, pp. 57-58. Florovsky's treatment of the XVII c. as seminal, as one of enormous change, as one of contrast, contradiction, and innovation, needs much more attention and emulation.

When the government agreed to return the escapees to Sweden he categorically refused to comply and fought until he won. The government ultimately paid Sweden in money for incurred losses.[54]

Such facts make any discussion of religious toleration and xenophobia impervious to casual formulation. As in so much else in the XVII century Russian contacts with westerners, the practical aspects and the case example are the most instructive. It should not be surprising that the degree of religious toleration is highest among the traders and the commercial people.[55] In Arkhangel'sk, where there was always a good number of foreigners living, special problems could arise. Thus, the foreign merchants complain in 1686 that the Archbishop Afanasii (of Kholmogorsk) has unjustly accused them and forbidden them their former privilege of hiring Russian servants. The action of the bishop was occasioned by the fact that some women working in foreign homes had given illegitimate birth and that, with the presence of two foreign churches there, many Russians were seen in them. Doubtlessly the good bishop felt that by limiting the areas of contact such abuses would be lessened. In handling the case the Posol'skii Prikaz (office of foreign affairs) first gave orders that Russians be taken out of foreign homes and not live there. But, this was gradually rescinded for practical reasons. Foreigners needed the manpower to take care of their goods, load and unload, watch and clean their homes while they were away.[56] It was not likely that several cases of illegitimate birth, nor the appearance (perhaps even due to conversion) of a number of Russians in the foreign churches would stand as hindrance to trade and commerce.

---

54. This discussion is based on Zenkovsky, *Staroobriadchestvo*, pp. 201-02.

55. M.P. Alekseev, Iavleniia Gumanizma v Literature i Publitsistike Drevnei Rusi (XVI-XVII vv)," ftn. 40, p. 196, in A.N. Robinson (ed.), *Issledovaniia po Slavianskomu Literaturovedeniiu i Fol'kloristike* (M: Akademiia Nauk SSSR, 1970).

56. D.V. Tsvetaev (compiler), "Pamiatniki k Istorii Protestanstva v Rossii". *ChOIDR*, 1883, bk. 3, sect. I, part 6, pp. 85-103.

An interesting sidelight to speculate on is the degree to which conversion to Orthodoxy was motivated by the restructuring of one's faith or by more mundane and practical reasons. There seems to have been a practice (it is difficult to determine to what extent) at this time of rewarding foreigners (presumably ones whose services could be useful) for converting to Orthodoxy. Thus, in 1680, the Dutchman Ioan (Johann?) Pangoin, requests permission from the Tsar to convert. He is, of course, allowed to do so and upon taking the sacrament is given a number of gifts, including 10 rubles, two sable furs, and broadcloth.[57] One army officer named Demont converts (1681) and some government office being slow in allotting him his reward, he petitions the government, complaining that he has yet received nothing. The petition draws a response and material reward is his.[58] This corresponds, in a sense, to rewards such as trade privileges (like those granted to the Dutchman Vinius) though these cannot always be tied to religious conversion.

Of a specifically different nature was the relationships of Russia to another group of foreigners — the Orthodox under Ottoman domination. The Russian attitude had been one of duality, especially since the Union of Florence in 1439 in which the Greeks by (though temporarily) casting their lot with the Latins, had also cast themselves into the well of Russian infamy. Much had happened since then, of course, and the very high degree of Russian contact with their Middle Eastern brethren in the XVII century (especially in the time of Tsar Aleksei) certainly attests that, in the very least, much had been forgotten.

Contact was either personal, or by exchanges of messages and both kinds were numerous. Many an Eastern prelate or a lesser Church official made the long trek to the northern empire which was viewed as the sole and logical protectress of Orthodoxy. Traffic was so heavy that a modern historian has referred to it as of "epidemic proportions".[59] A special entry

---

57. Ibid., pp. 42-45.
58. Ibid., pp. 46-48. Other examples along this line follow, pp. 48-69.
59. Zenkovsky, *Staroobriadchestvo*, p. 162.

point was set up at the border and ukazy (decrees) of 1645, 1646, 1649 forbade passage within until the necessary papers were cleared.[60] One suspects that the frequency of these ukazy reflects a practical failure of the measures instituted.

These visits were not usually mere exchanges of good will or just extended leaves of absence. Their practical side was always underlined by the constant seeking of aid (monetary and other) by the Near Easterners. Very frequently they were successful in their endeavors which thereby only fueled their desire to count on Moscow's generosity. At other times, along with matters concerning aid, various other questions were raised. In the 1640's such points as the possibility of a Greek school in Moscow, the establishment of a printing press, and determining the correctness of one edition of the Fathers were discussed.[61] Discussions of this type were facilitated by the fact that the Greeks had a number of their people in Moscow. In 1649 when Patriarch Paisios of Jerusalem arrived in Moscow he soon noted the importance of Nikon (then still Metropolitan of Novgorod). A number of meetings were held and some important points on the rite and the question of correcting service books were raised.[62]

Paisios left Russia in June of 1649 loaded with gifts and money for the Holy Sepulchre. He had no cause for complaint having been satisfied with the accomplishment of his intended task. Positive reports about Russian treatment are readily apparent in the writings of other prelates who made the northern trek. For example, Makarios, the Patriarch of Antioch, and his son Paul, archdeacon of Aleppo, when on their long Russian visit (1654-1656) find that treatment of them was indicative of a high

60. Zenkovsky, Ibid.

61. Pavel F. Nikolaevskii, *Iz Istorii Snoshenii Rossii s Vostokom v Polovine XVII Veka* (SPB: 1882), pp. 8-9. Hereafter cited Nikolaevskii, *Iz Istorii Snoshenii...*

62. Nikolaevskii, Ibid., pp. 9-13; Zenkovsky, *Staroobriadchestvo*, pp. 170-78.

level of care for their comfort and needs.[63] As stated previously, visitation to Russia was constant throughout this century and at its very end, in 1698, when the trial of Iiushka Mikliaev (for holding religious service while unordained) takes place there are foreign prelates from Georgia, Serbia, and Greece present.[64] They were all temporarily in Moscow for one reason or another and were asked to participate in the adjudication.

Aside from personal contacts, whether on formal terms as official visits or otherwise, written contact was maintained in a considerable degree with most areas and prelates of Near Eastern Orthodoxy. A pertinent example may be cited. In the period between March, 1651, and July, 1652, some sixty five messages and letters were sent by Near Eastern prelates to Moscow. Twenty four of these were from Patriarch Ioannikii of Constantinople (then holding that position for the second time) and in his, as in the others, are frequent calls for aid.[65]

Some contacts should not have been, given better means of communication, accepted. Afanasii Pateliarii had been Patriarch of Constantinople for a few days through crooked machinations (he had promised much money to the vizier). He made his way to Moscow (April 1653). There it is not clear exactly what he did or in how many Church discussions and meetings he participated. He did compose a tract titled "Chin Arkhiereiskago Soversheniia Liturgii na Vostoke" (Ceremony of the Hierarchical Liturgy in the East) which was immediately translated. By October he was holding services in the palace church in the presence of the Tsar

63. N.V. Rozhdestvenskii (ed), "Makarii Patriarkh Antiokhiiskii v Rosii v 1654-1656 gg. Dokumenty Posol' skago Prikaza". *ChOIDR*, 1906, bk. 4, sect. I, i-vi, & 1-120.

64. Pavel F. Nikolaevskii, *Iushka Makliaev: Epizod iz Tserkovno- Bytovykh Otnoshenii Kontsa XVII Veka* (M: 1888?), p. 4. Hereafter cited Nikolaevskii, *Iushka Mikliaev.*

65. P.V. Bezobrazov (ed.), "Gramota Konstantinopol'skago Patriarkha Ioannikiia k Tsariu Alekseiu Mikhailovichu ot 1 Marta 1652 goda", *ChOIDR*, 1888, bk. 1, sect. III, pt. 1, p. 4. This particular letter from Ioannikii to Moscow deals with problems in the diocese of Sofia (Bulgaria), showing the poor state of that diocese. The source contains the original Greek and the Russian texts.

(the choir was Greek in this case). He was given 1200 rubles (in sable) on this occasion and 2,000 more in December when he had a farewell audience with the Tsar. In leaving he presented the Tsar with a long letter in which the purported right of Moscow to Constantinople was stated.[66]

Items from the Near East always welcome in Muscovy were relics. Comments on authenticity must obviously be held in abeyance. Some of the relics were of an incredible nature (and, doubtlessly, part of that enormous, uninhibited, and false traffic). Among the relics sent were a piece of the true cross, a piece of the cross of Constantine, part of the remains of St. Ignatius, and the head of John Chrysostom![67] The gullibility of Russians in these matters was much like that of medieval man.

This, like so much else in our period, is witness to a religious intensity. The penchant for building and ceremonial was strong. The general sense of heightened religiosity was reflective of many undercurrents in Russian life. This has also been called a state of religious tension.[68] There was a series of canonizations between 1649-1652 (strongly supported by the Zealots of Piety). Regarding the canonization of the three most notable figures, Iov, Filip, and Germogen, George Vernadsky has written: "The matter was important not only because of the zealots historical consciousness, but also because of their conceptions of the Christian state in which lay rulers were to assist the church, not dominate it."[69] Muscovite society was, in Billington's formulation "... ruled by custom rather than calculation,"[70] but, in keeping with Florovsky's ideas on the prevalency of contrast and contradiction in this century, it was also a society where "... least of all there

---

66. For this interesting episode see Nikolaevskii, *Iz Istorii Snoshenii...*, op. cit., pp. 26-34.

67. Ibid., p. 41.

68. Zenkovsky, *Staroobriadchestvo*, pp. 87, 98, 100 and passim.

69. George Vernadsky, *The Tsardom of Moscow* (A History of Russia, 5 vol., New Haven and London: Yale University Press) vol. V (1949), part 1, p. 419.

70. James H. Billington, *The Icon and the Axe* (New York: Random House, Vintage, 1970 ed.), . 123.

was spontaneity and simplicity. All was too forced, too calculated. People begin to resound and be troubled regarding the indestructibility of their national traditions and bases precisely when their way of life commences to crumble. And in the social pathos of the XVII c. we more nearly see a belated defense against the commencing crumbling of a way of life ..."[71].

71. Florovsky, op. cit., p. 57.

Chapter 3

Religiosity: People and the Church

In the Nikitnikakh area of Kitai-gorod in Moscow is the Church of the Holy Trinity. Its model is quite impressive.[1] Between the years 1628-1653 the structure gradually grew under the watchful eyes of the rich gost'[2] Nikitnikov, who sponsored the church and paid for its construction. It was a personal monument, a memorial, and not to be thought of as particularly unusual for the time. Perhaps it is the supreme physical manifestation of the desire to be known as religious benefactor.

Merchants with money to spend were well known for this. And the period under discussion here has many examples of their generosity. Such towns as Iaroslavl', Kostroma, and Murom had churches built by merchants that were not only larger in scale than some Moscow churches, but also, significant architecturally and artistically. The church of St. John Chrysostom and that of the prophet Elijah (both in Iaroslavl') are pertinent examples.[3] Regarding the churches of Iaroslavl' it has been said:

---

1. See model in *Istoriia Russkago Iskusstva*, op. cit., I, p. 133.

2. Gost' is a term used to denote one of the members of the richest merchants in Muscovy. It was an honorary title received from the Tsar. For more detail see *Historical Terms*, op.cit., p. 23.

3. See plates 72A, 72B, and 74B in *Istoriia Russkago Iskusstva*, op.cit., I, and p.. 133-34 in text.

"As in terms of composition, so in terms of exterior decoration, the churches of Iaroslavl' are distinguished by a light, optimistic spirit. This major aspect of the form was immeasurably enhanced by the bright frescoes which, like tapestries, covered the walls, arches, and columns, and the saturation of the richly illuminated interior by the varied works of applied art."[4]

Other monied groups such as the bishops, the nobility, and lesser personnel did much the same. Patriarch Nikon himself built three monasteries; the Iverskii, the Krestnyi (Monastery of the Cross), the Novyi Ierusalimskii (New Jerusalem). The stol'-nik (a service man of the Tsar) Ivan Verderovskii built a stone church for the Trinity Monastery (near Riazan') in 1685.[5] The monastery had been neglected and this was to serve to invigorate it. In 1666 Archbishop Ilarion of Riazan' gave Prince Mikhail Shchetinin permission to construct a stone church in Lagov.[6]

Moving eastward to the Polish lands, we have the example of the nobleman Mozeli. Getting on in years, he decided to build a small church for the brotherhood of Lutsk, a brotherhood founded in 1617 with the intended goal of maintaining Orthodoxy at some level of independence in the Catholic lands of Poland (such brotherhoods existed in other cities under Polish control. Permission to do this was granted in a certificate issued by King Vladislav IV (Dec. 1645).[7] And when two years later Mozeli died and left everything to the brotherhood, the legitimacy of the will was confirmed by King Vladislav.[8]

What these cases show is that the upper classes were not

---

4. Ibid., p. 134.
5. Dobroliubov, op.cit., pp. 50-53.
6. Ibid., pp. 64-67. Many more examples are cited here.
7. "Gramota Korolia Vladislava IV, na Postroenie Bogadel'ni Aleksandrom Mozeli pri Tserkvi Lutskago Bratstva", *Pamiatniki Izdannye Vremennoiu Kommissieiu Dlia Razbora Drevnikh Aktov.* (Kiev: 1846-1859, 2nd ed. 4 vol.), I, pp. 159-62.
8. "Gramota Korolia Vladislava IV, Utverzhdaiushchaia Zaveshchanie Aleksandra Mozeli Otpisavshago vse Svoe Imushchestvo Lutskomu Bratstvu", Ibi., pp. 163-66.

averse to supporting the religious institutions, even when it meant a significant expenditure of their own money. What is at center here is an attitude, a frame of mind, a will to have an external, physical manifestation of one's inner beliefs and motives.

One of the best examples to cite for piety is Tsar Aleksei himself. He attended the lengthy vespers and liturgical services assiduously and these were part of the day's affairs. Skipping religious observances in order to meet a diplomat was not done. At banquets and dinners instead of music one heard readings from the Lives of the Saints. Foreigners were always impressed with the Tsar's humility. Paul of Aleppo recalls how the Tsar personally served monks in a refectory and also the poor, the blind, and the lame at their special table.[9]

Kotoshikhin records how, at the time of the Tsar's wedding, Aleksei and the Tsaritsa went to poor houses and jails giving alms to people therein and to beggars and other poor. "And many thousands were thus spent in this manner," he states.[10] The same general routine was adhered to when a child was born to the royal family.[11] It would be incorrect to assume that only such major occasions were cause for philanthropy. Holidays were traditionally always accompanied by charity. And Tsar Aleksei, on the anniversary of his father's (Tsar Mikhail's) death, always granted amnesty to a whole series of criminals put up for minor crimes.[12]

Tsar Aleksei's religiosity has been frequently attested to. His approach was essentially a simple and practical one and no hint of the pejorative is implied here. If the documents are true witness, then we can surely attest to an intensely personal reli-

---

9. Paul of Aleppo, *The Travels of Macarius: Extracts from the Diary of...*(London: Oxford University Press, 1936) p. 71. Hereafter cited Paul of Aleppo.

10. Grigorii Kotoshikhin, *O Rossii v Tsarstvovanie Alekseia Mikhailovicha* (SPB: 1906, 4th ed.), p. 14.

11. Ibid., p. 157.

12. Zenkovsky, *Staroobriadchestvo*, p. 135.

giosity. We have testimony for this from Tsar Aleksei himself. He is not ashamed to admit (in a letter to Nikon) the great fear which he felt when he paid his last respects to the Patriarch Iosif (d. 1652), or when he first learned of the Patriarch's death. It was during vespers. Candles flickered in the dark church. Shadows played on the icons and the priest's voice would sound from the altar's depth. Rushing into the stillness came the cellarer of the Spaskii Church and he sought the Tsar with the sad news. While he was telling Aleksei of Iosif's death, the bell struck above, its metal sound suddering in the damp darkness. And Aleksei himself shuddered, and so did the cellarer... but let us hear the Tsar's own words: "... and the great bell rang at just that moment, and such fear and horror befell on us that we could barely commence singing and even then, with tears..."[13]

The same type of intensity was frequently apparent on the mass level. Special days would bring outpourings of people. Such a day was the entry of the relics of the saints Germogen, Filip (who suffered martyrdom under Ivan the Terrible), and Iov (Job), Russia's first Patriarch. These relics were being brought from the Solovetskii Monastery by Nikon, at that time still Metropolitan of Novgorod. They were to find resting place in the Uspenskii Cathedral in Moscow. The cathedral, then being renovated, was deemed worthy of new additions and the relics were greeted with tumultuous warmth, spirit and joy. On the journey south in that spring of 1652, the relics were shown to villages and towns along the way and the people paid benediction all along the route. When the party reached Moscow that summer, the same thing occurred but on a greater level as the city of a thousand churches rose in greeting and prayer. Aleksei wrote: "...there were so many people that there was no room from the gate of Tver' to the Neglinskii gate. The people climbed unto the roofs. Even an apple could not have fallen into the streets..."[14]

---

13. Tsar Aleksei Mikhailovich, *Sobranie Pisem Tsaria Alekseia Mikhailovicha* (Moscow: 1856), p. 167.
14. Ibid., p. 157.

It would seem of moment to recall Fedotov's keen observation that Russians came to religion with the five senses. He phrased it thusly: "Coming from hypotheses to historical facts we find that from early Christian times to the present, the Russian has been finding his way to God through the bodily senses, all five of them; not only through sight be means of icons, and hearing by means of the Church chant, but also through touch by kissing, smell by means of incense, cypress, and mother of thyme, and taste by sacred bread, water, and all kinds of consecrated food."[15] The bringing of relics was religion, and pageantry, and inner excitement. The personal involvement must be stressed. It is even quite apparent at institutional levels. Parishioners would bring their own icons to church and pray to them, thus creating certain problems in disciplining the flock. Many boiars and merchants had so-called "house churches" (domovye tserkvi) on their properties, they being personally responsible for their support and maintenance.[16] This is a rather unique form for an existing church for they were sanctioned by the diocese and the priests were appointed and assigned by the diocesan bishop. It is also instructive to observe the large number of petitions requesting the privilege of building churches.[17]

We have already observed a number of ways in which the Church manifested itself in the life of the people and the nation. With the idea of philanthropy (and attendant humility) still prevailing, it was no surprise to have many poor living off the Church.[18] Most monasteries had special provisions for handling the indigent. The monastery as a place of refuge for the poor or the fallen is practically as old as the history of the Church in Russia.

---

15. G.P. Fedotov, *The Russian Religious Mind* (New York: Harper Bros., 1960, v. I), pp. 196-97. This whole approach to religion has also been strongly affirmed by Pierre Pascal. *The Religion of the Russian People* Crestwood, N.Y. St. Vladimir's Seminary Press, 1976.

16. Perov, op.cit., pp. 38, 41.

17. See for example, Dobroliubov, op.cit., I, II, throughout.

18. Ibid., II, pp. 296-98 for a pertinent example.

The whole notion of lay involvement in monastic life is most fascinating. We have already noted the vastness of monastic land holdings and we have seen why the monastery's role could extend into finance, administration, and national defense. For each of these there is much historical precedence.[19] Hence, lay contact was frequent, nay, inevitable, unless the house in question was truly a hermitage of the ascetic. And this extensive lay contact over the centuries gave rise to the phenomenon of lay persons living within a monastery or under its protective wing.[20]

The motivations for "entering" a monastery on these grounds (and taking monastic vows was not required) were many — old age, sanctuary, escape from the tribulations of a brutal world, inner peace. A significant reason also was the very Russian wish to pray for the forgiveness of a lifetime's sinning. Thus, when approaching old age, an individual would frequently give up the worldly in order to spend his last years cleansing his soul and preparing for the next life.[21] Or, if especially moved, an individual would enter a monastery because his life was too full, too generous with both meretricious and valuable gifts.[22]

Of course, the reasons for entry were not often so exalted and pure. For sometimes the entry did not correspond to the individual's desire. Such would be the cases of the "barren wives" sent to nunneries to leave behind their stigma on the tongues of village women.[23] Or witness the case of the dissatisfied husband of one Anna Osakina, one of history's faceless.

19. Gorchakov, *Monastyrskii Prikaz*, p. 116

20. Russian Orthodox monasteries, including those in the U.S.A. maintain this practice to this day.

21. P.V. Nikol'skii, op.cit., p. 15.

22. This aspect was ably brought out by the V. Rev. Alexander Schmeman in a guest lecture at the New York University Catholic Center titled "The Spirit of Eastern Orthodoxy", Spring, 1966.

23. V.I. Savvich, *Vklady i Vkladchiki v Severno Russkikh Monastyriakh XV-XVII v.* (Perm: 1929), pp. 68-69.

Her husband Klimentii, it appears, beat her regularly, took all her goods, sold their house, and left her with nothing but despair. He then went to the Arkhangelskii Monastery to live unfettered by responsibility.[24] And peasants, dissatisfied with their master, their land, or both, would run away and commit themselves to the care of brethren. Thus, Tsar Aleksei writes the voevoda of Ustiug ordering a search for some peasants reportedly to have taken refuge in near-by monasteries.[25] Interestingly enough, the alleged run-aways are referred to in the order, on the basis of their village's report to the Tsar which prompted his intervention, as the "best ones".

Perhaps the so-called "vkladchiki" provide us with the best example of lay monastic life. The term "vkladchik" means donor or contributor (one who pledges), and because the word loses accuracy in translation, I shall use the original. The "vkladchiki" were people that were preparing to enter a monastery to end their days (and here the connection with old age must not be made). To facilitate their impending upkeep at a monastic establishment, these people would, years in advance, constantly give money to the monastery of their choice, and whatever sum was given, it was in effect, "credited" to that individual. This must be carefully distinguished from the outright gift, for the gift was not used for the donor's support. The idea behind this was simple: the money deposited in a monastery (and each monastery kept a minute record of this) by an individual would accumulate and hence when he was ready to enter, his support would not be dependent on monastic coffers. Two apparent reasons may be offered for this: 1) one's independence would be assured, and 2) not all monasteries were well off. Thus, they could not possibly support a sometimes considerable body of "vkladchiki" — a body that occasionally made up one half the total of a monastic house.

The sums donated were, at times, considerable. It is shown

24. *RIB*, op.cit., XXV, col. 305-06.
25. *RIB*, op.cit., XIV, col. 971-75.

that in some years 16% of the yearly income of the well to do Solovetskii Monastery was accounted for by these contributions ("vklady") though occasionally the proportion dropped to 2%.[26] Money, however, did not always serve as the "vklad", for the poor had little of it. Thus, contractual labor was substituted; a peasant working for the monastery a certain number of years would, upon completion of the obligation, be allowed to stay and live out his life.

And there were cases of those destitute who had not even labor, let alone money, to offer. Such is the story of T. Novikov, a Cossack from the Voronezh area. In 1652, he was sent out on a scouting mission to the south and was captured by the Tatars who kept him prisoner for a year. He was then sold to the Turks who kept him at slave labor for sixteen years. Finally he was able to escape and upon returning home and finding out that two of his sons had been killed in battle and a third was away at war, he not only had no place to go, but was too broken physically to work. So, he petitioned the local officials for permission to enter the Borshov Monastery without a "vklad".[27] There were actually monasteries specifically for invalids. Such a monastery was the Semilutskii Preobrazhenskii in the Don area. Founded in 1620 it was, during this time, almost exclusively inhabited by old Don Cossacks who no longer could fight[28] — and for whom the life of a warrior had given the reward of pain, of loss of limb, of body' scars. Old now, unable to move with former speed or drink with former abandon, they could sit back in the quiet sun amidst the sunflowers or in the chapel's shadow, and in their mutual solitude, exchange stories of how they had fought the Tatar, Turk, and Pole.

The "vkladchiki" took active interest in their monasteries. Their own money and efforts were partly responsible for a

---

26. Savvich, op. cit., ftn. 5, p. 71.
27. Nikol'skii, op. cit., pp. 15-16.
28. Ibid., p. 39-40.

brotherhood's well being, and participation to insure continued well being was only practical. Sometimes they had a voice in the election of a new hegumen.[29] Or, they would be sent on missions for the monastery, missions that took the forms of representation at some minor church council, a monetary investigation, a judicial proceeding. And these "vkladchiki" shared the spirit of their monastery, a spirit often founded in the independence of a monastic house. With the monastic heads they often shared the idea that only the Tsar had jurisdiction over them.[30]

The rich and the well placed could also be, and often were, "vkladchiki". The Stroganovs made bequests to the Nikol'skii Koriazhemskii Monastery. Bishop Aleksandr of Viatka likewise made "vklady" to this monastery, and Patriarch Filaret made bequest to the Siiskii Monastery.[31] Collective "vklady" were similarly not unknown.[32]

James Billington has discussed the ringing of church bells in Muscovy as a sacramental act (bringing the word of God into man's presence). Bells also lent color and solemnity to Church proceedings he adds, noting that this was heightened by the general prohibition on the use of musical instruments in the Church.[33] Some foreigners, such as Paul of Aleppo, were occasionally unmoved or irritated by their "incessant" tolling.[34] All of them were probably surprised at the length of services, at the fact that there were no seats in the churches, and the general daily demands of religion. They might have wondered at how the Western recognition of Our Lady of Loretto had carried over

29. Savvich, op. cit., pp. 83-85 shows the various "rights" they possessed.
30. Gorchakov, *Monastyrskii Prikaz*, p. 36.
31. Savvich, op. cit., p. 75. Bishop Aleksandr's total 'vklad" at the time he entered the monastery in 1674 was 3261 rubles, 13 altyn, 1 denga!
32. Ibid., pp. 76-77. Incidentally, Professor Billington makes a brief, very negative comment about the institution of "pledging", referring to it simply as "a form of tax evasion..." I find this simplistic. Billington, op. cit., p. 126.
33. Billington, op. cit., p. 39.
34. Paul of Aleppo, op. cit., p. 27.

into Orthodox Muscovy[35] or been interested in describing Russian religious customs.

Reutenfels does the latter. Easter is witness to firings of cannon, constant ringing of church bells, the exchange of eggs (he explains this as an expression of Christian love), and the kissing of each other in greeting in church. On the day of the Epiphany the Patriarch and the Tsar lead the people to the Moscow River. There the blessing of the water takes place amid the multitudes. Multicolored tents dot the shore line and the Tsar's sleigh is even the more resplendent with six white horses pulling it. On Palm Sunday there is, again, much pageantry. The Tsar leads the Patriarch on a horse to the churches of the Kremlin. In front of them all is the huge carriage pulled by horses bedecked grandiosely. On it are artificial trees generously hung with fruits and flowers. On the branches sit several young boys dressed as angels who greet the crowd with hosannas. The whole path of the procession is laid with green and red broadcloth which is then removed by soldiers who follow the boiars in stead.[36]

Reutenfels was so interested by Russia in his two year stay there (1671-73) that he later presented several notes, via a cardinal acquaintance to the Pope with proposals for converting Russia to Catholicism. Some of the points he deems pertinent for such a project are notable. He states that the person/s chosen for this task should know well the character, tastes, and needs of the Muscovites. They should have a very religious Slav with them so as not to depend soley on a translator. The whole

---

35. A.I. Kirpichnikov (ed.), "Russkoe Skazanie o Loretskoi Bogomateri", *ChOIDR*, 1896, bk. 3, sect. II, part 1, pp. 1-18. This is quite an interesting example of cultural cross flow. A broadly based book on Russian culture that does not fail to treat the multiform aspects of Russian religion is Suzanne Massie's *Land of the Firebird: The Beauty of Old Russia* (N.Y.: Simon & Schuster, 1980).

36. Iacobus Reutenfels, "Skazanie Svetleishemu Gertsogu Toskanskomu Koz'me Tret'emu o Moskovii (Padua 1680)", *ChOIDR*, 1906, bk. 3, sect. III, pp. 173-75.

retinue must consist of morally acceptable people who must also be very friendly. Daily distribution of alms is considered to be a necessity as are prayers and services. Also, among other points, is the belief that missionaries should be there constantly, even if in secret.[37]

The more than casual observer also would have noted the Russian habit of keeping time by holidays. Thus, some of the materials that have come down to us from the area of Kholmogor and Velikii Ustiug (in the N. Dvina River area) attest to this. A peasant receives a loan from a church elder (1671). He is told to pay it back by the Feast of the Intercession of the Virgin.[38] Another case (1647) shows that the money borrowed to facilitate the proceedings in a murder case is to be returned by a specified holiday.[39]

Evoking a multiplicity of personal emotions and religious meanings was the icon. Theologically, for Orthodoxy, the whole question had been resolved as a result of the Iconoclastic controversies of the eighth and ninth centuries. Icons were (in Zernov's phrase) "a vehicle for the spirit". They could act as intercessors in time of dire need and Russian history is full of such intercessions. One need not be overly versed in Russian religious history to note the enormous number of miracle working icons. Some were of national significance, others of a purely local.[40] They served as inspiration, guide, and example to the individual. Icons, in providing a spiritual intimacy, as Tamara Talbot Rice rightly observes, were accompaniment to

37. Pavel Pirling (ed.), A.I. Stankevich (transl.), "Novye Materialy o Zhizni i Deiatel'nosti Iakova Reutenfelsa", *ChOIDR*, 1906, bk. 4, sect. II, part 1, pp. 1-24. An English rendering and discussion of some of these may be had in Nickolas Lupinin, "The Project of Jacob Reutenfels", *Trans. Rus.-Amer. Scholars*, vol. VI, 1972, pp. 300-05.

38. *RIB*, op.cit., XII, col. 81.

39. *RIB*, op.cit., XIV, col. 395-97.

40. This is referred to frequently in general works. Here note Miss Rice's brief comments on this. Tamara Talbot Rice, *Russian Icons* (New York: Marboro Books, n.d.), pp. 8-11.

fact.[41] They were symbols of faith and so considered rather early in the development of Orthodoxy. If a pagan asks you to show him your faith said John of Damascus, take him into church and place him before the icons.[42]

Icons were everywhere — in peasant homes, at court, in taverns. The making of icons was a function of considerable importance. Not only were icons made and painted in isolated monasteries, they were also commissioned to workshops, be they royal or private (e.g. that of the Stroganov family). Merchants were well noted for their generosity in commissioning new icons. Interestingly enough, the icon, in artistic terms, lost some of its value in the eighteenth century, for up to that time hackneyed artists had not yet managed to break into the circle of iconographers. For the preparation of an icon was not merely a question of oil or tempera and wood, but one of spirit, and the monk who painted them went through spiritual rituals of moral cleansing before commencing his holy task.

It is for such reasons that, for instance, oil could not be used for icons. Even the techniques were prescribed, though not, in terms of direct corollary, thereby limited. I do not propose to delve into various technical aspects and reasons for them. This is done excellently in Nataliia Schaffer's book.[43] The purpose here was to draw attention to the spiritual nature of the work. And it is indicative how in the budding secular interests of the mid-seventeenth century, the old still retains its grasp for with the rise of portraiture one finds that the first Russian portraits were essentially iconographic in nature.[44]

This is the background to how icons tied in with daily life.

---

41. Ibid., p. 8.

42. Ware, op.cit., p. 41.

43. Nataliia Schaeffer, *Russkaia Pravoslavnaia Ikona* (Washington, D.C.: 1967).

44. E.S. Ovchinnikova, "Siuzhet Knigi Esfiry v Russkoi Zhivopisi XVII v.", pp. 371-91; in N.V. Ustiugov (ed.), *Russkoe Gosudarstvo v XVII Veke* (Moscow: 1961).

Illustrative is the fact of their domestic and familial importance for they were intricately bound up with all family functions. Hence, upon the birth of a child an icon, depicting the saint whose name the child was to receive, would be ordered. This icon would accompany the person through life and be placed in his grave upon death. The bride and groom would be blessed by icons of the Virgin and Christ; a son going to war by an icon of St. George, Dimitrii, or Feodor. The ailing were frequently presented with an icon of St. Panteleimon. And, notable days in the life of the family would be inscribed in an icon.[45] These manifestations were nationwide and saw few exceptions. From the Tsar to the peasant, from noble to lowly peddler, the icon was an inherent part of the religious conscience — an object always to be venerated.

"Holy fools" (iurodivye) were a very Russian phenomenon. These were men who took upon themselves the cross of suffering, of pain, and self abnegation to make their religious mark. The common man's reaction to them was a blend of respect, fear, abuse. He could not quite comprehend the necessity of such severe self-punishment and self-denial and, in a peculiar sense, this inability to cope in effect helped to insure the hold of the holy fools over the people.[46] We cannot forget that often the upper classes reacted in the same way, with the same sense of reverence and fascination. It was a reverence that was sometimes deserved for the lay saint is not uncommon in Russia, and canonization of these "fools for Christ's sake" is not a sporadic occurrence. In the sixteenth century there were fourteen such canonizations and in the seventeenth century, seven.[47]

Tsar Aleksei, we know, esteemed these "holy fools". One, "Vasilii the barefoot", who is mentioned in several of the Tsar's

---

45. Schaeffer, op.cit., pp. 16-17.

46. Pushkin's play Boris Godunov and Mussorgsky's opera based on it give well known prototypes. Countless literary examples exist.

47. G.P. Fedotov, *The Russian Religious Mind* (Cambridge: Harvard University Press, v. II, 1966), p. 315.

letters, was given the honor of going with Nikon for the holy relics of Iov, Germogen, and Filip to the Solovetskii Monastery. This despite at least one assertion that Nikon considered all "holy fools" to be crazy.[48] And it was a "holy fool" (most likely) who was the "old man" sitting next to Aleksei himself during the triumphal procession into conquered Vil'na (1655). This bedraggled man, worn and dirty, walked before the Tsar from the city's gate to its court on red broadcloth and suede.[49] The Tsar had deemed the "fool" worthy and the "fool" had led.

The fool could make himself out to be practically anything — the nation's conscience, the sage, the confessor, the pure spirit, the symbol of ultimate humility, and so forth. But, in general terms, certain broad characteristics may be traced as Fedotov has done. He lists: 1) an ascetic repression of vainglory with a concomitant aim of provoking vilification from men; 2) service to the world in the form of a special mission; 3) radicalism of asceticism (an asceticism, moreover, practiced while living in populated areas, especially cities), and 4) the ir-rational motivation.[50]

The fools, despite these general traits, were occasionally in-volved in matters not purely ascetic. They are ascribed, for example, a role in the spread of the raskol (schism). Such "holy fools" as Kiprian, Fedor, and Afanasii were quite successful in this endeavor. Fedor, as well as Kiprian, were known to the Tsar and Kiprian frequently presented the Tsar with the many petitions of Avvakum.[51] Feodor, too, was one whose eyes had been opened to old belief by Avvakum.

The "holy fools", individuals and with no institutional ties, were left pretty much to ramble about, seeking holiness in

48. Andreev, op.cit., p. 71.

49. *Sobranie Pisem Tsaria Alekseia Mikhailovicha*, op.cit., p. 162.

50. Fedotov, op.cit., II, pp. 319-22. Also see comments by Billington, op. cit., pp. 59-60.

51. P.S. Smirnov, *Istoriia Russkago Raskola Staroobriadchestva* (SPB: 1895), p. 56.

their own fashion. Movement was more restricted within the institutional setting. Monks, for example, were not allowed to change their monasteries (whether within the same diocese or otherwise) without the permission of the local bishop. This permission was called the "otpusknaia" or the "blagosloven-naia" or gramota.[52] And it was not overly effective, not being readily adhered to. Time and time again there are complaints against the peripatetic monk. The metropolitan of Rostov, Iona, writes to Archimandrite Ignatii of Velikii Ustiug regarding two "runaway" monks.[53] And the Council of 1667 again had to include this provision. But, seemingly, to no avail.

Seen on the background of pilgrimage, which was very popular and whose benefits were always sought, one should not really be surprised. It was not just the beggar and the monk who criss-crossed the countryside. There is the steady image of the Russian pilgrim who sought out famous monasteries and churches, the man or woman who sought remission of sin by religious exploit. There were many of these pilgrims and a decent sized village would likely have at least one who had made a trek. The fact that he had done so insured him a special place in the village for he was at least thought of as a person of courage, dedication, and will, a person whose reaction to the transcendental had motivated a self-denial, another, higher confrontation with the religious experience.

We cannot delve into an exegetical analysis of the psychology behind this. But the range of people who so committed themselves was as broad as the whole spectrum of Russian society. Pilgrimage was a facet of Don Cossack life also. And these acts of humility rendered by these warriors may have had incalculable personal and spiritual effects. The seventeenth century is still a turbulent era for the Cossacks and their

52. Perov, op.cit., pp. 55-58.
53. *RIB*, op.cit., XII, col. 292-94.

pilgrimages, especially to the Solovetskii Monastery[54] which was particularly esteemed by them may have been a crying of the soul for that contact with peace and humility which they could not, or were not allowed by the circumstances to cultivate.

It would have been well had abuses within the Church been restricted to wandering. Unfortunately, priests themselves were too often guilty of unexemplary behavior and their exhortations to the populace to shed bad habits were frequently mere velleities. So, immorality, laziness, excessive drinking were frequent companions of the ecclesiastic, as even some of the poems of Simeon Polotskii, the leading poet of the age show. The priest of a village church reports, for example, that his deacon had twice tried to choke him to death.[55] Or, a trader lodges complaints in which he demands that the local officials and priests return the 2,000 rubles they owe him.[56] Then, perhaps it was a priest's own ineptitude or poor handling of peasants that led to an attack on his person by them.[57] Perhaps the fact of a very pronounced contact of priest and flock helped to foment acerbities that less frequent confrontations might have softened.

The law's and the authority's concern for improvement in this area was constant. Directives of bishops to their lower clergy repeat again and again the need for a higher morality, for more exemplary behavior. They lament the fighting and drinking. Bear baiting is forbidden. Admonitions go out to monastic leaders to keep a closer eye on their subordinates, to make sure they did not entertain the fair sex in their cells, sneak in alcohol or tobacco, or support their relatives by means of

---

54. Nikol'skii attests to this widespread Cossack practice of pilgrimage. P.V. Nikol'skii, op.cit., p. 16. Also, Pushkarev, *Trans. Rus.-Amer. Scholars*, vol. II, pp. 21-22, and the notation in "Otpiska Meshcherinova Gosudariu s Rosproshymi Punktami Solovetskago Vykhodtsa Startsa Pakhomiia", p. 80 in: "Akty Otnosiashchiesia k Istorii Solovetskago Bunta", *ChOIDR*, 1883, bk. 4, sect. 5, part 1.

55. *RIB*, op.cit., XXV, col. 337-39.

56. Ibid., col. 245-46.

57. *RIB*, op.cit., XII, col. 243-44.

monastic funds which were, on occasion, appropriated or that purpose.[58] The Council of 1667 passed further laws on these ill doings, but it is instructive to observe, with the great churchman Makarii, that few of its prohibitions were new.[59]

It should not be surprising, therefore, that the civil administration did step into local Church affairs from time to time even though the voevodas (administrators in the provinces, frequently military) and other officials were often berated for their unsolicited interference.[60] Doubtlessly they overstepped their bounds enough times to warrant complaints, but it is sometimes difficult to see how intervention could be detrimental. We know, as one reference point, of the particularly turbulent history of the Pecherskii Voznesenskii Monastery (in the Nizhegorod area). In the early 1640's the hegumen of this monastery led a raid of his monks upon a neighboring village. The monks were armed with slingshots, muskets, bows and arrows, axes, and evidently used them all. The ensuing brawl was severe with some men killed. More than some of the women were dishonored.[61]

The latter is, to be sure, an extreme case, though this monastery found little peace in the years following. It seems to have run an uncanny streak of ill luck. Its heads always seemed susceptible to corruption. Thus, one Dionisii Omachkin, who by 1662 headed the monastery, ruined the good reputation he brought with him by stooping to corruption and arrogance. The brethren, in their petition against him (1674) accuse him of

58. For various aspects of this see Perov, op.cit., pp. 32-33, 48-50, 60-61.
59. Mitropolit Makarii, *Istoriia Russkoi Tserkvi* (SPB: 1883, 12 vol.), XII, p. 792. Hereafter cited Makarii, *Istoriia*.
60. Gorchakov, *Monastyrskii Prikaz*, p. 46.
61. A. Titov, "Cherty Monastyrskago Byta v XVII Veke. Kelar' Dionisii Omachkin", *Russkii Arkhiv*, vol. 42, part 2, pp. 604-05.

arbitrary use of power, falsification of the account books, and blatant support of his children and nephews with monastic funds.[62] However, because Dionisii enjoyed the protection of the Metropolitan Filaret of Nizhnii Novgorod, his iniquitous dealings continued to find free play.

What is lamentable here is that this was a relatively high churchman, one whose example was bound to have pernicious effects on the brethren. And the incident is not singular. The monk Gerasim Firsov of the Solovetskii Monastery (d. 1666) was a brawler, a drinker, a crook. He was punished several times for dipping into the monastic till and the beatings he sustained in his many fights were often severe. What is noteworthy here is that despite these extra-religious activities Gerasim was a talented writer of tracts and the Solovetskii Monastery frequently made use of his pen for official petitions, decrees, and polemics.[63] These cases are typical of why aspersions on the Russian Church could be cast.

Certain forms of irresponsibility with attendant lack of critical perception were also apparent in popular religiosity. A good example is the stream of pilgrims from the Near East to Muscovy. There were so many that the Russian government imposed restraints on entry several times, but with little success. One of the reasons was the indiscriminatory help given, whether in the forms of alms, goods, or otherwise. Moldavian and Ukrainian towns along the route had a flourishing trade in forged letters of recommendation, false signatures of Patriarchs, false relics, imitations of ancient icons, etc..,[64] Fraud seemed not to be a hindrance. The poor whom the average Russian saw (Fedotov has shown) as sacred, being in the image of the

---

62. Ibid., pp. 609-11.

63. N. Nikol'skii, "Sochineniia Solovetskago Inoka Gerasima Firsova po Neizdannym Tekstam", *Pamiatniki Drevnei Pis'mennosti i Iskusstva.* CLXXXVIII, 1916.

64. Nicolas Zernov, *Moscow the Third Rome* (London: Society for the Promotion of Christian Knowledge; New York: Macmillan, 1937), pp. 55-60.

humiliated Christ,[65] could legitimately expect alms and aid, but the unscrupulous were too often similarly blessed.

Certain other laxities were also apparent. Such was the case (late 1690's) of Iushka Mikliaev, a deacon in the Novgorodian eparchy. Mikliaev decided that the rewards of his office were too limited and that the priesthood would serve him better. His petitions in this regard were rejected by Metropolitan Iov of Novgorod. Mikliaev then promtly proceeded to give himself the priestly orders and served as a priest for one and a half years before being deposed. The arm of Muscovite justice was also slow at times. But seen pradigmatically, this could be repeated many times. Who knew how many self-proclaimed priests served the Russian vastness? It seems that in this period of ferment there were too many.

In the case of Mikliaev, in whom there was no hint of heresy, it seems that the official hierarchy was not aware of his self-elevation. Action was taken when the people in the parish became too worried and turned to Metropolitan Iov himself. They were afraid that the sacraments of christening, marriage, and last rites perfomed by Mikliaev were invalid.[66] What, of course, was needed to insure the priest's ecclesiastical legitimacy, aside from ordination, was a "stavlennaia gramota" (the legal paper without which a priest could not officiate). When a new bishop assumed his post, these documents might have to be renewed (and a resultant fee paid). Lower church officials, such as the deacons and the ponomars (sextons) received their certificates from members of the bishop's staff.[67]

Despite all, exact determinants for the religious aspect of the age are not ultimately easy to come by. The furher the investigation proceeds, the more aspects appear, positive and negative. Seventeenth century Russia is full of them and all cannot possibly be traced. The rise of the oral sermon is impres-

---

65. Fedotov, op. cit., II, p. 61.
66. Nikolaevskii, *Iushka Mikliaev*, pp. 2-3.
67. Perov, op. cit., pp. 42-43.

sive and has immediate effects on the religious consciousness.[68] Didacticism flourished, even in one of the most enlightened, most Western, and best educated men. Simeon Polotskii is insistent on using the moral tone in his work.[69] The theme of the beauty of the liturgy and the Church is a common notion in the religious thought of the time.[70] How far down to the masses did it go? When people entered a monastery, what ultimate motives prevailed? Certainly we cannot accept that all could be as dramatic as Nikon's who took vows upon the sudden death of his three sons.[71]

The diversity, the multi-dimensional aspects of the religious elements (or trappings thereof) are intricately entwined in Russian life of this period. It is apparent as much in the efforts of noblemen on behalf of the Church as in what may be called the mass reaction of the people. The latter were most apparent in major holidays or special events such as the exhibition of newly acquired relics. Less spectacular, but just as steady were the daily manifestations such as the considerable lay involvement in monastic life. This worked in reverse fashion also: The monastery, through its land holdings, as the best example, was a prime factor in Russian administrative and agricultural life. The indigent, having less recourse to standard means of support, did as often as not, depend on the Church for their sustenance. All this is not the whole picture, and various abuses within and without the Church, relating to religious affairs have been pointed out. These must stand not only as a corrective, but also as the factor which helps us draw a far more composite drawing of the whole.

---

68. A.S. Arkhangel'skii, "Bor'ba s Katolichestvom i Zapadno-Russkaia Literatura Kontsa XVI — Pervoi Poloviny XVII Veka", *ChOIDR*, bk. 1, sect. I, part 1, pp. 122-25.

69. A.S. Eleonskaia et al (ed's), *Istoriia Russkoi Literatury XVII — XVIII Vekov* (Moscow: 1969), pp. 189-91.

70. Zenkovsky, *Staroobriadchestvo*, p. 116.

71. Vernadsky, op. cit., V, part 2, p. 558.

Chapter 4

Church and Society

Traditionally and popularly the seventeenth century has long been held to be nascent in character — a mere prelude to the dynamism of Peter and the introduction of Western influence into Russia. Increasingly this formulistic approach is being held suspect, and properly so. For the degree of change in the XVII century is quite considerable. The nation was brimming and it was Peter who applied more flame to the cauldron to make it boil over.

It is really best seen as a transitional period[1] and we cannot limit the idea to just a few areas of investigation such as religion, literature, mining, etc. Ferment began to reach most stratas of Russia endeavor, most areas of Russian culture, not to speak of the religious. Scholars are familiar with the fact of greater foreign travel abroad and contact, the influx of foreign personnel into Russia, the rise of towns, the increase in commerce and in the

---

1. Our concern will not be to focus on this question in toto. In fact, a separate volume should synthesize and interpret (especially the last part of) the XVII century in this light. We will view only some elements which turn upon certain religious and cultural phenomena and are integrally linked with the total picture.

commercial class.[2] It is an age called a turning point in the history of Russian culture[3] as a whole and the same may be applied to most of its parts. Vodovozoz states, in regarding literature that: "In the new, rapidly changing conditions on the eve of imminent and inevitable reforms, before Russian literature of the late XVII century arose, in all definitiveness, the question was how to live further, how man, who was breaking with traditions and traditional relationships, was to find the correct way in life".[4] Such a statement is indicative of the scope involved. We will focus here on religious and parallel points and hope to show more clearly how not only were they intertwined but also how the Russian Church was affected by the new and disturbing trends.

It should be pointed out at the outset that we are not, in discussing certain literary aspects, providing an interpretation or a history of Russian literary activities of this period. The goal is to show the flux in the literary pursuits of the time and, since they were still quite Church oriented, they were bound to have a strong effect on the religious consciousness. For, as Prof. Zenkovsky states, this was a period that witnessed the breakdown of a purely spiritually orientated culture, a period where State

---

2. Sakharov, *Obrazovanie i Razvitie...* see for the latter two points, pp. 148-49, 209-10; on the variety of Moscow crafts, p. 143. James Cracraft points out much of this as preparatory background material for Peter in James Cracraft, *The Church Reform of Peter the Great* (Stanford, Calif.: Stanford University Press, 1971), chapt. 2.

3. Sakharov, *Obrazovanie i Razvitie...*, p. 201. Also, A.N. Nasonov, *Istoriia Russkago Letopisaniia XI — Nachala XVIII Veka* (Moscow: 1969), p. 478. And, most brilliantly, Florovsky, op. cit., esp. chapt. 3. It might also be pointed out that pre-revolutionary Russian historians were well aware of this. Sergei Platonov's works could be especially mentioned. Modern historians of Russia in the West, not fully aware of XVII c. materials, do not yet make the pertinent conclusions. The still prevalent tendency to view Russian history from the beginnings to Peter as "medieval" — and Petrine and post-Petrine as "modern" is lamentable.

4. N.V. Vodovozov, *Istoriia Drevnei Russkoi Literatury* (Moscow: 1962), p. 358.

and Church control over literature was relaxed.[5] This reinforces the concept of the transitional age that is also a whole in itself.

Fedotov, in discussing the Izmaragd,[6] notes the old Russian belief in the wisdom of books. He states: "book reading in Ancient Russia was, certainly, not contemplated from the point of view of theoretical knowledge; it was the school of practical conduct".[7] (Witness later examples like the **Domostroi**). And even tough he speaks of Ancient Russia, it was a tradition unhampered until the XVII century. For it was not until then that new currents flowed in.

The new currents took many forms. The erotic and love element appears. It is significant in that it is an admission of realism in literature, idealism in life. The relaxation of State and Church vis a vis literature allowed newer themes and protagonists who are not of the old mold. There are drunkards, corrupt clerics and monks, jealous husbands, inefficient administrators. There are satires on the Church (such as The Tale of the Rooster and the Fox), criticisms of monasticism (such as the Kaliazinskaia Chelobitnaia — the Kaliazin Petition), and countless references to adultery.[8] It is a period when tales of courtship, prevalent in the West centuries before, finally begin to appear. Zenkovsky writes: "No traces of innocent romantic courtship can be found in Russian chronicles or tales until the seventeenth century".[9] Also, the purely personal expression begins to take

---

5. Zenkovsky, *Epics*, p. 37. This is a point made with Professor Zenkovsky's customary perspicacity. The phrasing is such that we may understand the significance of 'purely''. For what this means is *initial* breakthrough in the facade of a spiritual culture.

6. The Izmaragd (The Emerald) is an anthology of devotional literature that originated in the XV century and remained very popular thereafter. For background and descriptive analysis see Fedotov, op. cit., II, pp. 37ff.

7. Ibid., pp. 41-42.

8. See on these general points Zenkovsky,*Epics*, p. 37; Miliukov, op. cit., II; Also, A.L. Zhovtis (ed.), *Drevne-Russkaia Literatura* (Moscow: 1966, 2nd rev. ed.); Eleonskaia et. al. (ed's), op. cit., and many more.

9. Zenkovsky, *Epics*, p. 13. The only exception, as he notes, is the Tale of Peter and Fevroniia of Murom.

hold with the very notable example of Avvakum's *Auto-biography*. Likhachev goes so far as to claim that: "Not one of the Russian medieval writers wrote so extensively of his feelings as did Avvakum".[10]

The lives of the saints, so popular in previous times were, from the beginning of the XVII century, gradually replaced by secular biography, autobiography, and the first-person confession.[11] The lives of St. Dionisii, Abbot of the Holy Trinity Monastery, of Ivan Neronov, a leader of the Zealots of Piety and later the Old Believers, and the boiarina Morozova, who was to die for the old belief, are, in Zenkovsky's determination, essentially secular biographies of people of exemplary religious life, though there are traditional hagiographic features.[12] "The emergence of secular biography, autobiography, and the literary confession signals the end of the medieval literary patterns. With the secularization of life, literature turned away from purely religious-historical biography. New ways of life, together with freer cultural and spiritual criticism, demanded a new type of letters, greater realism, and a more penetrating portrayal of character and human psychology. A fictional hero replaced the historical or hagiographic one, and the novella and satirical tale made their appearance."[13] But we must not lose sight of historical perspective. For it is of an "emergence" that we speak and we must not be forgetful that, as Slukhovskii observers, the Church continued to be the chief guardian and propagandist of the book.[14]

It is instructive to observe briefly the state of books and literacy. It has been cited that "The art of writing for practical purposes, for the writing of various documents was sufficiently

---

10. D.S. Likhachev, *Chelovek v Literature Drevnei Rusi* (Moscow: 1958), p. 157.
11. Zenkovsky, *Epics*, pp. 31-32.
12. Ibid., pp. 33-34.
13. Ibid., p. 35.
14. Slukhovskii, op. cit., p. 108, in his superbly researched work.

66

widespread in the second half of the XVII century, even among the posadskii and the rural poor. Here was a group of professionals who had special permission from the authorities to make their living by the pen..."[15] This group of professionals may have been fairly wide spread. Certainly the rise of commerce, among other developments, is one obvious example of how the spread of the written word was facilitated. It has been stated, in discussing the documents of this period that "Documents were written and distributed in huge numbers. They derived not only from professionals but also from literate people in general..."[16] The concusion drawn from this is that: "Only a population with a substantial degree of literacy could create a whole class of writing specialists who were scattered in all the towns from the Western borders of the government of Muscovy to its Siberian borders".[15] And Slukhovskii, who has written a superb study on books and libraries in Old Russia, explains that the basic circle of book lovers and collectors was grouped in towns. The 'feudalists" he notes, "were rich and frequently very well educated people".[18] He points out, likewise, that the work of the central governmental apparatus forced bureaucrats to come to the book and to written documents for aid. "The use of the book was becoming a necessity of work."[19]

Later he observes that: "In the period under dicussion the book played a big role not only in terms of enlightenment, but in all facets of the social life of the nation. It developed national conciousness and it helped the Russian people in their struggle with foreign invaders. The literate and the illiterate population

---

15. Vodovozov, op. cit., p. 319.

16. A.A. Nazarevskii, *O Literaturnoi Storone Gramot i Drugikh Dokumentov Moskovskoi Rusi Nachala XVII Veka* (Kiev: University of Kiev Press, 1961), p. 6.

17. Ibid., See Nazarevskii's more detailed comments regarding this; also points such as artistic methods in the writing of documents, religio-rhetorical devices, etc., esp. pp. 4-8.

18. Slukhovskii, op. cit., p. 104.

19. Ibid., p. 86. Also Sakharov, *Obrazovanie i Razvitie...*, p. 207.

of Russia reacted to the written word with the utmost respect."[20]

It is interesting that the term "enlightenment" is used. And if we do not burden the term with excessive connotations, it may be substantially useful. Sakharov, another modern historian, uses the same term in citing reasons (not wholly adequate or exhaustive) for the growth of 'enlighthenment" in this period:[21] 1) the development of town life with its attendant crafts and commercial endeavors, 2) the first appearance of manufacturing, 3) the growth in size and complexity of the system of government, and 4) the growth of foreign contacts. All these, he claims, correctly, demanded a rise in literacy. The rise of literacy was abetted by such items as the publication, in 1651, of the "letter book" (literally, from the word "azbuka") or grammar. It came out in an edition of 2400 copies.[22]

The publication of books is an indicator of the growth of

---

20. Slukhovskii, op. cit., p. 126. Some may object that this is all too generous a view. I suspect not and the idea tht pre-Petrine Russia, especially of our period, was festering in pains of almost unanimous illiteracy, is a gross, popular misconception. This is not, by any means, to imply that literacy was particularly common. Certainly so when viewed in terms of schools, the impetus for which on anything approaching a mass level did not come until Peter. But it is definitely to suggest that a class was coming into being for whom literacy was a necessary fact of life and that progressive factors would not thereby be (or, conservatively speaking, would be less) impeded. More suggestions along this line follow in the text. Of course, in discussing documents and literacy, documents that have been destroyed by fire can also be mentioned, at least simply as means of adding to the written corpus. See, e.g., such notations in *RIB* op. cit., XIV, col. 975-77, XXV, documents numbered 196, 212, 213, 231, et. al., XXV, appendix, pp. v-vi.

21. Sakharov, *Obrazovanie i Razvitie...*, p. 207.

22. Sakharov, Ibid. He states also that this sold out in Moscow in one day, though unfortunately, he gives no citation. One aspect, re circulation, is supported by Zenkovsky, *Staroobriadchestvo*, p. 95, where he cites figures of more than 300.000 for the sale and distribution of primers in the second half of the XVII century and some 150,000 for the readers and the Hours. He attributes it partly to cheap book prices, noting that a kopek often could buy a book. The first book store, incidentally, in Moscow, opened in 1672.

literacy and the following breakdown may be given of books published:[23]

	No.
1601-1620	23
1621-1630	45
1631-1640	71
1641-1650	74
1651-1660	62
1661-1670	45
1671-1680	33
1681-1690	63
1691-1700	69

It is curious that the number dips at the time of the ultimate ascendancy of the reformers though, of course, Nikon's striving for reform cannot really be seen as a regressive manifestation. Likewise, such elements as his refusal to ordain illiterates into the priesthood must be seen in this light.

Many of the books were religious and oriented towards the Church. Curious again is the fact that immediately after 1654, when the impetus for reform peaked, the majority of the books issued did not, as Professor Zenkovsky points out, contrive to fill out the list of volumes available to the Russian Church and the schools, but primarily replaced previous editions (that the reforms stated to be wrong!). This changed soon after though many of the published works were still religious in character. Much of the literate population was still Church connected and this is readily understandable historically.[24] But literacy rose, and with

23. Zenkovsky, *Staroobriadchestvo*; table taken from p. 93. Discussion of various aspects regarding publishing, pp. 91-95.

24. Zenkovsky, in citing statistics from Sobolevskii, gives the following figures: the "white clergy" — completely literate; "black clergy" — 75%; the dvoriane — 65-78%; the merchant class — 75-96%; the posadskie (generally towns-peple) — 16-43%, and the peasantry, abut 15% (all figures are for males). Zenkovsky, *Staroobriadchestvo*, p. 95.

it the variety of books, though such traditional forms as the compilation of chroniles continued late into the XVII century.

The people who owned books varied as to ccupation but the most educated and wealthy generally had the best collections. Among these were the okol'nichii Vasilii Sobakin, the boiar Bogdan Khitrovo (a personal friend of Tsar Aleksei), the princess Nastasia Vorotynskaia (whose collection was exclusively religious), Ordin-Nashchokin (of whom it is not surprising in that he knew Latin, German, and Polish), the boiar Matveev, Prince Golitsyn (who is shown in portraits with a book), and others. Men of lesser station with large collections were the voevoda of Mangazei, Andrei Palitsyn,[25] the diak (secretary) Ivan Timofeev, the diak Feodor Griboedov (who also wrote a short version of Russian history to his time in 36 chapters for which he received fifty rubles, forty sable furs, an atlas and other gifts from the Tsar) and others. Additionally there were the churchmen, especially Nikon, who had an extremely rich collection. Others were Metropolitan Paul of Sarsk and Podonsk, the Siberian Archbishop of Tobol'sk, Ignatii, the Metropolitan of Rostov, Dimitrii, the Archimandrite Afanasii of Kholmogorsk, the monk Eleazar of the Anzersk hermitage, the Moscow priest Vasilii (who owned 80 hand written manuscripts), and others.[26] And, it is said that the lower clergy also had a number of secular works.[27]

On a wider scale, libraries as such made their appearance in Russia at this time. The fact that the government was increasingly dependent on the literate, on the ability to gather facts, etc., was one of the fators that led to their growth. Another was the greater availability of and interest in books. This development

---

25. He was the nephew of the famed Avraamii Palitsyn who wrote his Skazaniia in Tsar Mikhail's reign.

26. The material in this paragraph is based on Slukhovskii, op. cit., pp. 104-09.

27. Slukhovskii, Ibid., p. 108, with attendant examples. The author also believes that the circle of readers and the thematics considered were higher than generally thought; pp. 109-10.

also aided in the process of gradually lessening Church guardianship of the written words.

Reflecting practical needs, many specialized "libraries" came into existence. A considerable number of these were centered in the Prikazy. The Pushkar'skii Prikaz (Artillery Department) had military books but also those dealing with surveying, geography, arithmetic, architecture. The Aptekar'skii Prikaz (Office or Department of Medicine) had a varied collection including works far removed from the apparent subject matter. The Posel'skii Prikaz (or Foreign Offie) had the most famous library. In our period, in 1673, it had 112 published and 6 manuscripts that were foreign, plus the Russian volumes. And it grew quickly by various means. When the boiar Matveev was exiled in 1677, seventy seven of his books, in many languages, were placed in this collection. Transfer of books from other departments was not uncommon. And Russian diplomats often sent or brought books with them from abroad, many prikazy being the grateful recipients. The so-called patriarchal collection (not to be confused with Nikon's private one) was also quite large in size. It was not connected specifically to a particular department but served as a repository of books for the Russian Church as a whole.[28] Perhaps the most positive element in regarding this development is the functional aspect of the books and the implicit and explicit understanding that they were ever increasingly used.

Foreign translations now began to make their way to Russian soil. Finally, after many years, many Western classics (Greek and Roman) came to be read (primarily in the late XVII.).[29] Increasing foreign contact and travel, combined with developments within the country, were the primary movers in this regard. The number of books translated were: years 1600-1650 — thirteen; in the second half of the century — one hundred

---

28. For detailed discussion of the points here mentioned on libraries and for extensive examples see Slukhovskii, op. cit., pp. 86-98.

29. Zenkovsky, *Epics*, p. 4.

fourteen (a huge jump), and of these only approximately one fourth dealt with religious topics.[30] This is considerably mitigated, however, by the fact that many of the works translated, and which found wide popularity were those that were essentially didactic and moralistic. Even thought many of these dealt (frequently satirically) with realistic situations concerning the life of townspeople, peasants, churchmen, and ladies of leisure, a moral was invariably drawn, frequently in religious terms.[31] Some of the more popular ones were such tracts as the "Velikoe Zertsalo" (a translation of the Latin "Speculum Magnum Exemplorum")[32] which was purely religious, the Acts of the Romans (which, in addition to many religious stories also included some from Roman times), and the facetiae (compilations from the Polish, of anecdotes, novellas, and satirical stories).

The position of the Church in all this cannot be brought down to mere formula. We have already cited examples of churchmen with extensive book collections. We should also note those who were negativistic in their approach to new works be they domestic or foreign. Such was the case of the work of Ioann Bleu (Johan Bleu?) on the heliocentric nature of the universe. This appeared in Moscow in the years 1655-57 (though only in manuscript form). The reaction was negative and, in general, was indicative of an anti-naturalistic approach. However, in other areas the West could make headway. A

---

30. Zenkovsky, *Staroobriadchestvo*, p. 254. In all of the XVI century 26 foreign books were translated into Russian.

31. Eleonskaia et. al., op. cit., pp. 203-12. See also the comments on some of the effects of this type of literature in later centuries. Vodovozov does the same in his work. His discussion of some of the various works produed in Russia in this period such as The Tale of Frol Skobeev, and The Tale of Savva Grudtsyn, is very fine; Vodovozov, op. cit., pp. 354ff. Also Zenkovsky, *Epis*, pp. 312ff. Of course, to get the truest flavor, the works themselves should be read.

32. The original of the "Speculum..." in Latin was written/compiled in 1481: The later edition (also in Latin) by the Jesuit Johann Maier, in 1605. The Poles made translations of it in 1621, 1628, 1633, and 1690-91. The Russian translation (1677) used the Polish edition of 1633; Eleonkaia et.al., op. cit., p. 204.

notable case is the usage of a Czech Bible to aid in the correction of the holy books. This Czech Bible had gradually come into Russia via Poland (one of the L'vov religious brotherhoods had it) and then Belorussia.[33] Several of the Moscow libraries did, in fact, have foreign Bibles (Latin, German, and Polish in the main), though this should not be surprising.

Within the Church hierarchy there were elements both reactionary and progressive and, when seen in terms of a transitional period such as this one was, it is not difficult to find examples of either. Certainly much of the controversy regarding the Old Believers versus the "reformers" can be viewed in this light and we shall see this further in the text. What is of moment, though, is to carefully take heed of Zenkovsky's observation that as the conservative Old Believers were gradually alienated from the Church hierarchy (and the State) the cause of the pure traditionalists within these circles weakened and diminished in influence. Thus, the cultural, government, and religious elites were, in the main, gradually left to the more progressive and Western orientated elements. The secularizaiton and the modernization of Russia was thereby facilitated.[34]

Simeon Polotskii (1629-80) was an intellectual and poet who could be held up as paradigm, a man whose work and career typified many contemporary developments.[35] In the least he was at the center of many intellectual movements in Moscow such as theater, the formation of a press in the Kremlin (1678) and the rise of poetry (for which in Russia he introduced the syllabic principle).

Polotskii was born in the Polish lands (city of Polotsk) and

33. A.V. Florovskii, 'Cheshkaia Bibliia v Russkoi Kul'tury i Pis'mennosti", *Sbornik Filologiky*. III. Trida Ceske Akademie Ved a Umeni. Svazek XII, 1940-46. pp. 164-65.

34. Zenkovsky, *Epics*, p. 31.

35. The facts of his life and activity are well known and available. For the reader's (brief) referene here, see: Eleonskaia et. al., op. cit., pp. 180-203; Vodovozov, op. cit., p. 324ff; Vernadsky, op. cit., V, part 2; etc., A good biography of Polotskii in English would be a welcome historiographic addition.

upon completion of his education, came east to Moscow. He soon made a name for himself due to his varied intellectual capacities. In 1667 he became tutor to the Tsar's children and, at the time of the Councils of 1666-67, made formal and official statements and attacks against the old belief. He even sparred verbally with Avvakum. His written work falls into three major categories:[36] a) homiletic and publicistic, b) poetic, and c) pedagogical treatises. He is the first poet in Russia to have had his verses published during his lifetime.

Much of his work is extremely moralistic; much of it is religious in character; much of it is also new for Russia. He was much concerned with the role of the ruler and his relationship to the people he governs and in many of his works (e.g. the poems "The Bishop" and 'Love for the Citizenry") he presented the image of an enlightened ruler. Much of the image was taken up with the concept (based on Classical and Byzantine models) of a proper and respectful attitude toward the Church. But, he was not one sided and satirized the ecclesiastical body when he saw fit. Thus, e.g., in the poem "The Monk" he scorned that clergy which was lecherous and drunken and which acted contrary to religious ideals.

Polotskii was also much concerned with furthering education. He headed the Zaikonospasskii School when it first opened in 1665 and also taught there.[37] He was aware of what was needed a further education and conscious of current inadequacies. He understood the necessity of knowing foreign languages and in a homily delivered in church on Dec. 25, 1667, uttered dismay at the

---

36. The categories may be further divided. For example, his poetry can be broken up into that dealing with sociopolitical themes, satires, the didactic, the reworking of legends, and the religious. However, since we are not presenting literary analysis as such, I have deemed such detail to be outside the scope of this work.

37. This school was at the Spasskii Monastery though its purpose was to train administrative personnel. In fact, the Church monopolized education and learning until Peter's time. Even the more famous Slavo-Greco-Latin Academy (inaugurated in 1687) had as its primary motif '...to strengthen the Orthodox faith and protect it". See Vernadsky, op. cit., V, part 2, p. 737.

negligent state of the Greek language in Russia. He stated that Greek had been the vehicle of the faith and that those dwelling in the West, even the enemies of Orthodoxy, highly esteemed the Greek tongue for the wisdom of it. In conclusion, he invoked the Church to create a school that would teach Greek, Slavonic, and other tongues.[38] This homily shows simultaneously Polotskii the religious defender and Polotskii the educator pressing for a new academy.

The XVII century is one where there appears a striving for a greater degree of secular knowledge even though this was opposed by the Zealots of Piety,[39] the Old Believers, and other groups. Avvakum railed against those interested in philosophy and astronomy and wrote diatribes against Plato, Aristotle, Diogenes, etc. And Patriarch Ioakim (1674-90 — Joachim) who wrote tracts against the Old Believers also waged a campaign against the Westernizing elements. He had serious disagreements with Polotskii on this score.[40] An Old Believer poem laments the new in the following (given literally, free verse):

"Oh what depravities upon the holy things,
Things have become as in Rome
Where can one run from the innovations,
Everywhere leadership has weakened,
Everywhere the old things grow cold...'[41]

---

38. Eleonskaia et.al., op. cit., pp. 184-85.

39. Not surprising for the Zealots of Piety were essentially concerned to enhance the prestige of the Church. In this they are to be commended (for their work in the 1630's and '40's) for many of their programs saw at least some measure of implementation. They wished to expand the publication of liturgical and devotional literature, impose stricter clerical discipline, popularize the sermon, urge morality, curtail the sale of liquor. How else could they look upon the growing secularization except with suspicion? Zenkovsky, *Staroobriadhestvo*, p. 8.

40. N.V. Ustiugov and N.S. Chaev, "Russkaia Tser'kov v XVII v." in: N.V. Ustiugov (ed.), *Russkoe Gosurdarstvo v XVII Veke* Moscow: 1961), pp. 324-25.

41. T.S. Rozhdestvenskii, "Pamiatniki Staroobriadcheskoi Poezii," in: *Zapiski Moskovskago Arkheologicheskago Instituta*, v. VI, 1910, XLI, poem #38. Hereafter cited Rozhdestvenskii.

But the tide was approaching irreversibly. The sands of Russian life were to be washed.

Some of the newer tendencies were also apparent in art. Harbingers of the new were such artists as Ushakov, Vladimirov, and Khitrovo. Simon Ushakov (1626-86) and Iosif Vladimirov were the authors of the first Russian treatises on the theory of art. Vladimirov's the *Poslanie...* was written in 1665-66;[42] Ushakov's in 1667. It is interesting that both essentially call for newer, more realistic forms in painting. Vladimirov recommends that man be drawn the way the artist sees him in life. These were not isolated artists but men who were in the forefront of Russian art. Ushakov headed the iconographic workshop at the Oruzheinaia Palata (Arms Hall or Armory) which was the center of Russian art in this period. Iconography was still the major concern and Ushakov himself was responsible for many beautiful icons. Even in the icons we have new elements such as the inclusion in icons of historial and political figures. And with the rise of more realistic depiction portraiture moves forward quickly and finds considerable interest and response.[43]

Little of this (or less than in other cases) is due to foreign influence for this seems to have been more of an indigenous development. It is claimed that the number of foreign artists (especially those not working in decoration) was incidental and that they could not have played a determining role; similarly that the pedagogical significance of the foreign artists has been overstated for not one Russian artist of the XVII century can be wholly classified a student of any of the foreign artists then working in the Oruzheinaia Palata.[44] (It should be pointed out

---

42. See the text of the tract in V.N. Lazarev, O.I. Podobedova, V.V. Kostochkin (ed's), *Drevne-Russkoe Iskusstvo XVII Vek* (Moscow: 1964), pp. 24-62. A discussion of the text precedes it and is by E.S. Ovchinnikova, pp. 9-24.

43. On Ushakov, Vladimirov, and other artists and artistic developments see, Ibid,; also, E.S. Ovchinnikova, *Portret v Russkom Iskusstve XVII Veka: Materialy i Issledovaniia* (Moscow: 1955), esp. pp. 14-24 and the plates in back; Eleonskaia et.al., op. cit., pp. 9-13; *Istoriia Russkago Iskusstva*, op. cit., pp. 146ff.

44. Ovchinnikova, op. cit., pp. 24-26.

that Vladimirov defended foreign artists and thought their lessons to be worthwhile). This is an interesting sidelight though our main concern is different — to show elements of change. Some of the evidence of change is indirect: the greater number of orders for portraits, the drop in the number of apprentie iconographers. More direct is the evidence of the work itself, the written material, the fact that by 1683 a separate school (or workshop) for painting (secular) also at the Oruzheinaia Palata, had come into existence.[45]

Certain specific pecularities in XVII century art may be cited and it will be seen how the new and the old intermix: 1) mixed techniques, i.e. iconographic and other painting methods used in the same work; 2) with the new portraiture and greater realism of the face, old compositional schemes were still used;[46] 3) the face would be realistic, but the feet and hands would be traditional, etc...[47]

Many similarly new developments also occurred in the field of ornamentation where foreign influene was more pronounced. "The years of Tsar Aleksei's reign left a noticeable effect on the development of Russian ornament. Not a little of it was facilitated by the building of a whole series of palaces in the kremlin and in the Moscow suburbs".[48] New developments (especially in the second half of the century) are also attested in architecture[49] and in music[50] which was expereincing the influence of the poly-

---

45. Ibid., pp. 26-31.

46. For example, a three-quarter head turn is shown whereas the body generally would be given frontally.

47. These and others are discussed in Ovchinnikova, op. cit., p. 58.

48. N.N. Sobolev, *Russkii Ornament* (Moscow: 1948), pp. 8-9. Also the plates in back.

49. Vodovozov, op. cit., p. 338; *Istoriia Russkago Iskusstva*, p. cit., pp. 126-67.

50. Billington, op. cit., p. 147; Eleonskaia et.al., op. cit., pp. 11-12; it is noted therein that music was becoming more secular in character and more interest was shown to secular music. Toward the end of the XVII c. a school of music was founded in which Western influence was substantial.

phonic baroque, but these are beyond our purview.

Much of the artistic work was directly connected to the government, whether to the art workshops of the Oruzheinaia Palata or the commissioning of artists. This was the case for all fields of artistic endeavor, from painting to the decorative arts. Many of the projects were large, such as those commissioned to the iconographic sections: The Uspenskii Cathedral in Moscow (1642-1644), the Church of the Savvino-Starozhevskii Monastery in Zvenigorod (1650), the Arkhangelskii Cathedral in Moscow (1652) and others. They would be worked on by a group of artists or a school, with the head artist doing the most demanding parts and supervising the rest. Smaller projects like portraits obviously demanded less manpower, even if they were elaborate iconographic types such as "The Tree of the State of Musovy" (painted in 1668 by Ushakov). Other famous examples are the portraits of Tsar Aleksei (1670 and 1671, the latter done from sittings) and many others.[51] These could be quite profitable to the artists. Remunerations of 100 rubles per assignment were not unknown. Other benefits could also accrue. The master Bezmin was granted entry into the ranks of the dvoriane in 1679 due to his talents.[52]

Commissions for works were not just governmental. Many of the richer nobility and merchants also commissioned paintings, carvings, and so forth, for our period witnessed a growth in the appreciation and collecting of art objects. It must also be remembered that not all the work was centered in Moscow. Provincial iconographic schools were not at all uncommon. There were treatises on the painting of icons. Among these was that by Nikodim Antoniev, a monk of the Monastery of Siisk

---

51. See Ovchinnikova, op. cit., thruout for listings and examples.

52. Ovchinnikova, op. cit., pp. 45-46. This same Bezmin was later exiled (in 1685). He had been ordered by the Tsaritsa (Nataliia Kirillovna Naryshkina) to go to her brother's house and to paint his son who had just died. Instead, he sent one of his students to do the job. Moreover, when it was finished, he took it to the Empress Sophia and stuck it in a store room. In 1690 he returned to his job at the Oruzheinaia Palata.

in the North. The northern school was strict — and Byzantine and old-Russian models occupied places of honor. But Niko-dim's treatise was not a call for the status quo; it was an example of why the progress of Russian art was not limited to the environs of Moscow.[53] Among other schools of iconography were the Novgorodian and the Stroganov.

This meant that the icon painters came from many areas. The Tsar's painters, so to speak, and the Oruzheinaia Palata never hesitated to go to the provinces to seek out and bring artists to Moscow. In 1668, Feodor Zubov was taken from Ustiug; in 1669 Vasilii Ivanov from Kholmogory; in 1668 Georgii Terentiev, a student of Ushakov but also a serf of Gavril Ostrovskii, was bought from his master for 100 rubles and made a chartered iconographer. He was to receive bread and money for his work plus daily food allowanes.[54] Others were hired contractually and released to their own towns when the job was completed. Still others, who worked on a full time basis, did not get bread and money on a yearly basis. But all of them received special awards for their namesdays and on holidays. In 1666, on Easter day, they were given "a bucket of wine, two buckets of beer, a ham, three slabs of corned beef, five tongues of beef, five pieces of goose meat, and a measure of wheat flour per man".[55] Special gifts like these

53. "Vypiski Nastavlenii o Tserkvakh Kamenykh i Drevianykh i o Ikonakh i o Reznitse i Knigokranitil'ne i o Prochikh Tserkovnykh Potrebakh", text # XVII in: *Pamiatniki Drevnei Pismennosti i Iskusstva*, #161. SPB: 1906, pp. 185-90. Nikodim began his compilation even before Ushakov. He made it a point to make sure that his own work and that of his predecessors was saved for future use. Coming from the same circle as Nikodim was Paisii, a master calligrapher, a man who was to become Patriarchal treasurer. He left as bequest to the Siisk Monastery four trunks. In the first was a gospel in Moroccan binding. Each page (934 in all) was decorated with miniatures in the border and with gold and other colors within the text. There were close to 3,000 drawings altogether. This is the famous *Gospel of Siisk* (see pp. 192-93).

54. D.A. Rovinskii, *Obozreniia Ikonopisaniia v Rossii do Kontsa XVII Veka* (SPB: 1903), pp. 43-47.

55. Ibid., pp. 46-47.

were also given at completion of projects or on special occasions such as the birth of a son to the Tsar.

Sometimes the iconographers were used for other work: they made plans of cities, did gravures, worked at the mint, and did many more things. The State utilized their talents where and when needed. For large projects, such as the work on the Uspenskii Cathedral, icon painters were called in from all Russia. After Moscow the following cities provided the most: Novgorod, Iaroslavl', Ustiug, Kostroma, Balakhna, Viazniki, Nizhnii-Novgorod, Rostov, Vologda, Romanov. In Iaroslavl' each monastery had its own iconographers and monasteries were a primary source over all. The Holy Trinity Monastery housed up to twenty men who were in some way connected to the production of icons.[56] Interestingly enough, the icon painters did not, as such, make up a separate class. They could be gardeners, serfs, gunners, clergy, or practically anything else.[57] This explains why it was so easy to use them in other capacities when necessary.

Within the Church itself (certainly in the hierarchy) there were trends that portended of change. It cannot be denied that more was discussed, more items brought to communal attention, more problems recognized. If such a thing as critical spirit can be defined in the circumstances, and can be instanced, then we can allege to its growth. The case of Anna of Kashin is a case in point.

In the early years of Tsar Aleksei's reign, in the town of Kashin, the Archbishop of Tver' (with the Tsar's permission) opened the coffin of the good lady Anna of Kashin, princess and wife of the Grand Prince Mikhail Iaroslavovieh of Tver' (himself a martyr). She had been dead 280 years but her body was recognized to be unspoiled. Soon the Tsar and Tsaritsa arrived in Kashin with their retinue and in triumphal procession Anna's coffin was transferred to the cathedral. She was soon canonized by

---

56. Ibid., pp. 47-48.
57. Ibid., pp. 49-52.

a sobor (council). By 1677, however, some doubts had crept in. The Church was not sure that her holiness and sainthood were properly attributed. A sobor convened by Patriarch Ioakim (Joachim) came to this conclusion and steps were taken to disallow veneration of her as a saint.[58] A later sobor (of 1679) followed in the footsteps of the first and basically upheld the resolutions.[59]

The case of Iushka Mikliaev has previously been cited (chapt. 3) and it is to be recalled that it dealt with a self-ordained priest. A council session that examined this case (and which had such figures as Patriarch Adrian, Metropolitan Iosif of Pskov and Izborsk, Archbishop Nikita of Kolomensk and Koshirsk — in addition to three foreign hierarchs from Greece, Serbia, and Georgia, though these happened to be in Moscow at the time and were not expressly called in for the trial) was especially concerned with the ramifications of illegally administered sacraments. The Moscow priest Andrei, one of the council members, did however, argue that some sacraments, such as baptism could be accepted in this case;[60] it was certainly an unusual pleading for the time.

An interesting by-product, which can at least partially be seen in terms of a greater critical spirit, were works in defense of the old belief. As the reform movement took on greater scope, the defenders of the old belief were continualy forced into presenting better reasoned and more detailed works. They had to counteract textual criticism (and reform) with textual criticism of their own.

---

58. Conclusions in this regard were based on textual evidence such as disparities between chronicle accounts and the Life of Anna of Kashin. One of the compilers of the Life, the diak Nikifor, even admitted that he based much on mere hearsay (for this he was sent to do penance to a monastery unto his dying days). Another participant also paid penalty. The sobor was likewise not sure whether the remains were actually hers. Aleksandra Dimitrieva, "Po Povodu Stat'i G'na Kostomarova: Tserkovno-Istoricheskaia Kritika v XVII Veke" ChOIDR, 1871, bk. 4, sect. 1, pp. 39-44.

59. See the text thereof: "Moskovskii Sobor o Zhitii Blagovernyia Anny Kashinskiia", ChOIDR, 1871, bk. 4, sect. 1, p. 45-62.

60. Nikolaevskii, Mikliaev, p. 6-8.

This was not something (excepting, to an extent, the previous cirle of the Zealots of Piety) that had been done seriously before. New, Old Believer writers such as Feoktist, Aleksandr of Kolomna, and others do this as a matter of course. Nikita Dobrynin of (Suzdal') dissects in detail all the changes in the texts and rituals brought about by the Nikonian corrections.[61] Such works were part of their defense of the old belief.

"In the system of the fundamental laws of the Ulozhenie the defense of Orthodoxy as the spiritual basis of the Tsardom of Muscovy was placed in the first plane — before the defense of State honor. On the other hand, the Church as organization was moved to a secondary plane when compared to the State and State authority. This was the natural result of boiar politics after the death of Patriarch Filaret".[62] And it resulted in the Monastyrskii Prikaz, formed in 1649.[63] In a disussion of Church and society, the Monastyrskii Prikaz is of moment for here is an example where the State takes active measure to limit the power of the Church. It did so by essentially placing all lay matters involving clergy (and their peasants) under the jurisdiction of lay courts.[64] There was outcry from the clergy and the more powerful were granted some dispensations. Most notable is that given to Nikon, then Metropolitan of Novgorod. He was vigorously opposed to this measure — and was given immunity in his whole eparhy (i.e. he had the right to retain as previously, the Church court in these matters). This privilege followed him to the Patriarchy.

_____

61. Zenkovsky,*Staroobriadchestvo*, pp. 262ff. Nevertheless, at this stage, the 'textual criticism" of the Old Believers was extremely polemical and not truly critical. Points which might contradict old belief views were not generally included, so the criticisms were narrowly focused.
62. G.V. Vernadsky, "Tser'kov i Gosudarstvo v Sisteme Sobornago Ulozheniia 1649 Goda", in: N.P. Poltoratzky and P.A. Sorokin (ed's.), *Na Temy Russkie i Obshchie* (New York: 1965), p. 85.
63. Lest there be confusion it should be noted that the Monastyrskii Prikaz was part of (i.e. written into) the Ulozhenie (or Code of Laws).
64. Gorchakov, *Monastyrskii Prikaz* pp. 69-72 and, in general thruout; Makarii, *Istoriia*, XII, pp. 227-28.

The Monastyrskii Prikaz was not formally to last long and the Council of 1667 revoked many of the stipulations. The Prikaz itself was abolished in 1676 but its effect did not suddenly become nugatory. From this time until Peter's Church measures, a state of flux existed. In 1697, practically on the eve (a three year eve be it) of Peter's initial moves vis a vis the Church, Patriarch Adrian issued an "Instruction to the Priestly Elders", reaffirming clerical immunity from civil jurisdiction. Yet, eparchial authorities still allowed lay participation; e.g., in 1697 and 1698, the civil authorities had to send a circular to Siberian towns instructing district governors to protect the populace from the aggressions of the Metropolitan's "boiarskie deti" (lesser gentry), who were disrespectful in their behavior to women (using the excuse of investigating adultery) and who also bled money from the people.[65] Paper pronouncements were not always immediately translatable into reality, even twenty years after the fact.

Church and society, continued to intertwine, though separate developments and more delineated paths for each began to be charted. Increasing secularization was a fact not to be denied whether in the rise of drama, of non-religious and more technical interests, or the search for books in the West under the aegis of the Russian State.[66] The still overwhelming impact of religion and the Church, however, whether seen microcosmically in, e.g., cases of asking permission to marry from archimandrites,[67] or macrocosmically in the nationwide ramifications of the Old Believer movement and its multiple attendant discords, cannot be denied. The land which saw a greater number of Europeans admitted into the dvorianstvo during Tsar Aleksei's reign[68] also was the land where the Tsar still used much religious language in the seemingly purely civil honor of granting entry into the ranks of the "dumnye dvoriane," (dvoriane who were members of

65. Gorchakov, *Monastyrskii Prikaz*,pp.95-98.
66. For the latter part see Slukhovskii, op. cit., p. 110.
67. Dobroklonskii, op. cit., *ChOIDR*, 1888, bk. 1, sect. 1, pt. 3, pp. 121-24.
68. Andreev, op. cit., p. 14.

the boiar duma). The case of A.L. Ordin-Nashchokin is descriptive. "We the great ruler have granted thee, Afanasii, for your many services to us, that you, remembering God and His holy commandments, feed the indigent, give drink to the thirsty, clothe the poor, give shelter to the traveler, attend the sick, visit the jails, and that you wash the feet (of your fellow man, symbolically speaking — author's note), and that you perform dutifully your oath to us, and that you attend to our (i.e. the State's — N.L.) matters bravely and with manliness... entry into the dumnye dvoriane".[69]

These contradictive elements point again to flux, to a change in society's mode of life, to new currents constantly surfacing. If it is not stretching the point, perhaps it might be advantageous to set up an analytical framework and view this century in terms of the penetration of humanistic ideas (readily done for literature) or, at least, in the similarities of the seeking of the new in Russia and outside its borders.[70] I suspect more clarification than obfuscation will result, though to view it as an absolute key is to be far off the mark.

69. "Gramota Tsaria Alekseia Mikhailovicha A.L. Ordinu-Nashchokinu o Pozhalovanii Ego v Dumnye Dvoriane", *ChOIDR*, 1896, bk. 3, pt. V, p. 32.
70. See the judiciously suggestive article of M.P. Alekseev, "Iavleniia Gumanizma v Literature i Publitsistike Drevnei Rusi XVI—XVII vv." in: A.N. Robinson (ed.), *Issledovaniia po Slavianskomu Literaturovedeniiu i Folkloristike* (Moscow: 1960), pp. 180ff.

Chapter 5

Patriarch Nikon

In a life of Patriarch Nikon (written no earlier than 1731) the author of the tract "wonders how such a nasty individual could attain such a high position..."[1] and goes on to portray Nikon as a beast. The boiar Streshnev, an opponent of the Patriarch, despised him enough to call his dog "Nikon".[2] The head of the Russian Church was accused of taking bribes, of beating the clergy, of being a heretic (by the ludicrous assertion of Avvakum that he had the cross sewn on the sole of one shoe and the image of the Virgin Mary on the other)[3] and a plain robber.[4] The list

---

1. Nikanor, "Povest' o Rozhdenii i Vospitanii i o Zhitii i Konchine Nikona, Byvshago Patriarkha Moskovskago i Vseia Rossii", in: *Opisanie Nekotorykh Sochinenii Napisanykh Russkimi Raskol'nikami v Pol'zu Raskola* (SPB: 1861), p. 186. This life of Nikon is incomplete and full or error, in addition to serving as a diatribe. Even basic biographical facts are frequently false.
2. "Pis'mo Patriarkha Nikona k Tsar'gradskomu Patriarkhu Dionisiiu (1666 G.)", in: *Zapiski Otdela Russkoi i Slavianskoi Arkheologii Imperatorskago Russkago Arkheologicheskago Obshchestva* (ZORSA), v. II, 1861, pp. 527-28. For this Streshnev was damned and excommunicated by Nikon (but ineffectually). Also, Andreev, op, cit., p. 56.
3. The charges, cited respectively, in Andreev, op. cit., pp. 53, 56, 71. Other "charges" to be seen in S. Maksimov, *Razskazy iz Istorii Staroobriadstva Po Raskol'nich'im Rukopisiam* (SPB: 1861), pp. 12, 14, and throughout.
4. "Oblichenie na Nikona Patriarkha, Napisannoe Dlia Tsaria Alekseia Mikhailovicha", in: *Letopisi Russkoi Literatury i Drevnosti* (Moscow: 1863) vol. V, part 2, pp. 158-159.

could be worthlessly extended though the degree of hate Nikon engendered in his opponents is clear enough. It might not be worth mentioning except that it is an inescapable conclusion that personal animosities played perhaps a disproportionate role in this period, when spirits of excessive ardor, passion, and hate sharpened the scythe that reaped discord.

These were the detractors. The supporters were often as adamant in support, citing Nikon's great intelligence, his fairness, his ultimate rectitude as assets not to be denied by vituperations. There is more than one note of his alleged miraculous and healing powers[5] (perhaps not surprisingly arising during his period of exile), certainly the other extreme of the callous heretic. It was easier for his contemporaries to have extreme views of Nikon and it is the historian's task to strike a balance. Even so, strong judgements are not unusual and Zernov compares Nikon only to Peter the Great in terms of effect on Russian history.[6]

Nikon was born of peasant stock in the village of Val'demanov in the area of Nizhnii-Novgorod in 1605. At the age of twelve he left home to enter a monastery (leaving his stepmother's house). At the age of twenty he left the monastery, not yet having taken the vows, married, and soon was ordained a priest and received a parish. The parish was in the village of Lyskov. The trading fairs of a neighboring village, Makar'evo, on the left bank of the Volga were attended by many Moscow merchants. Nikon had become known, and they facilitated his transfer to Moscow. By 1634, after having served for ten years in Moscow, he and his wife took monastics vows, partly motivated by the sudden death of their three sons. Nikon chose the Anzerskii "skit" (hermitage) and there he remained in solitude for several

5. V.I. Savva, "Ob Odnom iz Spiskov Zhitiia Patriarkha Nikona", *ChOIDR*, 1909, bk. 3, pt. 4, p. 13. For another exalted view see Ia. L. Barskov (ed.), "Pamiatniki Pervykh Let Russkago Staroobriadchestva", in: *Letopis' Zaniatii Imperatorskoi Arkheograficheskoi Kommissii za 1911 God.* (SPB: 1912, vol. 24), part 6, #1, p. 1-6.

6. Zernov, op. cit., pp. 63-64.

years. After some misunderstandings with his fellow monks[7] he left this hermitage to join another, the Kozheozersk (as the Anzersk, on the White Sea). Here he was soon elected hegumen and proved himself an able administrator while, as at Anzersk, continuing his very strict ascetic and religious regimen. As before, he also continued his extensive readings. When business demanded his presence in Moscow in 1646 some of his reputation had already preceded him. The confessor of the Tsar, Archpriest Stefan Vonifatiev presented him to Aleksei and both were impressed by the new man. They made him archimandrite of the Novo-Spasskii Monastery in Moscow. It was the burial place of the Romanovs, was often attended by the Tsar and his retinue, so frequency of contact was sought and inevitable. The two became close friends, despite their disparity in age, though it is generally conceded that Nikon's function was also, though not expressly, that of tutor, guide and consultant. When the see of the Metropolinate of Novgorod became vacant in 1649, Nikon was the one and logical choice to accede to this signigicant post.[8] From this moment on his and Russia's destinies were intermingled in a way not yet clear, not yet expected. Just three years hence Nikon was to assume the Patriarchate of Moscow, The Third Rome, and neither the Patriarchate, nor The Third Rome, nor for that matter, the body politic, would ever be the same.

Nikon's rule over the Novgorodian eparchy was highly successful, highly dynamic, and highly efficient. He firmly engrained himself in the esteem of the Tsar, Vonifatiev, and others whose say in Church affairs had weight. Before considering his ascendancy to the Patriarchy in 1652 it should be observed that by 1652, Nikon was already well formed in his

---

7. Andreev, op. cit., p. 46.

8. These general biographical facts are widely known. For some reference, however, see Zenkovsky, *Staroobriadchestvo*, pp. 108-10; Vernadsky, op. cit., V, part 2, p. 557-62; A.V. Kartashev, *Ocherki Po Istorii Russkoi Tserkvi* (Paris: 1959), vol. I, pp. 133-35.

views and policies. He was protective of the Church and quite impatient with any hint of encroachment. For this he drew the enmity of the boiars who, since the death of Patriarch Filaret were pursuing a policy of forestalling any further intervention of the Patriarchy into state affairs. They wished to take measures to gradually establish certain controls over ecclesiastical administration and courts.[9] They succeeded in considerable degree with The Code of Laws (Ulozhenie) of 1649 and Nikon penned attacks on Prince Odoevskii, a principal mover behind this. Yet, Nikon already showed his adamancy in requesting, and getting approval from the Tsar for exemption. This actually occurred even prior to his ordination as Metropolitan of Novgorod. "Before he would accept ordination, Nikon asked the Tsar to exempt the diocese from the regulation of the new Code of Laws which subjected the population of the church and monastery lands to the newly created Monastery Department (Monastyrskii Prikaz) and the clergy to the lay courts. The Tsar granted the exemption, and Nikon was ordained".[10] This shows the great degree of faith in Nikon by Tsar Aleksei and the depth of the relationship may be gleaned from the Tsar's letters to Nikon. He speaks kindly, gently, humbly and solicits the prayers of the strong metropolitan.[11] The enmity of the boiars was relegated to the background with the Tsar's support, a situation that would change drastically in less than a decade.

Nikon firmly believed in the traditional educational functions of the bishopric and strove to implement many of the measures advocated and pushed through by the Zealots of Piety. In fact, he himself was an adherent of this group and enjoyed

9. Vernadsky, "Tser'kov i Gosudarstvo..." (Poltoratzky & Sorokin, ed's), op. cit., pp. 84-85.

10. Vernadsky, op. cit., V, part 2, p. 560.

11. *Sobranie Pisem Tsaria Alekseia Mikhailovicha*, op. cit., pp. 210-12 is one good example; given and discussed in English in N. Lupinin, "A Letter from Tsar Aleksei to Nikon: Commentary and Translation", *Trans. Rus.-Amer. Scholars*, V, 1971, pp. 184-87.

their support. It is one of the major ironies of this period that two parties initially so closely aligned could break so decisively and cause irreparable rupture. This will be touched upon later.

Here, it is necessary to note Nikon's attitude to Church and State. His refusal to accept the provisions of the Ulozhenie is evidence of his unwillingness to have the State dictate any Church affairs. He believed in the Byzantine notion of the dyarchy (as, e.g. expressed in the Epanagoge of the IX c.), a symphony of the temporal and clerical spheres, where the two would be supreme in their own spheres. It is, however, rather common (and correct) to view him as a theocrat; more as a Medieval Pope with the attendant notions of the supremacy of Church vs. State.[12]

The difference in interpretation arises legitimately, partly because of Nikon's later dominance, partly because of the development of his more far-reaching and grandiose concepts. These dealt with the role of the Russian Church in the whole Orthodox world. Somewhere in his studies and meditations (and, it is generally conceded, perhaps with the prompting of the Patriarch Paisios of Jerusalem, who, while in Moscow in 1649, met frequently with Nikon), Nikon came to view the role of the Russian Church as paramount in the Orthodox sphere. He was not narrowly nationalistic and, as Zenkovsky observes, his actions as Patriarch were to be stimulated by a deep feeling

---

12. This is frequently stated. Zenkovsky, *Staroobriadchestvo*, pp. 227ff; S. Runciman, *The Great Church in Captivity* (Cambridge: Cambridge University Press, 1968), p. 336, states Nikon's kinship to the Medieval Papacy as being closer than that of Byzantium's; very insistent re this is the somewhat tendentious work of N.A. Kapterev, *Patriarkh Nikon i Tsar' Aleksei Mikhailovich* (Sv. Troitskaia Sergievskaia Lavra, 1909-12, 2 vol.) Also Serge Bolshakoff, *Russian Nonconformity* (Philadelphia: The Westminister Press, 1950) who stated, p. 53, that Nikon "looked upon the patriarchal power with the eyes of a medieval pope". Others believe that, in the absence of indisputable evidence, Nikon was an adherent of the notion of the symphony of powers. For this, see Vernadsky, op. cit., V., part 2, pp. 56-61; Zʸ⁻' in, op. cit., 1, pp. 7-11, & passim.

of responsibility for Orthodoxy beyond Russian boundaries.[13] He would consider other Orthodox within the context of Russian involvement and it is frequently suggested that the urgency of his reforms, aside from the question of correction and cleansing ritual from accrued obfuscations, are partly explainable in this light. It would be difficult to participate in aiding the Greek Church, for example, if there were major disparities between the Russian and the Greek Church. On a less ecumenical level, it is under Nikon, as Makarii notes, that the unification of the Western (Kiev) and the Eastern (Moscow) parts of the Russian Church commences.[14]

When Patriarch Iosif died in April, 1652, the Tsar's choice to fill the vacancy was Nikon. The only other candidate was the gentle Vonifatiev who had the support of the Zealots of Piety. However, Vonifatiev refused the candidacy and Nikon was left as sole candidate.[15] This time, as at his ordination as Metropolitan of Novgorod, Nikon again refused the office pending acceptance of his demands. He wished, upon returning to Moscow, (on July 6, 1652; he had been on the forementioned trip for the relics from the Solovetskii Monastery) that before he would consent to the Patriarchy, the Tsar, boiars, and the people would swear allegiance to him in all ecclesiastical matters, that he be, in a word, granted full power in his sphere.[16] Only after the assembly convened for the election did

---

13. Zenkovsky, *Staroobriadchestvo*, pp. 197-98. He draws a parallel between Nikon's views and those of Boris Godunov who, when still a regent pointed to Moscow's universal role in the matter of protecting the Orthodox world. Godunov supported the Eastern Patriarchs and in the 1590's moved forces to protect Georgia against the Muslims. Interestingly, Polotskii entertained notions of freeing the Eastern Christians; Vodovozov, op. cit., pp. 341-43.

14. Makarii, *Istoriia*, XII, pp. 9-10.

15. Once Vonifatiev removed himself from consideration the Zealots supported Nikon. Even Avvakum, later to be an implacable and fierce enemy, did so.

16. S.M. Solovier, *Istoriia Rossii s Drevneishikh Vremen* (Moscow: 1959-66, 29 vol. in 15 books), X, p. 523.

so swear did he accept, again with a precondition. Nikon's authority was not to be doubted.

Nikon, now Patriarch, continued to retain privileges previously obtained. For now, in the vast Patriarchal domain, as in the Novgorodian when he was Metropolitan, the clergy and people belonging to the Church were exempt from the jurisdiction of lay courts. He was also immune to that section of the Ulozhenie which forbid the hierarchy (and the Church) further acquisition of immovable property. Nikon was allowed to buy whatever votchinas (hereditary properties) he wished and did so when he wished.[17] This exemption from the general laws enabled Nikon to greatly indulge in his passion for building. He himself was responsible not only (among major projects) for a new Patriarchal palace (to enhance Patriarchal prestige), but for three new monasteries. One, the Iverskii, was completed in 1656 and became very rich. The second, the Monastery of the Cross, the Krestnyi, (like all three, with a stone church), near Lake Onega, had by 1661, become the third richest in the North. And the third, the Novo-Ierusalimskii, forty-five versts from Moscow and on the land of a village (the Voskresenskii) bought by Nikon from the boiar Roman Bobarykin for 2,000 rubles, also became quite wealthy.[18] The monasteries belonged (formally) to him personally.

Nikon, as Patriarch, if anything, increased in his autocratic ways though it might be said he was generally fair. He applied to himself the strictures he expected others to adhere to[19] and was not the type to gather about him cliques and favorites[20]

---

17. Regarding some of these privileges, see Gorchakov, *Monastyrskii Prikaz*, pp. 53ff, 69, 89-91; also, Makarii, *Istoriia*, XII, p. 247.

18. Makarii, *Istoriia*, XII, pp. 247-63.

19. This is admitted even by writers generally anti-Nikonian, e.g. Andreev, op. cit., p. 65.

20. N.A. Gibbenet, "Patriarkh Nikon po Vnov Otkrytym Materialam", *Russkaia Starina*, vol. 43, Aug., p. 254. Hereafter cited Gibbenet, Patriarkh Nikon.

even though he understood intrigues against him. In this there is a basic honesty and pride in the man. He continued in a high-handed manner against the boiars, a personal policy it may be said, that was not far sighted. He was overbearing to much of the higher clergy, something that was even apparent to foreign observers such as Paul of Aleppo.[21] Sometimes this attitude led to unnecessary arbitrariness as when Nikon burned a shipment of musical instruments destined for the boiars.[22] Another example is the raids he authorized (late 1654, early 1655) on the homes of the higher circles in order to confiscate "Frankish" icons, i.e. those of newer, more Western iconographic methods.

Such actions were not likely to ingratiate him in the eyes of the nobility. It was galling enough that in the Tsar's absence it was Nikon who received ambassadors, took care of affairs of State, and served as regent. He increased the role of the Patriarchate to a position the boiars, after Filaret, had hoped never again to countenance. He even presided over the boiar duma in the Tsar's absence.[23] With him, the practice of calling the Patriarch "most holy" began and he was now the Patriarch of Great, Little and White Russia. Meanwhile, he maintained his pressure on the lower clergy to improve themselves morally so people could respect them, to observe the requirements of the Church and its calling, to refrain from wandering. He took punitive measures at reports of poor behavior and wrong doing.[24]

Of course, the upper clergy took its share of punishment (as will be especially seen in the fate of some of the opposition to the reforms). Sometimes it was in behalf of others that Nikon intervened. The Archbishop of Siberia, Simeon, was forbidden to serve one year (1656-57) for his unfair damning of one diak and for his cruel attitude to the son of the boiar Beketov.[25] The

---

21. Paul of Aleppo, pp. 34-35.
22. Andreev, op. cit., p. 50.
23. Bolshakoff, op. cit., p. 53.
24. A. Shchapov, *Russkii Raskol Staroobriadchestva* (Kazan': 1859), p. 63.
25. Makarii, *Istoriia*, XII, pp. 299-300.

elders of the Solovetskii Monastery, Gerasim and Iona, were sent by Nikon to the Korel'skii Monastery because of certain excesses. Nikon ordered that "they be held under strong guard", be assigned manual labor, and not be allowed to leave the monastery.[26] Generally, Nikon tried to support the clergy and, in some degree, during his rule, freed them from lay control. But this was not permanent and was further injured by the autcratic flaws in Nikon's own character. As the Metropolitan Makarii noted: "Unfortunately, in Church matters, having granted the diocesan bishops a measure of independence from civil rule, Nikon used the very same lay powers to subject them to his own rule and thereby still further violate their rights in their own eparchies".[27] The general characterization of Nikon as administrator, given by Gibbenet, is one of strictness. As a human he is shown to be kind, without guile, plain. He was proud, cognizant of his intelligence and aware of his moral superiority.[28] It is not a characterization leading to uniform portrayal.

Nikon began his patriarchate energetically, setting into motion numerous measures designed to improve the state of the Church and the people. He pushed through and implemented a plan to decrease the sale of alcohol and, thus, to combat drunkenness. There were limits placed on the intermingling of non-Orthodox foreigners with the Muscovites. Western influences in iconography were fought. Edinoglasie continued to be upheld.[29] He elaborated church ceremonials, processions, and the patriarchal function therein. Kievan church melodies were

---

26. "Gramota Patriarkha Nikona v Korel'skii Monastyr' o Prisylke Tuda Pod Nachal, za Bezhinstvo, Solovetskikh Startsev Gerasima i Iony", *RIB*, XIV, col. 414-15.

27. Ibid., p. 267.

28. Gibbenet, *Patriarkh Nikon*, p. 254.

29. Edinoglasie is the term referring to the measure, passed in February 1651, under Patriarch Iosif, but with Nikon's active prodding, forbidding more than a single prayer to be read or chanted at a liturgy at one time. Previously, several could be read simultaneously by different clerics with the result of garbling the service. Gibbenet, *Patriarkh Nikon*, p. 224.

introduced.[30] But most important were the reforms. These occurred on two levels, that of correcting the church books (to bring them in line with Greek practice) and changes in ritual as first appearing in the Psalter (published February, 1653) and followed by a circular later that month. The changes were two, as follows: "The new form of making the sign of the cross, (troeperstie i.e. by means of three fingers, not two) was prescribed for all, and the number of genuflections in Ephraim the Syrian's prayer was reduced to four".[31] (We shall view both levels in more detail in chapter 7). Here it is imperative to note Nikon's abrupt way of forcing change and the ire it drew. The Zealots, who had supported him were now his enemies, as if it were not enough to have the boiar faction constantly, and ever more effectively, scheming against him. An interesting sidelight to the Nikonian reforms is the number of books deemed necessary to serve as guides for the proper collation of the texts. Many monasteries, especially those such as the Kirillo-Belozerskii that had sizeable collections, were required to submit many of their books to the patriarchal offices. This had the dual effect of furthering two developing processes in Muscovy; the increasing exchange of books, and the sifting out and "cataloging" of extant collections.[32] This process of wholesale solicitation of books for a specific purpose was again repeated in the early 1680's. At that time the goal was to collect sufficient materials to aid versus the many antischismatic tracts that were then being produced.

In the second part of Nikon's rule, 1655-58 (there had been a tacit agreement between Nikon and the Tsar in 1652 that Nikon serve three years and then, pending the cooperation and obedience to his dictates, he would decide on continuing his reign; Nikon decided on another three years), the rumblings and

---

30. For a fine summation of these see Vernadsky, op. cit., V, part w, pp. 56-74.

31. Ibid., p. 570.

32. Slukhovskii, op. cit., pp. 91, 96ff, 112-113.

dissatisfactions grew louder as the boiars, with a series, ever more insistent and prolonged, of complaints against Nikon, more often than not engendered by his activity within the State apparatus, tried to seal the Tsar from the Patriarch. They began to make their point[33] and Aleksei himself, more mature due to personal involvement and command in two wars (with Poland 1654-55, with Sweden 1656) was less inclined to take constant heed of the Patriarch's counsel. This is a period of cooling in their relationship, less a case of major confrontations but more a series of small, constant misunderstandings and, on the Tsar's part, positional realignment. One major case may, however, be cited. This concerned the 1657 death of Sil'vester, Metropolitan of Kiev. The Ukraine, now having become a part of Russia, it was thought appropriate by the Tsar, the boiars, and a number of the Ukrainian hierarchy to install a candidate acceptable to the Tsar. Nikon, however, refused to ordain the man without prior agreement from the Patriarch of Constantinople. The Kievan see was still, ostensibly, under Constantinople's jurisdiction, and Nikon refused to act counter to the canons. For a man, who, as has been stated, "in spite of his dictatorial instincts, was consistently anxious to present his reforms as an expression of the mind of the entire Orthodox Church and not of the Russian hierarchy alone"[34] this was a step in keeping with his principles. For the Tsar (and the boiars) it was another step ultimately indicative of insubordination, of inordinate stubbornness. For Nikon, even Nikon, who was, as we are reminded, ultimately dependent on the Tsar's good will,[35] it was another omen of the erosion gradually working at the patriarchal crest.

---

33. Gibbenet feels these constant boiar attacks against Nikon were, in fact, the first causes of the growing rift between Tsar and Patriarch. N. Gibbenet, *Istoricheskoe Izsledovanie Dela Patriarkha Nikona* (SPB: 1882-84, 3 vol.) I, P. 25, thereafter cited Gibbenet, *Izsledovanie*.

34. Frederick C. Conybeare, *Russian Dissenters* (Cambridge: Harvard University Press, 1921, Harvard Theological Studies, X), p. 56.

35. Makarii, *Istoriia*, XII, p. 306.

In July, 1658, when Nikon left the patriarchal seat in a dispute, we see how the Tsar's will fails Nikon. On July 6, 1658 the Georgian prince Teimuraz came to visit Russia and was met by large crowds of people. In the tumult one of Nikon's men, Prince Meshcherskii was struck by the okol'nichii, Bogdan Khitrovo, one of the Tsar's men. When Meshcherskii complained to Nikon he sent a protest to the Tsar, demanding redress for the grievance, but this this was not forthcoming.[36] On July 8, on the feast of the Miracle Working Icon of Our Lady of Kazan', the Tsar did not appear at the service, thus breaking normal precedent for this feast. When Nikon invited him to appear at another Church feast on July 10, the Tsar again refused to come[37] and Nikon decided on a bold measure. He took off his patriarchal robes, donned monk's garments and prepared to leave the cathedral. The people were shocked and begged Nikon to stay, preventing him from leaving. When he did, later in the day, manage to leave, he left for the Voskresenskii Monastery where he was to stay, probably longer than he expected and where he soon immersed himself in the building of the monastery.[38] There are differences of opinion among contemporaries as to Nikon's alleged terminology in announcing his withdrawal. Metropolitan Pitirim of Krutitsk, the Archbishop Iosaf of Tver', and Prince Trubetskoi differ in their stories, especially regarding the question whether Nikon had promised not to return to the Patriarchy.[39] Nikon, in fact, had not renounced or abdicated the patriarchal seat and this was

36. This was all the more galling in that Nikon also had not been invited to the festivities in honor of Teimuraz.

37. In refusing to come at this stage he sent the boiar Romadonovskii, who brought with him the Tsar's complaint that Nikon improperly used the appellation "Great Sovereign" and thus drew the Tsar's ire. Nikon replied, correctly, that this had not been instituted by him but was a title, in fact, granted to him by the Tsar back in 1653. For this reason he had used it regularly.

38. For the best treatment of the immediate circumstances of Nikon's withdrawal see Gibbenet, *Izsledovanie*, I, pp. 26-35.

39. Gibbenet, *Patriarkh Nikon*, pp. 229-30.

duly recognized by the Tsar and all officialdom. Otherwise, there would have been no need for a whole series of attempts to formally depose Nikon, a deposition effected only at the Council of 1666. One other thing must be recognized: the boiars and the Tsar's retinue, in that brief five day flurry of July 6-10, successfully forestalled any possible personal meeting of Tsar and Patriarch. They greatly feared even a hint of reconciliation, certainly a distinct possibility in view of the long friendship between the two. Even a foreign observer noted how gradually, by the efforts of others, Aleksei's "heart was long since gradually being cooled toward Nikon". He notes that the courtiers had so surrounded Aleksei that he was practically inaccessible.[40]

From this point, Nikon's relations to the Tsar were dualistic, sometimes adamant, sometimes solicituous of aid.[41] In essence, it mattered little for the Tsar was not now willing to change and, as time went on, was ever more desirous of disposing of the matter by somehow legally eradicating Nikon's still extant claim to the Patriarchy. Much effort was therefore geared in this direction.

Without going into minute detail and looking analytically Nikon was now subjected to steady harassment. He was visited by court officials and conversations were held attempting to entrap him by hoping to elicit an inadvertent admission to the effect that he had refused the Patriarchy as a future consideration. Visits by others were forbidden and in 1663 he was placed under house arrest. His personal belongings were impounded and a complete inventory made. It is a fascinating item for over 1,000 books (many in Latin and Greek) are listed.[42] No incri-

40. "Puteshestvie v Moskoviu Barona Avgustina Meierberga", *ChOIDR*, 1874, No. 1, sect. IV, p. 171.

41. Ustiugov & Chaev in: Ustiugov (ed.), op. cit., p. 319.

42. "Perepisnaia Kniga Domovoi Kazny Patriarkha Nikona, Sostavlennaia v 7166 Godu po Poveleniiu Tsaria Alekseia Mikhailovicha", *Vremennik Imperatorskogo Moskovskago Obshchestva Istorii i Drevnostei Rossiiskikh*, No. 15, 1852, pp. 1-134. The lists of books are given on pp. 8-15, 79-82, 117-32.

minating evidence was found. He does write the Tsar from time to time as in 1662 in an effort at reconciliation.[43] It does not work.

More serious and more dramatic were his occasional ventures into Moscow, none advertised aforetime. These occur in 1659, 1662, 1664. The latter actually saw Nikon in the cathedral, attempting to officiate, but forced out by the Tsar's officials once they had heard the news. The news had spread with the quickness of a Moscow fire, and the Tsar acquiesced in reminding Nikon that his place was no longer in the capital. The boiar Ziuzin, one of the few who were pro-Nikon, had summoned him to Moscow this time, evidently feeling the moment propitious for such a move. But Ziuzin paid for his misguided interest by being sentenced and exiled. His wife died from the tribulations and trials.[44]

Serious, likewise, was the sobor of 1660, undertaken to depose Nikon. It was thought to depose him as Patriarch or defrock him as bishop or even thirdly, to forgive him because in leaving the Patriarchy he sinned as a man, and did not sin against the dogmas of the faith. In the end it was decided to depose him as Patriarch and cancel his priestly calling but neither was done. The rules did not allow for a Patriarch to be judged by subordinate and lesser clergy. Other hierarchs of similar stature had to be present.[45] To allow for the implementation of this clause, it was decided (in 1662) that a wider council, to include patriarchs from the Near East, be held.

---

43. Gibbenet, *Patriarkh Nikon*, p. 237.

44. This episode is detailed in Gibbenet, *Izsledovanie*, II, pp 114-141. Ziuzin had kept Nikon abreast of various developments in Moscow since Nikon's departure. See a letter from Nikon to Ziuzin: *ZORSA*, v. 2, 1861, pp. 581-90.

45. This sobor is discussed more fully in Gibbenet, *Izsledovanie*, I, p. 69-89. In addition to the Tsar, the more important churchmen present were the Metropolitans Makarii of Novgorod, Lavrentii of Kazan', Iona of Rostov, Pitirim of Sarsk, Michael of Greece and Archbishops Markel of Vologda and Filaret of Smolensk.

Originally scheduled for the following year (1663) it did not convene until 1666. Insofar as the election of a new Patriarch was concerned, Nikon maintained that he was not averse to it, provided he was privy to the process of selection. He claimed that any election of a new Patriarch without his blessing and approval would be invalid.

At this time too, the boiars and other opponents felt free to charge Nikon with numerous wrongdoings. The boiar Bobarykin complained of Nikon's alleged misdemeanors regarding certain land problems. When the complaint was dismissed in court, he claimed that Nikon had **defamed** the Tsar.[46] The boiar Sytin filed charges against the peasants of the Voskresenskii Monastery (Nikon's) but that, too, came to naught.[47] The hounds, seeing the game at bay, barked ever more fiercely, but the game proved resilient and fraudulent grievances drew no retribution.

More subtle were the methods employed by the journeying prelate, Paisios Ligarides who was residing in Moscow. Though a scholar, and ironically one who was invited to Moscow by Nikon himself in 1657, Ligarides was a totally undependable man. Bolshakoff describes him well: "A clever but utterly unscrupulous Greek adventurer, Paisios, Metropolitan of Gaza in Palestine, who was sometimes an Orthodox and sometimes a Uniate, became the Tsar's chief adviser in the Nikon affair".[48] It

46. Gibbenet, *Patriarkh Nikon*, p. 238.

47. The text of this petition in *ZORSA*, v. 2, 1861, pp. 530-81. Both Bobarykin and Sytin also, incredibly, accused Nikon of conspiring to murder; Gibbenet, *Izsledovanie*, pp. 99ff.

48. Bolshakoff, op. cit., p. 54. Briefly, Ligarides' background is: born in Chios, 1612. Studied in Rome (St. Athanasius College founded by Gregory XIII for Uniate Greeks) from 1625-36, graduating with top honors. In 1641, sent to Constantinople as a missionary by the Congregation of Propaganda. Left Constantinople 1644 because of complaints of the Patriarch. Went to Moldavia. Admitted into Orthodoxy 1651 by Paisios, Patriarch of Jerusalem and ordained as Metropolitan of Gaza in 1652. Never went to diocese. When Nikon sent the invitation in 1657, Ligarides was in Wallachia, still sendig reports to the Congregation of Propaganda and drawing salary from it. See Vernadsky, op. cit., V, part 2, pp. 589-90.

is not clear how he ingratiated himself with the Tsar so quickly, but his immediate assumption of an anti-Nikonian stance helped immeasurably. With the boiar Streshnev he formulated a series of questions such that Nikon would be incriminated.[49] This was done on the supposition that Nikon's answers would prove to be self-incriminating. In regarding the questions, Ligarides judged Nikon guilty on all counts. He was also a chief proponent for the invocation of a new council, a measure decided upon by Aleksei in December, 1662, and for consulting with the Near Eastern patriarchs. When the Russians asked Ligarides to contact the Near Eastern prelates concerning the Nikon case he did so, but in a form never mentioning Nikon's name. Ligarides had to be very careful for Nektarios, Patriarch of Jerusalem, had once anathemized Ligarides himself. In replying to the Tsar (1664) Nektarios warned him not to pay heed to envious men whose chief interest was intrigue and who pretended at a clerical calling.[50]Nektarios, not sure that his message would reach the proper people, sent his own emmissary. He told the Tsar to seek reconciliation and asked Nikon why he escaped his duties. But, he affirmed that only Nikon had the right to the Patriarchy at the moment. Nektarios' message was generally ignored in Moscow.[51] It did not correspond to the plan long since drawn.

Nikon himself tried to get in touch with another Patriarch. He wrote Dionisios, Patriarch of Constantinople (1666) outlining all the troubles that had occurred since the generous

---

49. Nikon himself was not to see these "questions" untl 1664. His answers to these "questions" are detailed in Gibbenet, *Izsledovanie*, II, pp. 178-249.

50. Ibid., II, p. 149. Also, Zyzikin, op. cit., II, p. 220.

51. There were other things in Nektarii's message quite unpalatable in Moscow; e.g., he wrote, in reference to an accusation, "But if Nikon does accuse the people of being insubordinate, then give him what is due to a builder of spiritual prosperity". Nektarii, in asking that Nikon's demands as shepherd of the flock be adhered to was asking the impossible. Gibbenet, *Izsledovanie*, II. p. 149.

times of his advency to the Patriarchy. Included were complaints against the Tsar for interference in Church affairs, descriptions of boiar attacks, and allegations of the grim mood of the people.[52] The letter was intercepted and brought to the Tsar. It greatly angered him and the court officials for they viewed it as having potentially damaged (had it reached the intended source) the international prestige of the Tsar and the State. This letter became one of the charges against Nikon at his trial.[53]

The trial itself came not long after, in that very same year, 1666. The Council of 1666, already convened since spring of that year in judging the Old Believers, was waiting to resume its session. After the two Near Eastern Patriarchs, Paisios of Alexandria and Makarios of Antioch arrived in Moscow in November, the Council was ready to turn to Nikon's case and did so on December 1. He would not come easily and two sets of messengers who had come to bring him were rebuffed. The third time it was ordered that Nikon, if he refused again, be brought by force.[54] This time he came.[55]

The trial of Nikon was, in essence, a showpiece, a formali-

---

52. For the text, see " Pis'mo Patriarkha Nikona k Tsar'gradskomu Patriarkhu Dionisiiu (1666 g.)," *ŻORSA* v., 2, 1861, pp. 510-30.

53. Ustiugov & Chaev, Ustiugov (ed.) op. cit., p. 321.

54. Arkhimandrit Leonid, "Diakon Lugovskoi po Tatishchevu Pisatel' XVII Veka i Ego Sochinenie o Sude nad Patriarkhom Nikonom", *PDPI*, No. 54, 1885, p. 26. Also, Gibbenet, *Izsledovanie*, II, p. 309.

55. Two items should be mentioned here. Only two of the four Near Eastern Patriarchs came, Dionisious of Constantinople and Nektarios of Jerusalem declining (in support of Nikon). Parthenios IV of Constantinople (successor of Dionisios), when hearing of Makarios' and Paisios' departure to Moscow, declared their sees vacant and new patriarchs were appointed to their sees by a synod convened for that purpose, Zyzikin, op. cit., II, p. 84; Vernadsky, op. cit., V, part 2, p. 601. Technically this meant that both Makarios and Paisios could have no legal say in the proceedings. Secondly, by this time word of Ligarides had come to Moscow that he was, in truth, a Catholic and also, not the exarch that he had been posing as. The govenment, with the cover removed from their chief prosecutor, so to speak, chose to sweep the information under the rug. The role of Ligarides at the Counil was not limited. It seems that some members of the Council had managed to lift the corners of the rug and peek under it. Yet, their knowledge was in no way instrumental at the Council.

ty. He was accused of labeling people heretics, of leaving the Patriarchy, of persisting in calling himself Patriarch, of anti-governmental statements (as in the letter to Dionisios), of exiling Bishop Paul of Kolomna, and so forth. In defense, Nikon was not allowed to present his "Refutation" (written in reply to the "questions" of Ligarides and Streshnev). Some of the meetings disallowed his presence. When he was predictably judged guilty on December 12, he took it calmly. He was not only stripped of the Patriarchy but also of any clerical office. He was now where he had started his brilliant and courageous career, a simple monk. The Ferapontov Monastery would be his abode.[56]

The boiars, struggling for so long to rid the nation of Nikon's presence, could now feel exhilirated. It had not been easy; the stern Patriarch was not a pliable man. Tsar Aleksei, though pursuing his policy to its conclusion was, nevertheless, not too happy. He and Nikon had been too close to allow the callousness to take permanent hold to the complete exclusion of the past. He avoided the last day (December 12) of the trial when the sentence would be read. The Tsar of Great, Little and White Russia did not wish to countenance pain, to see his former friend, mentor and regent suffer the indignity of a pre-determined defeat.

When the people heard of the sentence they came out in crowds into the street. Nikon was sent by a different route and those who came to see their Patriarch were left disappointed. When he arrived at the Ferapontov Monastery, Nikon again had to settle down to a quiet sedentary existence. He still attemped

---

56. Regarding Nikon's trial see "O Nizlozhenii s Prestola Byvshago Patriarkha Nikona", *Materialy*, II, p. 166-81; Gibbenet, *Izsledovanie*, II, pp. 309-74; Vernadsky, op. cit., V, part 2, pp. 601-04; Zyzikin, op. cit., III, passim. Nikon maintained to the end that his departure from the patriarchy was merely expressive of his belief, and of the oath taken to him, that the dictates of the Church were not being upheld properly, as promised to him. It was another example of his constant attitude on Church-State; he did not wish to tolerate State interference in spiritual affairs. On the "Reputation" see: Valerie A. Tumins, ed. (with George Vernadsky). *"Patriarch Nikon on Church and State: Nikon's Refutation."* (The Hague: Mouton, 1982).

to vindicate himself as in his letter to the Tsar in 1667. In it he replied to all charges against him, righteously claiming his innocence and and stating that there were not enough direct faults for him to be castigated. "All had already been decided by them", he notes correctly. He describes the conditions — the mud, bugs, darkness, etc., but does not complain. Yet the tone is one that asks the Tsar's pity. He even recalls how he had selflessly worked for the well-being of the Tsar's family during the cholera outbreak in 1654. "Like an old dog, I'v been discarded and locked up, and I shall die, devoid of food."[57] In 1671 Nikon writes again, and in a sense, repeats the general attempt at vindication. He describes how he had initially become Patriarch, the agreements reached between Aleksei and himself, the reminiscences of former friendship, the discord sewn by Bobarykin and Sytin. But now (after five years of dreary exile) the lordly former Patriarch leads a forlorn existence, a daily reminder of the heights that had been his. He was sick, he said, Even a cross was not given him to wear for three years. His hands ached and he could not lift the left one. He brought his own water, chopped his own wood. Reeking blood flowed from his gums.[58] But he had his pride and spirit and both were unshakeable. When the Tsar, upon the death of the Tsaritsa, requested Nikon to pray for her, he sent with the request a gift of 1,000 rubles. Yes, he would pray for the deceased, said Nikon, but he refused to accept the gift.

By the middle of the 1670's, access to Nikon, by now an old man, was seemingly easier and many people came to him. It seems that despite Nikon's letters to the Tsar in this period, he was treated reasonably well. A gramota of January, 1668, dictated by the Tsar, orders that all of Nikon's needs and wishes be taken care of. In any case, while in exile in the Ferapontov

---

57. "Pis'mo Patriarkha Nikona k Tsariu Alekseiu Mikhailovichu" *Letopis' Zaniatii Imperatorskoi Arkheograficheskoi Kommissii Za 1911 God,* No. 24, 1912, pp. 93-104.
58. Ibid., pp. 105-16.

(until 1676; in that year he was transferred to the Kirillo-Belozerskii monastery), Nikon kept himself busy praying, reading, fishing, working in the garden, caring for some livestock.[59] He also built a small island of rocks and put a cross on it. There he went frequently for prayer and meditation.[60]

There is little left. The young Tsar Feodor, after succeeding his father, wished to elevate Nikon again but the boiars were still adamant. When Feodor heard that Nikon was sick (1681),he recalled him from exile but it was too late. Nikon died on the way. The Tsar himself sang at his funeral and all the hierarchy was present. Feodor requested, and received the permission of the ecumenical patriarchs to nullify his deposition.[61] It was a justification that was due.

59. Arkhimandrit Varlaam, *O Prebyvanii Patriarkha Nikona v Zatochenii v Ferapontove i Kirillove Monastyriakh* (Moscow: 1858), pp. 3ff, 9-11, 13-17.
60. V.T. Georgievskii, op. cit., pp. 6-7.

61. Andreev, op. cit., p. 57.

Chapter 6

The Old Believers

The good elder Kornilii was in the Nilovsk hermitage when some Moscow officials arrived there. With them was an order that the services now be held according to the new (i.e. corrected) books and a new priest was assigned. When he attempted to start the service, Kornilii thrice interrupted him thereby stopping the service. The priest was wont to commence and continue the service and his insistence completely exasperated Kornilii. He grabbed the censor and struck the priest in the head, drawing blood. The friends of the new priest ran into the altar and, in turn, beat Kornilli's head against the floor until he too was bleeding. A general fight ensued and in the uproar Kornilii ran away to safety.[1] Another blow had been struck for the old belief.

The incident recited is quite unimportant. It is simply a very graphic picture of the intensity of feeling that was very fre-

---

1. "Povest' Dushepolezna o Zhitii i Zhizni Prepodobnago Otsa Nashego Korniliia, Izhe Byst' na Vygu Retse Bliz' Ozera Onega", in Maksimov, op. cit., p. 20. This was the same Kornilii who was one of the founders of the famed Old Believer settlement on the River Vyg; see Robert O. Crummey, *The Old Believers and the World of Antichrist: The Vyg Community and the Russian State 1694-1855* (Madison, Milwaukee, London: The University of Wisconsin Press, 1970), pp. 33-36, 59, 64.

quently reached at basic levels of the ecclesiastical structure in response to accursed innovations. We shall see (later in this chapter) intensity on a more exalted level, that of religious disputation, and coevally, as a response to it, an intensity of persecution. One seemed to breed the other and the facts do not have to be strained to see why.

The Old Believers (Starovery, Staroobriadtsy) or the schismatics (raskol'niki)[2] derive their appellations from their negative responses to the Nikonian reforms. The very term "old belief" was used by writers of this period who talked of the "old belief" vs. the innovations. By the late 1650's it is safe to say that the Old Believers constituted a distinct opposition group, one growing steadily in popularity, power, and adherents, though in the years immediately preceding they were frequently mixed up with such dissenters as the Kapitony.[3] The confusion stemmed in part from the irony that many (future) old believer leaders had had Nikon's assistance in their mutual efforts as members of, or on the behalf of, the Zealots of Piety. Until the split became more pronounced and cemented in reality, the tendency may have been to view the discord as an internal, household affair.

The question of what the old believer movement really represented has always drawn attention. The modern Soviet tendency is to view it as social in character.[4] That is a partial truth only, though it must be admitted that as the movement grew, and as it voluntarily or involuntarily took in other dissidents, and as the movement, partly due to increasing govern-

---

2. In the context of our period the two terms may be used interchangeably. Later, when more schismatics appeared, the term "raskol'niki" came to have a broader, more inclusive meaning though the identification with old belief was never lost. The term "old ritual" is basically synonymous with old belief. In a decree of April 17, 1905, on religious tolerance, the old term "raskol'niki" was replaced by "Staroobriadtsy", *Historical Terms*, p. 146.

3. For background on the Kapitony see Zenkovsky, *Staroobriadchestvo*, pp. 144-56.

4. e.g., Sakharov, *Obrazovanie i Razvitie*, p. 180.

mental persecution, became increasingly associated with an anti-governmental stance, the social element is less to be discounted. Other views have been many, attempting to tie in the raskolniks with the history of the zemstva in Russia,[5] or with the defense of "the rights of the locality and of the individual".[6] Both are far too limited. The most accurate of all is to view it as principally a religious movement for whatever other elements accrued over the years, the root was here. Smirnov notes that "the protest arose exclusively on religious grounds, without any admixture of elements foreign to the domain of faith and the Church",[7] and Zenkovsky supports this reasoning: "The Russian seventeenth century dissent developed as a purely religious movement aimed at satisfying the spiritual needs of believers."[8]

What molded the Old Believers into a group was their uncompromising attitude toward the innovations of Patriarch Nikon and Nikon himself. Though initially they supported some of his measures, as for church discipline and better behavior of priests, they could see no need for the new way of making the sign of the cross, the need to correct standard service books that their forefathers used, and so forth. It was all dangerous entanglement that, they felt, had no precedent nor a positive function. And to go along with the Patriarch merely because of his whims? It was not to be.

Their firm belief in the interconnection of ritual and spirit[9] or, as has been phrased differently, "their confusion of rite or ceremony with dogma"[10] made it even more impossible to

---

5. Andreev, op. cit., p. 6.
6. Conybeare, op. cit., p. 22.
7. P.S. Smirnov, *Vnutrennie Voprosy V Raskole v XVII Veke* (SPB: 1898), p. CXXVI.
8. Zenkovsky, *Staroobriadchestvo*, p. 12. Kartashev also notes that in Old Believer tracts of this period there is only the religious question under discussion.
9. V.P. Riabushinskii, *Staroobriadchestvo i Russkoe Religioznoe Chuvstvo* (France, Joinville: 1936) p. 8.
10. Conybeare, op. cit., p. 6.

countenance the spectre of change. They felt that capricious change in the books would, by virtue of the changes themselves, make the ritual replete with deep spiritual abysses. And the fact that the changes imposed by Nikon were geared to correspond to Greek practice made them even more capricious in their eyes.

This is not to imply that the early Old Believers were mere reactionaries, satisfied to preach the banalities of fundamentalism. On the contrary. We must recall that many of them had actually been at the forefront of Church reform, as members of the Zealots of Piety or otherwise. They felt, as Mel'nikov suggests, citing Khomiakov's dictum, that ritual is an artistic symbol of inner unity, that ritual was not so lightly to be tampered with. Regarding the Old Believer he writes: "We cannot demand of him that he drop ritualism and become inner meaning without external form, a thought without an image or expression in words".[11] And further: "It is not ritualism that is at the pinnacle of importance for Old Believers, but the inner essence of external action. Here ritualism is not outside but inside. Reigning here is not the external form, but inner psychic powers and moods."[12]

The Old Believers, in their myriad defenses, did not consider the question of what constituted the basis of the old faith. Though the Nikonites claimed that their corrections were in line with the ancient, original texts, and thus not to be hastily prejudged as thoughtless impositions, the Old Believers antagonistically maintained the opposite — that Russian Orthodoxy was being travestied. They knew full well that many corrections were included only insofar as they coincided with contemporary Greek models. The Old Believers essentially adhered to the strictures of the Stoglav Sobor of 1551, a past of not long duration. They were able to make polemical headway by pre-empting this whole question. The problem of textual authenticity was foreign to them. If, as Avvakum asked, the

<hr />

11. A. Mel'nikov, "Samobytnost' Staroobriadchestva", *Russkaia Mysl'*, May, 1911, Sect. 2, p. 79.
12. Ibid., p. 80.

ancient texts (as he understood them) and service books were wrong, then where did that leave the saints of old Russia? Would they not be saints then? These saints, he notes, were aso "old believers", and not possibly heretics. The rhetoric of this argument was formidable, one that invariably had mass effect. It was far easier to suppose that the Nikonian party was in error and leave the Russian saints unimpeached in their glory.

Michael Cherniavsky, in discussing this aspect of their thought states as follows: "The logic of schismatic thought is extremely simple, deceptively simple, for it does not convey the enormous painfulness of the whole issue, the shock of the logically necessary deductions, and their revolutionary significance for the Old Believers.

There was only one general conclusion possible: If Moscow, the Third Rome, had instituted religious changes which required the condemnation of itself, in its own past, then Moscow had accepted heresy — and the end was at hand. The end was not something vague or ambiguous. It was the apocalypse, described in greatest detail by St. John of Patmos and St. Cyril of Jerusalem."[13]

There were other strains in old believer argumentations, however, that aside from purely questions, were unpalatable to many people. Among them were an insistence on their own moral and theological rectitude, a belief in their own perspicacity, an unwillingness to consider opposing viewpoints and measures.[14] This intransigence was to prove detrimental to any possibility of reconciliation. As one historian has noted, the Old Believers were prone to disavow discussion; they were more intent on determining who was for and who was against.[15]

13. Michael Cherniavsky, "The Old Believers and the New Religion", *Slavic Review*, vol. XXV, no. 1, March 1966, p. 13. Hereafteer cited Cherniavsky, op. cit.

14. This is apparent from many sources. See *Materialy*, I, passim.

15. Andreev, op. cit., p. 78. And this from a writer generally sympathetic to the Old Believers. Qualifications must come, however, in the form of some finely argued tracts later composed by raskol'nik writers.

Their continuous railings against secular knowledge and growing interest therein also tended to impede their cause. In view of the ever growing interest toward secular knowledge (or Westernism) the Old Believers found themselves athwart history.[16]

When the Old Believers turned to writing, many of the same characteristics appeared. And the writings were generally effective, being spread among the populace whenever the opportunity arose. Among many others, Avvakum, the deacon Feodor, the priest Feoktist, and the Moscow archimandrite Spiridon were instrumental in writing very many tracts. While the writings were basically religiously oriented, it is curious to observe how, by the beginning of the XVIII century, they began to display ever greater attacks on the State.[17]

A great weapon in their hands was the oral sermon, formally reinstituted by the sobor of 1651 after a desuetude dating to the end of the XVI century. This is not to suggest that the sermon was not in use prior to 1651. The Zealots of Piety, especially Ivan Neronov, had used it extensively with notable success[18] and were, with Nikon, instrumental in its reintroduction into the church service. Now the Old Believers merely continued a habit many of them had acquired as Zealots. And they, especially in such leaders as Avvakum, Neronov, Login, and others, had preachers who were fierce in their vituperations against the encroachments on truth, in their loyalties to their adherents and friends, and fierce in their faith. Their honesty and personal integrity were real, and so was their selflessness.

---

16. Incidentally, it should not be construed that this trait is solely attributable to the Old Believers. Nikon took anti-Western measures, as did, at times, the government itself. Witness, for example, the creation of the Nemetskaia Sloboda (or foreign quarters) outside Moscow. Also, the anti-Western tendency found strong and strenuous support in the figure of Patriarch Ioakim (1674-1690) who intensified the struggle. It is to be noted that Ioakim was a severe persecutor of the raskol'niks.

17. Maksimov, op. cit., pp. II-III.

18. Borozdin, op. cit., p. 10.

When preparing for the trials against them at the Councils of 1666-67, the Old Believers, in their defenses, almost invariably begged for the Church, not for themselves.[19] It was an example of spiritual fortitude that left an indelible mark on Russian history, and these traits, so constant and real, make for admiration and respect, irrespective of the final position taken. The Old Believers preached throughout the breadth of the land, whether wandering themselves, escaping sentence, or even if in exile. The message was starker in its call and imagery when spoken with the fervor demanded of it.

Help in propagating the old belief came from a somewhat unexpected quarter, the 'holy fools". A number of them are known, especially Kiprian, Feodor, and Afanasii, and they served various functions as go-betweens, propagandists, prophets of doom. Feodor had been "converted" to the old belief by Avvakum. After hearing the impassioned exposition of the archpriest, Feodor whose eyes were now opened, "grabbed the book and immediately threw it into the fire proclaiming damnation on all innovations".[20] Kiprian, who like the other two lived (at least for a time) on the palace grounds and was known to the Tsar,[21] frequently ran after the Tsar's carriage asking in desperation that the old faith be restored,[22] that the piety forgotten in the growing darkness of the world be made vibrant. Kiprian, unfortunately, did not realize when his agitation had become dangerous, when the totality of his commitment made him patent to the martyrdom of which his kind always spoke.

---

19. Smirnov, *Istoriia Raskola* p, 61; a similar example is to be found at the sobor of 1660, convened to discuss and to take action on Nikon's leaving of the Patriarchal see. Neronov, a leading opponent of Nikon who had severe disputes with the Patriarch and could be expected to press for Nikon's deposition and punishment, protests that the sobor should not really be concerned with handling Nikon's case but should involve itself with the troubles of the Church: p. 54.

20. Ibid., p. 56.

21. Zenkovsky, *Staroobriadchestvo*, p. 269.

22. Plotnikov, op. cit., p. 51.

And so, from the hem of the Tsar's robe which he touched to get attention, he rose to the scaffold where his chained, decrepit, sore-infested body hung tremulously surveying the holy city that had so abused him.

Whereas the sobor of 1654 had proved a catalyst in drawing Old Believers together, Nikon's self-willed departure from the Patriarchy proved another. Neronov now openly took up the verbal cudgel. Previously, when in exile (because of his opposition to the decrees of 1654) he had been the silent leader of the anti-Nikonian campaign. Nikon later forgave him, had him recalled, and allowed him to serve according to the old books. But it was not a solid compromise for Neronov took the opportunity to intensify activity. He had visions of God (a number of Old Believers such as Lazar', who saw the prophet Elijah, and Avvakum also had visions) who in the visions ordered him to serve according to the old books. Furthermore, with Nikon's absence, their actions could gather more fruit for there was a temporary suspension of retaliatory measures.[23] It was a time (1658-60), as Borozdin states, in which "it was very easy for a substantial raskol'nik literature to arise". It was then (1658) that Spiridon Potemkin's influential book appeared detailing much of the antichrist and the end of the world.[24] This type of thought found ever greater response and expression in Old Believer ideology.[25]

Neronov's compulsion to speak out and be active reflects all of his adult life. As the motivating force behind the movement (organization of priests in Russia up to that time, i.e. 1630's, had not been common at all) of the Zealots of Piety he was largely responsible for the anomaly of moves for betterment of the Church coming from the ranks of the priests and not the

---

23. For these points see *Borozdin*, op. cit., pp. 8-101, 122, 173.
24. Ibid., pp. 104-06.
25. It is a curiosity of the first order that not a single dogmatic difference ever arose between the establishment Church and the proponents of the old belief.

episcopates (as had usually been the case).[26] Through what we might now term street work he and his adherents became influential enough to draw the response of the Church hierarchy. In the 1640's he, the gentle Vonifatiev, and others were actually in a position to have almost a permanent say in Church policy. As Makarii notes, Neronov, Vonifatiev, and friends got used to having a voice in administrative and juridical affairs of the Church.[27] It is a matter of conjecture to what degree was Neronov's opposition to Nikon dependent upon the circumstance of influence lost.[28] Neronov even had access to the Tsar (at least an epistolary one). He wrote him regarding the necessity of the participation of lay people and priests in the administration of the Church, and in Church sobors.[29]

It is all the more ironic, in view of the background of unmitigated and constructive work for the Church by the Zealots, that those first exiled by Nikon were not done so because of their "old belief" but because of their alleged violations of standard church discipline.[30] In this case the god truly did not smile.

The freedom for propagation, as mentioned above, was now relatively high. The raskol'niki worked without external

26. Zenkovsky, *Staroobriadchestvo*, pp. 86-87.

27. Makarii, *Istoriia*, XII, p. 3.

28. The role of personalities with attendant animosities is frequently mentioned as major factors in the rise of the schism. Even such authorities as Kliuchevskii feel very positive about this. V.O. Kliuchevskii, *Kurs Russkoi Istorii* (Moscow: 1956-59, vol. 1-8), III, p. 308.

29. Zenkovsky, *Staroobriadchestvo*, pp 131-32. Zenkovsky, in this work, gives much treatment to Neronov, and properly so, who comes off very well in his analysis. I do think, however, that there could be an addenda to the assertion made (p. 79, in talking of efforts to make people more religiously responsive). He writes, regarding Neronov's experience: "This attempt to make civilians also to be carriers of God's word was completely unusual not only in Russian, but also in Western medieval practice and sooner approached the example of Protestant preaching". Such fully people orientated movements as those of the Bogomils, the Albigensians, of St. Francis of Assisi, the work of St. Catherine of Siena and countless others, to mention only Western examples, might be construed to involve civilians as carriers of God's word.

30. Ibid., p. 234.

pressure and freely entered into disputations (as at Rtishchev's house). Their fervor did not abate. They even (and this marks the degree of development and growth attained) called their own sobors. At one of them, the participants were: Spiridon Potemkin, Avvakum, Archpriest Daniil, the hegumen Dosifei, the priests Feodosii, Isidor, Lazar' of Romanovo-Borisoglebskii, the deacon Feodor, the monastic elders Avramii, Isaia, Kornilii.[31] All were to be instrumental in the spread of the old belief and the fact that such key men could all be gathered for a council proved the movement was substantial. It was approximately at this time that the leadership that had been Neronov's became Avvakum's. Neronov's authority was falling, he was aging, his effectiveness was diminishing. And, irrespective of his constant opposition to Nikon and the reforms, there was the suggestion that he had mellowed, at least to the point where he did not wish to be anathemized by the ecumenical patriarchs.[32] The Church still spoke to him with a voice that touched his being. A lifetime of service could not force the ultimate break; the revocation and denial could not be wrought from a tortured spirit.

Avvakum is the embodiment of the old belief, a man who through his fervor, his total inability to compromise, his brilliance, his strict compassion and, yes, sometimes his egregious folly, is often the generally accepted protagonist of the drama inherent in the rise of the old belief. Born in the village of Grigorievo (some 15 versts from the birthplace of Nikon)[33] in 1619 or 1620, he chose the religious vocation early and at the age of twenty became a deacon. Two years later (1642 or 1643) he was ordained a priest. From the beginning his priesthood is

31. Borozdin, op. cit., p. 133.

32. Ibid., p. 134. Though this seems quite plausible, its suggestion appears only here. My tendency is to accept it.

33. This area, in addition to Nikon and Avvakum, produced such principals in the struggle as Paul (eventually bishop of Kolomna, and to die in exile as an opponent of Nikon) and Ilarion (later to be archbishop of Riazan' and fierce defender of Nikon's reforms).

characterized by two things: a large number of spiritual children and an equal number of antagonists. Sometime in 1646 he came to Moscow as a serious altercation in his parish forced him to flee. He met Vonifatiev, Neronov, the Tsar. When more troubles occurred in his next assigment (Avvakum was severely beaten in a rioting by the parishioners)[34] he again came to Moscow (1651) and became an assistant to Neronov. He became known quickly, aided by his acquaintanceship with leading men of Church and State, and by his own strong-willed efforts on behalf of such projects as the institution of edinoglasie and the general platform of the Zealots of Piety.

In 1653, in protest against the exile to the Novo-Spasskii Monastery of Neronov (because of opposition to a new, shortened edition of the Psalter and anti Nikon activity in general) Avvakum and Daniil of Kostroma petitioned the Tsar for their friend. The petition was violently anti-Nikon in tone and it was turned over to the Patriarch. Daniil was defrocked and Avvakum was banished to Siberia. Along the way he continued his propagandistic efforts. Eventually, the success of these efforts drew an order that he be sent even further and Avvakum wound up in the Dauria region on the Lena River. His fortitude in the face of such gruesome adversity was unbending and he took the suffering stoically. Once when his wife asked him "how long will our suffering continue?" he replied, "until our very death."[35]

Fortitude was one of the many facets of his character, a character that Fedotov has most aptly drawn. Avvakum possessed great contradictions. A man of great soul and narrow mind,

---

34. This gives an idea of the polarization engendered by him. A reason for the rioting against him, and how ironical in view of the future, was a wholesale disgust and anger at the innovations he introduced. As Borozdin states: "With all his activities and innovations he rapidly set against him the local clergy and populace; he was initially asked to desist from the innovations..." when that failed, force was restored to and he was beaten very severely. Borozdin, op. cit., pp. 11-12.

35. As cited in his autobiography. *"Avtobiografiia Protopopa Avvakuma"*, *Letopisi Russkoi Literatury i Drevnosti* (Moscow: 1861), p. 138. Hereafter cited Avvakum, *Avtobiografiia*.

he was both violent and tender. Unable to distinguish between the essential and the secondary in religion he saw everything as the Law of God. He was constantly overwhelmed by the continuous presence of the Almighty. Avvakum felt he was sent by God to announce His will to sinful men. He was not a mystic, despite a sensual approach to religion. The image of the meek and loving Savior penetrated him deeply and an under-current of compassion and tenderness was never too far from the surface.[36] In his eyes the ideal man was basically quietist, a listener, a person who worked six days a week and on the seventh went to church to pray and sanctify his labors. "This is the poor man whom Avvakum asks his flock to respect: 'If you bow to the waist to a rich man then bow to the ground to the poor.' "[37]

In the more benevolent climate of 1658 to the early 1660's Avvakum was recalled (1660). The order did not reach him until 1662 and it was not till 1664 that he actually returned to Moscow. He immediately threw himself into the furious activity of the Old Believers assuming, in effect, the leadership that had become his even though he was in exile. His popularity ran high in Moscow[38] and with his presence it seemed easier to raise the pitch and tone of the struggle. Denunciations flew at every-body tainted with the stigma of Nikonianism. Tsar Aleksei, though wary, allowed leeway to Avvakum. His desire to some-how "reconvert" Avvakum and bring him back into the fold of Mother Church met with typical stubbornness.[39] By the end of

---

36. G.P. Fedotov (ed.), *A Treasury of Russian Spirituality*. (New York: Sheed and Ward, 1948), pp. 135-36.

37. Eleonskaia et. al., op. cit., p. 173.

38. Conybeare, op. cit., p. 63.

39. This desire was by no means new. Before Avvakum was exiled to Siberia Aleksei had resisted Nikon's efforts to defrock Avvakum. "The Tsar, evidently, understood better than Nikon what a powerful social and moral force was represented by Avvakum — the fiery preacher surrounded by the aura of martyrdom. He did not give up the hope to draw the archpriest to his side. This explains the multitude of attempts to talk Avvakum into returning..." etc... Eleonkaia et. al., op. cit., p. 127.

the year Avvakum had become too dangerous to leave free. He was again exiled, this time to Pustozersk in the far north.

While there Avvakum's activity did not cease. He wrote, he preached, he spread the faith and was able to easily maintain contacts with his far-flung adherents. It seems that his freedom was not fully proscribed. The degree of contact maintained by Avvakum has led to an occasional misstatement by historians claiming that all Russia came to him for advice and guidance,[40] but there can be no question as to his preeminence in the old belief and in its defense.

Among his adherents were such churchmen as the priests Nikita Dobrynin and Lazar', the elder Avraamii of the Iosif Volokolamsk Monastery, the archbishop Aleksandr of Viatka, of those not yet mentioned.[41] Of the nobility such people as Irodion Streshnev, Princess Anna Repnina, Prince Ivan Khovanskii, Prince Ivan Vorotinskii,[42] could be classified as adherents of the old belief though within their ranks in Moscow there were few who were thus committed.

It has been frequently pointed out that some of the most fervent Old Believers were women, for Avvakum had a particularly strong effect on them. It is even mistakenly asserted that the most uncompromising were the women, a view, unfortunately, that relies too heavily on the classic example of Feodosiia Morozova and Evdokiia Urusova (sisters, and wives of leading Muscovite figures) and their close friend Mariia Danilova (wife of a colonel). It is not too difficult to see why such an assumption is sometimes made for, until their imprisonment in 1671, their homes (especially Morozova's) had become active, semi-secret centers of resistance.[43] When they died

40. S.P. Mel'gunov, *Staroobriadtsy i Svoboda Sovesti* (Moscow: 1917, 2nd ed.). pp. 3-4.

41. For a more substantial listing see Episkop Makarii, *Istoriia Russkago Raskola* (SPB: 1855), pp. 169-71.

42. Vernadsky, op. cit., V, part 2, p. 594; Plotnikov, op. cit., pp. 50-51.

43. It should be noted that until the death of Aleksei's first wife Mariia Miloslavskaia in 1669 these ladies had an influential protectress at court.

in prison four years later their efforts and lives drew the halo of martyrdom and they became beloved figures among the faithful.

Another outstanding female personality of the old faith was the nun Melaniia (probably from Belev). Her role was that of a spiritual mother to many of Avvakum's female followers and it is suggested that she really was at the head of these. The woman's place in the home where "in matters of faith she was not pressed by anyone" may have played a greater role in furtherance of the raskol than generally recognized.[44] And in nunneries there was also activity on behalf of the old belief especially when there was an energetic and able sister to do the propagating such as Elena Khrushcheva in the Voznesenskii Nunnery.[45]

Avvakum kept in constant touch with his female followers. He wrote frequently to Morozova, Melaniia and the others admonishing them when he thought desirable (he was a strict master), urging them to retain their humility, and stressing the necessity of frequent prayer.[46] His relationship to Morozova, Urusova, and Danilova is a poignant one, filled with a tenderness and grace of feeling that knows no bounds. But we also see the very straightforwardness of the teacher to his pupils.[47]

One of the things that has struck scholars most about Avvakum is his very striking and genuine talent for writing. It is most apparent in his brilliant autobiography,[48] long held up

44. Smirnov, *Istoriia Raskola*, pp. 57-58.
45. Borozdin, op. cit., pp. 126-27.
46. Ibid., pp. 169-71.
47. Ibid., pp. 312, 314. Both aspects may be gleaned from some of Avvakum's letters; *RIB*, XXXIX, passim., and *Letopis' Zaniatii*, 1911 (Barskov, ed.), op. cit., pp. 33-35: Morozova's letter, pp. 41-42 is interesting in that, in addition to asking Avvakum to pray for her son's lawful wedding and her friends, she also asks his intercession with God so that He would give her the strength to bear tribulations and remain firm.
48. The edition I have used, as cited above, is to be found in *Letopisi Russkoi Literatury i Drevnosti* (Moscow: 1861), pp. 117-73. For an English version see Zenkovsky, *Epics*, pp. 322-70.

as a superb model of pre-Petrine Russian prose, though it is similarly apparent in the rest of his corpus (including letters, petitions, tracts). Professor N.K. Gudzii, a leading authority on old Russian literature, has noted the lively pace of his language, its simplicity and color, Avvakum's own statement that he likes to speak simply. The innovative element is that Avvakum took "the traditional life with its stylistic and thematic restrictions and transformed it into a polemically sharpened autobiography".[49]

His was a realism that stemmed from the folk and Makarii observes that Avvakum's words "seemed as if they were torn from the living speech of the people".[50] Even in his treatment of standard biblical stories and themes his writing strongly reflects its dependence on contemporary realistic speech. "Until Avvakum's *Life* there was no work of Russian literature where the individual personality was allotted so much attention and where it was portrayed in all its complexity so completely, multi-dimensionally, and fearlessly".[51] These literary qualities greatly enhanced his effectiveness as leader of the schismatic movement and he was aware, in a sense, of his special qualities. Perhaps some such awareness enabled him to be pleasantly presumptive in the title of a work such as "Poslanie Bratii na Vsem Litse Zemnon". — "A Message to Brethren in All of the World".[52] In Avvakum it was a forceful leader who dwelt in his actions, his oral teachings, and in his written word.

This is not all to describe the subject uncritically. Borozdin, who wrote an excellent study of Avvakum, notes in delineating the peculiarities of Avvakum's works items which take away from a purely positive appraisal. Specifically, he mentions that

---

49. Citation on p. 467. Other comments interspersed in chapter "Staroobriadcheskaia Literatura — Prototop Avvakum i Ego Sochineniia", N.K. Gudzii, *Istoriia Drevnei Russkoi Literatury* (Moscow: 1956, 6th ed.).

50. Makarii, *Istoriia*, XII, p. 607.

51. Eleonskaia et. al., op. cit., p. 128.

52. To be found in *RIB*, XXXIX, pp. 771-807.

the proofs of the correctness of the old rituals as presented by Avvakum are far from substantially true. Sources cited in this regard cannot be authoritative. There is the feeling that the force of the polemic is not so much in the incontrovertibility of proofs as in the realistic imagery used. And, not unexpectedly, he is, in the main, quite intolerant toward his opponents.[53]

The Councils of 1666-67, which, among other things, tried and condemned the Old Believers (we shall discuss these procedures in more detail in the chapter on the Councils) showed Avvakum to be remarkably steadfast in his positions. He was, like a number of others, exiled, this time for good. The condemnations of the old belief added fuel to the notion that by acts of persecution and anathema the government really forced the Old Believers to be different.[54] Though in the 1660's most Old Believers were not anti-government per se, that strand of their thought could not but be heightened by the wholesale condemnation by the Councils.

Old believer efforts to maintain their identity and to further propagandize their faith did not stop with a mere condemnation by the Councils. They continued to work in earnest wherever they were. Avvakum sent several petitions to the Tsar, reviling Nikon (who should be split into four parts, was a whore's son, etc.) with increasing desperation.[55] A certain dejection is sometimes apparent as in his first message where he states that he would have rather died in the Daurian tundra than hear calumny against the Church.[56] In this message (1669), Avvakum makes the interesting suggestion to the Tsar that he, the Tsar himself, bears the chief responsibility for the Church.[57] This

---

53. Borozdin, op. cit. Along with these points he discusses several others, pp. 320-21.

54. Cherniavsky, op. cit., p. 5.

55. Borozdin, op. cit., pp. 244-46; *RIB*, XXXIX, pp. 767-70. The latter petition under *RIB* is addressed to Tsar Feodor. Avvakum's petitions are steady through the years of his incarceration.

56. *RIB*, XXXIX, pp. 723-30.

57. Zenkovsky, *Staroobriadchestvo*, p. 315.

somewhat peculiar notion is not totally new for the Old Believers. Even in the very early stages of their dissent this idea appears. Neronov, at the sobor of 1653, in opposing Nikon also said that the Tsar should, in effect, take the upper hand for "any truth and proper belief is affirmed through the Tsar..."[58] Neronov re-asserts this in a letter to the Tsar in 1654 and similar notions are expressed by key figures in the raskol such as the deacon Feodor and the priest Lazar'. Zyzikin refers to this as the "Caesaro-papist tendency" in old believer thought.

This tendency should not be ascribed to any deeply held notion regarding the Tsar as head of the Church. The Old Believers were far from such an idea. But as the years went on and as it became more apparent that things would not revert to desired ways, the Tsar became increasingly seen as a symbol of last recourse. Once the Old Believers were finally convinced that the Tsar (and the State) could not be saved or returned to the traditional fold, the level of despair heightened greatly and the notions of antichrist and the forthcoming end of the world prevailed ever more.

The adherents to the old belief continued to grow despite the imposition of prohibitions. It was decided that punishments beyond just exile be meted out to the leaders. The decision was hastened when the monk Avraamii (formally a "holy fool" under the name of Afanasii) was arrested in February of 1670.

---

58. Zyzikin, op. cit., I, p. 201. The manifestations of this idea among Old Believers is discussed pp. 201-05. Though the role so ascribed to the Tsar was decisive, there grew feelings of discontent with him personally for Avvakum's view of the Tsar grew more uncertain, more dualistic in nature; Borozdin, op. cit., p. 247. Father Schmeman notes that (in the later stages of the development of old belief): "The Old Believers opposed not so much the Church itself as the State — but in the name of that theory of Tsardom which, no matter how it became narrower and less apparent, saw and wished to see in it, the State in service to Christ. Their opponents by now barely felt the approaching metamorphosis of Christian theocracy into absolutism"; A. Schmeman, *Istoricheskii Put' Pravoslaviia* (New York: Chekhov Publishing House, 1954), p. 378. See also Kartashev, op. cit., in the sections on the Old Believers.

Found in his possession were various papers which incriminated the exiles in Pustozersk. They clearly showed that Avvakum, Lazar', and Feodor were actively working for the raskol and that Avraamii was the link (one of many) between the exiles and Moscow. Ivan Elagin was dispatched to Pustozersk with orders to halt the underground operations (which in the North were quite overt). Were they to sign papers of submission they would be pardoned. But they did not and pardon remained a still gesture. Two followers were then hanged. Avvakum was put into an underground cell. Lazar' and Epifanii had their tongues and right hands cut.[59] A witness reports that the executioner could not cut out Lazar's tongue because of his shaking hands, so Lazar' helped him do so. Then, when a towel was bloodied from his mouth, he threw it to the sympathetic crowd saying "take it as a blessing on your house". The witness claims that even with their tongues cut out Lazar', Epifanii, and Feodor continued to talk, perhaps a concession to myth making.[60]

Punishment was also meted out in Moscow where Prince Khovanskii was flogged and at least one person burned at the stake. Meanwhile, a rebellion was in progress in the distant north, at the prestigious Solovetskii Monastery. There the monastery had unanimously rejected the rulings of the Councils of 1666-67 and remained firm in maintaining the old belief. Rejecting any compromises the monastery was besieged by government troops, a siege that was to last from 1668 until 1676, and the resistance to which made these Solovetskii monks a legend to later generations of Old Believers (see chapt. 8).

By the 1670's the old belief was multi-directional with many strands becoming constantly more obvious. The greatest

59. Vernadský, op. cit., V, part 2, pp. 705-06.
60. "Svidetel'stvo Ochevidtsa o Nakazanii Protopopa Avvakuma, Popa Lazaria, Diakona Feodora i Startsa Epifaniia 4 Aprelia 1670 g.v Pustozerske, "Letopis' Zaniatii Imperatorskoi Arkheograficheskoi Kommissii za 1913 God (SPB: 1914), pp. 17-19.

numbers were essentially followers of Avvakum and his co-leaders, and constituted the main grouping. Certain tracts had already been accepted as authoritative and as key explanations of their position. These were the "Words" of Spiridon Potemkin, the treatise of Feodor, (translated by Vernadsky as) "Reply of the Orthodox defenders of religion concerning the Creed and other dogmas" (1667), and the famed fifth petition of the Solovetskii Monastery to the Tsar composed by the treasurer and elder Gerontii. Zenkovsky suggests that this petition is so logical, broad, and detailed that it is at the foundation of almost all the following theological writings of Old Believers.[61]

The idea of antichrist was becoming more accepted, rising all the more now that active measures were being taken against the Old Believers. It was now somewhat easier to countenance, for with the gloom of increasing persecution it seemed the apocalypse was more imminent. The fact that earlier dissenters had predicted the antichrist and with it the end of the world (for example, 1666 was to have been such a year)[62] never stopped then from so assuming again. This strong grain of pessimism had initially, in terms of the old believer movement, been injected as early as 1658 by the deacon Feodor. Holding, as he did, a high position in their circles, his eschatological obsessions came to have a tragic influence on Old Believers. It is now in the 1670's that we begin to have evidence of mass immolations, of suicides, of many defections from the daily chores of life and desertion to deep forests and barren wastes. Miliukov attributed this end of the world idea to severe simplification on the part of the Old Believers for it envisaged only two possiblilities: either Orthodoxy was still preserved among them and must triumph or else it was lost and antichrist ruled the world.[63] Too

---

61. Zenkovsky, *Staroobriadchestvo*, pp. 310-11.
62. The "Book of Faith", published in 1648 had predicted Russia would abandon the true faith in 1666. The antichrist idea is very well discussed in Cherniavsky, op. cit.
63. Miliukov, op. cit., p. 46.

often in those early years the exacerbations inherent to the struggle were only fueled by false preachers and purveyors of the ultimate holocaust. Why wait to reach the perfect world, the present world being what it is. It was better to die, clean and purified, while antichrist had not yet taken full control.

The play of excessive pessimism appears not only in concrete acts but in writings as well. Some of the poems of Old Believers that have come down to us are illustrative. One states:

> "The years of the world pass by,
> The end of the world approaches,
> Evil times have come,
> Difficult years have come:
> The true faith has passed,
> The stone wall has crumbled,
> Strong pillars are no more,
> The Christian faith has perished..."[64]

Though the general tone of this is filled with dread of the Universe's iniquity and impending doom, sometimes there is a ray of light, a rendering of hope. This usually is most apparent when nature is mentioned. Nature will protect and harbor their homes, their souls. A poem reads:

> "I will hide in the forest depths,
> I shall dwell with the beasts.
> There will be my home...
> There the air is clean and pleasant,
> And I will hear the whistle of birds.
> Soft winds blow there,
> And streams of water gurgle."[65]

It was a vision of unmolested bliss that gave them strength and hope, and one which they clearly tried to implement in practice.

---

64. Rozhdestvenskii, op. cit., p. 4 (poem #2). I have rendered the poems literally with no attempt to rhyme.
65. Ibid., p. 8 (poem #5).

Curiously, with all of Avvakum's authority, he did not speak out against the radical manifestations of his followers. Immolation, the gruesome death by fire, was accepted by him as proof of dedication to the old, true values. Zenkovsky points out that Avvakum thought primarily, despite this, of the victory of old belief, not its defeat or of antichrist's ultimate rule.[66] I would perhaps suggest that the two are not exclusive of each other, that, viewing as he did, immolation as a sign of strength, he thought it a sign pertinent and encouraging enough for him to assume that given such fortitude his adherents must come out victorious.

---

66. Zenkovsky, *Staroobriadchestvo*, pp. 383ff. A fine anthology about Old Believers, with some excellent fictional renditions is A.S. Rybakov, K.N. Shvetsov, and P.G. Nosov (ed's), *Staraia Vera, Staroobriadcheskaia Khrestomatiia* (Moscow: 1914).

Chapter 7

Problems of Reform

The question of reforms is quite central to the controversies of this period, and is in itself a problematical one. It is not merely possible to ascribe all the reforms, or even the impetus for them to Patriarch Nikon. He was, in fact, a product of a movement (later to be called the Zealots of Piety) that since the 1630's was in the forefront of reform. Nikon, upon his ascendancy to the Patriarchate, accelerated many of the reformist tendencies.

By the middle of his reign as Patriarch, a number of innovations or reforms had come into ecclesiastical practice. There were measures for greater discipline and stricter morality of clergy and parishioner. These dealt widely along the range of popular transgressions, be they dunkenness or moral laxity. The oral sermon had been re-introduced and edinoglasie was (since its formal institution in 1651) becoming prevalent. None of these are attributable to Nikon.

Changes attributable strictly to him were the use of five breads, not seven, during the service, some alterations in choir singing, the change in the number of genuflections in the prayer of Ephraim the Syrian during Lent, the introduction of troeperstie (crossing oneself with three fingers, not two) and so forth. These were all measures that were introduced in the first two years of his ascendancy, and had (especially the issue of troeperstie) been enough to set off an opposition that was to culminate in schism. But after these "successes", Nikon pressed constantly further.

The point should be made that Nikon's reformist measures were essentially textological. This is what really set him apart from all other fellow reformers previously involved in re-educating the Church and its people. This is not to say that even here he was the lonely innovator, for textual improvement was also a feature of the program of the Zealots of Piety. Yet, they, in constrast to their normal fervor and impetuosity, were, in this matter, content to move with great deliberation and care.

Historiographically it has been common to view Nikon's reforms as arbitrary, too quick, and ill-prepared, though this reflects too much of the criticism of his contemporary adversaries. Several points tend to disqualify this notion. Nikon had already been in the forefront of the reform movement (recall that the more practical side of his reforms did not draw the ire of anybody) and the idea of reform was by no means foreign to his thought. Secondly, when already in a position of central power (as Metropolitan of Novgorod) he took to heart the admonitions of Patriarch Paisios of Jerusalem who, on his visit to Russia in 1649, constantly impressed upon his listeners the advisability of bringing Russian service books in line with those of the Greek. Nikon, whose view of the Russian Church did not adhere to purely local conceptions, was predisposed to accept this advice. If Russia was to lead the Orthodox world and if the Russian Church was to play an ecumenical role, then disparities in the texts could not be countenanced.

Arsenii Sukhanov, the learned Russian monk who ac-companied Paisios back to the Near East in 1649, found that the Greeks were rather truculent and intransigent on this point. The monks of Mt. Athos had even burned some Slavonic books that differed from the Greek on the presumption that seeds of potential heresy were contained. But Sukhanov was a scholar himself and in disputations such as those held in Jassy in the spring of 1650 he threw back at the Greeks the very point they had attempted to make to him. Why, Sukhanov wondered, did Greek texts published in Venice contain gross misrepresentations along Latin lines, especially the Creed which contained the filioque? But many Eastern hierarchs still wished textual uniformity (e.g. Patriarch Makarios of Antioch). It should be noted that Sukhanov, after returning to Russia in 1650, was shortly again (in 1651) sent to the Near East, this time to collect manuscripts of all kinds. This mission was authorized with Nikon not yet the Patriarch (but at the center of all decisions). These manuscripts would aid in the correction of Russian texts.

The question of correcting the Russian texts along Greek models had been discussed previously. After Paisios' departure in 1649 there were meetings discussing the desirability of maintaining contact with the Near East on Church related problems. Some questions were sent to the Patriarch of Constantinople immediately thereafter. they were: 1) when several hierarchs serve, can they use two poteras, 2) should edinoglasie be instituted, 3) what is the proper procedure in handling men or women who leave their spouses to enter monastic orders, and 4) should those men who have wed widows or serfs be ordained into the priesthood? Patriarch Parthenios replied, and it is noteworthy that he gave support to the most important of these four questions, that of instituting edinoglasie.[1]

The Kormchaia Kniga (the Russian version of the Byzantine Nomakanon) containing works of the apostles, the decrees of the Councils, writings of the Fathers, was published in 1650. Nikon's revised edition appeared in 1653. In it were two clauses, significantly added by Nikon: that concerning the development of the Patriarchy in Russia, showing the independence of the Church, and the famed Donation of Constantine.[2] Both reflected Nikon's idea of the Church's role in society

---

1. Nikolaevskii, *Iz Istorii Snoshenii*, op. cit., pp. 15-21. He maintains here that official relations with the Near East re Church matters recommence at this time.

2. Makarii, *Istoriia*, op. cit., XII, p. 229. *Historical Terms*, p. 40.

and further reflected Nikon's belief and insistence that he could act independently when necessary. This applies to the problem of reform.

What gradually emerges then is a picture of Nikon that properly leaves out most of the purely arbitrary elements in his moves for the correction of books. He used two basic principles here: 1) the employment of ancient Slavonic and Greek texts as proper guides for correction, and 2) in important points, consultation with Near Eastern churchmen.[3] We have already seen, in the case of Sukhanov, that systematic collection of manuscripts was begun. This was not relegated only to Sukhanov. In 1654, after the sobor of that year, Nikon and the Tsar ordered that Russian book collections be combed for usable ancient texts to help in collation. Monasteries such as the Troitsa-Sergievskii, that of Iosif Volokolamsk, the Iuriev, and many others supplied Nikon with numerous texts.[4] This was the continuation of a practice commenced by Nikon from the inception of his reign.

The several thousands manuscripts collected from the various sources could not all be checked and this has led to attackes on Nikon. They are partially justifiable for doubtlessly more exacting procedures would have yielded greater accuracy. Yet it is also argued that, given the necessity of textual reform, it took someone with Nikon's indomitable energy to effect it. And given the animosites of the principals, the longer Nikon was to wait, the more difficult the task would become. Nikon could hold the opposition at bay and hindsight shows how much more openly (and strongly) the Old Believers functioned after his departure (1658) from the Patriarchy. Avvakum's agitation at this juncture actually dealt far more with Nikon than with the reform of books.[5]

---

3. Makarii, *Istoriia*, op. cit., XII, pp. 113-14.

4. Makarii, *Istoriia Russkago Raskola* (SPB: 1855) p. 147-48. Hereafter cited Makarii, *Raskol.*

5. Ibid., pp. 159-68.

The reform of books needed men capable of working with ancient texts and new Greek manuscripts. In Muscovy there were few specialists who simultaneously knew theology, liturgics, Greek, and who could make proper comparative studies. Tho who did were a number of churchmen such as Arsenii Sukhanov, Arsenii the deaf, Spiridon Potemkin, and others.[6] But, theirs could not be a complete effort for their own duties demanded time. To create a staff of correctors, Nikon (and the government) turned to the southwest, to Kiev, for their chief help.

Some of this help was already in Moscow for Feodor Rtishchev, close friend and adviser to the Tsar, had, in building a school, brought some scholars from Kiev.[7] This had occurred in 1648-49. In the years 1649-50, notable scholars such as Epifanii Slavinetskii, Arsenii Satanovskii, and Damaskin Ptitskii came to Moscow.[8] And there were Greeks such as the Archimandrite Dionisios from a monastery on Mt. Athos and Arsenios the Greek who had come to Russia in 1649 and, after allegations of apostasy had been proved (he had already been a Roman Catholic and a Moslem) was doing penance in the Solovetskii Monastery. In 1653 Nikon recalled him to take advantage of his fine education (in Rome) and his scholarly abilities, a move, in view of his background that chagrined many of the purists. To all these figures must be added the Russias themselves and when taken in toto it is difficult to perceive how wholesale condemnations can be made of Nikon's lack of seriousness or his lack of system in propagating his reforms.

The southwest (Ukrainian) and the western (Belorussian-Polish) contacts must be mentioned briefly. It was at this time that a) the Russo-Ukrainian union was becoming a reality (to

---

6. Zenkovsky, *Staroobriadchestvo*, op. cit., pp. 100-01.

7. Kliuchevskii, op. cit., III, pp. 278-79; Makarii, *Raskol*, op. cit., pp. 142-43.

8. Zenkovsky, *Staroobriadchestvo*, op. cit., pp. 100-01; Kliuchevskii, Ibid., p. 275; Makarii, *Istoriia*, op. cit., XII, p. 155ff; Makarii, *Raskol*, op. cit., pp. 142-153.

culminate in the Pereiaslavl' Union of 1654) and b) Nikon was considering, in thought and practice, the greater ecumenical role of the Russian Church. Contact was thus desirable, especially the more so in view of the good reputation of Kievan scholarship (enhanced particularly by the theological school founded by Petr Mogila in 1632). The Kievan Church was not reluctant to send scholars to Moscow but, it was more cautious in pronouncing support for union. It did need material support from Moscow just as Moscow was in need of Kievan scholars. But the Kievan hierarchy preferred to have the Church remain, as previously, under the jurisdiction of Constantinople. For the Kievans this seemed desirable for this state of affairs was nominal and without any practical interference. Such would not be the case with Moscow though in de facto terms the metropolitanate of Kiev was already substantially linked to Moscow.[9]

The Western (Polish) lands were developing scholars in religious matters more quickly than Moscow. The Orthodox Church's position, being formally illegal after the 1596 Union (rights to its existence not reinstated until the Convocational Seim of 1632) led to severe problems. To not only maintain Orthodoxy at some level but also to polemicize on its behalf in the strenuous circumstances of foreign domination became the ultimately successful tasks of the various "brotherhoods" (combinations of monks, churchmen, burghers), that of L'vov becoming the most notable. Much serious work was done and it was from the school of the L'vov brotherhood that Petr Mogila

---

9. Makarii, *Raskol*, op. cit., pp. 51-83. He observes that in these contacts the Metropolitan Sil'vester of Kiev (who succeeded Mogila upon his death in 1649) did not actually petition for formal union with Moscow, even after the formalities of union in 1654. It is suggested that part of the reason for this caution is attributable to a desire to placate the former Polish masters to whom, of course, a Kievan-Moscow axis would be abhorrent. There was an attendant canonical problem for no one Patriarch could legally assume a metropolitanate from another. This meant that a church union of Moscow and Kiev demanded acceptance of the move by the Patriarch of Constantinople.

132

came (he was to complete his education in Paris). In these schools the seeds of a scholarly literature took place for they were demanding and strict. The famous Grammatika (Grammar) of Meletii Smotritskii was published in Vil'na in 1619 and for a long time remained the sole grammatical treatise not only in Western and Southwestern Russia, but also in the Moscow area itself and even among the Southern Slavs.[10] Mogila's major work, *Pravoslavnoe Ispovedovanie* (Confession of the Orthodox Faith) owes much to the training received here, interspersed as it was with Latinisms and a methodology more chatechetical than Eastern Orthodox churchmen were used to.[11] This is common to most of those working in the Western lands. A side effect of the need to polemicize and keep Orthodoxy solvent (and one having its Russian parallel) was the dramatic rise of the oral sermon. "All of the scholarly apparatus then available was freely used by the preacher" and many became famous. In the period of Aleksei's reign such men as Iovannikii Gouatovskii (d. 1688), Innokentii Gizel (d. 1684), Lazar' Baranovich (d. 1693), and Antonii Radivilovskii were known as able defenders of Orthodoxy in the West.[12]

---

10. A.S. Arkhangel'skii, "Bor'ba s Katolichestvom i Zapadno-Russkaia Literatura Kontsa XVI — Pervoi Poloviny XVII Veka", *ChOIDR*, 1888, bk. 1, sect. 1, part 1, pp. 106-09.

11. It should be noted that though these Western areas were able to supply Muscovy with some able scholars, the textological problem was perhaps even more serious there. The immediacy of Roman Catholicism, the greater degree of Westernization, the large number of disparate peoples, among other reasons, led to havoc in the texts. Catholic texts in, for example, the dialects of Illyria, Bosnia, Walachia, were common. In Orthodox texts (as also in Catholic ones) there were errors, grammatical and logical misrepresentations, the absence of key prayers, and much apocrypha. It was such a situation, in addition to the fact of Polish dominance, that led to attempts at correction by such men as the Bishop Gedeon of L'vov (d. 1607), and the ubiquitous Mogila (d. 1649). Ibid., pp. 72-79. It may also be observed that many church books in Slavic lands lacked organization and unity; a Slavic codification of the Bible came into being only at the end of the XV c. (the work of Archbishop Gennadii of Novgorod). See the excellent discussion of this and other aspects by Arkhangel'skii, Ibid., pp. 80-95.

12. Ibid., pp. 122-125.

As Nikon turned to the task of manifesting the reforms he took actions to facilitate his plan quickly. The amended Psalter (1653) that contained the troeperstie clause had created a storm and Nikon flung himself into the teeth of the gale. He chose to punish those in too unacceptable a disagreement, just as in the following year he punished those unwilling to adhere to the dictates of his council on reform. Being a former Zealot he knew how far a movement not upended in time could carry and he chose to proceed decisively.[13] Then, he knew full well the value of controlling the government printing house (pechatnyi dvor). The older more conservative elements (among them some Zealots) began to be phased out. By 1654 he had attained complete control and could proceed unencumbered by the tentacles of opposition. Personal animosities (and how strong they were!)[14] were temporarily in abeyance. Among Nikon's prime correctors in the printing house were such personalities as Arsenios the Greek, Evfimii, an elder of the Chudov Monastery, the elder, Matvei, the archpriest Adrian, and Epifanii Slavinetskii.[15] Arsenios the Greek, by virtue of his ambiguous background and foreign birth was particularly odious. The schismatics put much blame on his shoulders, saying on occasion that he (and other foreigners) bore primary responsibility for Nikon's loss of mind.[16]

The number of corrected books that began to appear soon increased. After the impetus of 1654 (and keeping in mind that editions of the Psalter and the Kormchaia had already been issued), allowing due time for corrections, there came in 1656 the Triod, the Hours, the Irmologii; in 1657, the Psalter, the New Testament, the Books of the Apostles, another edition of

13. This is a parallel drawn by Zenkovsky, *Staroobriadchestvo*, p. 211. As to punishments, it has long been observed that the dissenters bore them whether the measures were lenient or strict (throughout their history), Conybeare, op. cit., p. 1.

14. *Materialy*, op. cit., I, II, passim.

15. Zenkovsky, *Staroobriadchestvo* pp. 217-19.

16. Smirnov, *Istoriia Raskola*, op. cit., p. 64.

the Irmologii, in 1658, some service books, a new edition of the Psalter, and so forth.[17] It is not an insignificant list for the task was large in scope and demanding in nature. There was, as has been cited above, no question of dogma involved,[18] and the book as bearer of knowledge, of practical application, and veneration was a notion imbedded in Russian history.[19] Unfortunately, the Old Believers could not bring themselves to realize that corrections (even allowing for Nikonian impetuosity and imperfectibility) could actually enhance the texts. Such views were made easier by reality: the six Sluzhebniks published under Nikon were all different.

This was a serious problem and was a foundation stone of the dissent. Book correction was not new per se in Russia. Patriarch Filaret had, in the reign of his son, Tsar Mikhail, undertaken the editing and publication of Church manuals[20] and the Zealots of Piety, along with others in the printing house had from time to time made an effort here. Such notable figures as Vonifatiev and Rtishchev had also given their hand in correction but it should be observed in all these cases that mostly old texts were used for collation.[21] One charge against Nikon was that far too many modern Greeks texts, themselves subject to corruption, were used and the charge is not completely unfounded.

This charge was only one of many. Other allegations also bore substance. One was that of nibbling, namely, that given the huge quantity of texts ostensibly collected as vademecums and references for correction, the staff could not possibly use enough to insure thoroughness. The Nikonians were like mice, nibbling only at corners, not able to reach the center, one source said.[22]

17. See the list in Makarii, *Istoriia*, XII, pp. 198-99.
18. Some pertinent comments on this are in Makarii *Raskol*, op. cit., p. 9.
19. Fedotov, op. cit., II, p. 42.
20. Vernardsky, op. cit., V, part 1, p. 417.
21. Ustiugov, (Ustiugov, ed.), op. cit., p. 308.
22. Borozdin, op. cit., pp. 259-60.

Then, we have the serious allegations of Father Schmeman. He writes: "The correction of books was not so much inspired by a return to the spirit and essence of Orthodox faith as by a striving toward uniformity and, frequently, a flippant Greco-philism".[23] And Professor Cherniavsky observes that the Old Believers, in cognizance of the limitations on unimpeachable accuracy, were able to attack, from the very beginning the Nikonian changes at their most vulnerable point — scholarly foundation.[24] He goes on to note that the Old Believers were shocked at the "arbitrariness" and Nikon employed enormous police power to effect his goals.

Capriciousness was not foreign to Old Believers and textual analysis, as given by Kartashev, demands attention. Old Believers became fond of quoting books such as the "Kniga o Vere" (Book of Faith), the "Kirillova Kniga" (Book of Cyril), both, incidentally, containing concepts of antichrist and the end of the world later widely used by Old Believers, and the "Malyi Katekhizis" (Short Chatechism) of Petr Mogila. These books were among the "true" books of old belief.

The "Kniga o Vere" was compiled by Nafanail, hegumen of the Mikhailovskii Monastery in Kiev. In the introduction, Nafanail notes that he was inspired by a feeling of repentance to atone for the years of delusion in his youth. He borrowed some thirty chapters from books then circulating in the south-west regions, and another ten from the "Palinodii" of Zakharii Kopystenskii which had not yet been published. The book is profered against the Latins, and even more so against the Uniates. Curiously, it goes on to cite the text of the confession of faith given to the Pope in Rome in 1596 by Cyril Terletsky and Ipatii Potei. This confession was replete with capitulations to the Latin faith. Now, at Vonifatiev's request, it was translated into Church Slavonic to be used, as it turned out, as an anti-reformist symbol by Old Believers.

---

23. Schmeman, op. cit., p. 376.
24. Cherniavsky, op. cit., pp. 8-9.

The "Malyi Katekhizis" of Mogila was written in Polish in 1645 and translated, with some corrections, into Church Slavonic in 1649.

Perhaps the most paradigmatic case is the apocryphal "Feodoritovo Slovo." Prior to Patriarch Iosif, this had appeared only in the volume titled "Bol'shoi Katekhizis" of Lavrentii Zyzanii (1627). Russian correctors entered it into the "Kirillova Kniga," the "Kniga o Vere," and into the "Malyi Katekhizis." In so doing, they changed the Kievan original so that it would prescribe the two fingered method of making the sign of the cross, instead of the three fingered method. They also changed the clearly stated form for the use of "alleluia." Thus, Avvakum and Neronov, who were principally responsible for these altera-tions, insured when they could that their own predilections were entered into the texts. Their own acceptance assumed, the books unsurprisingly became hallowed texts of the old belief.

Thus, the charge of lack of scholarly foundation could as easily be leveled at the Old Believers also for their support of the Church was the Church of the Stoglav Sobor (1651), a mere hundred years old. And when looked at in terms of systematic approaches to the problems of reform and change their "method" left much to be desired.

The idea of the necessity of correction was not new. Large number of texts and manuscripts were used. But the underlying perceptions of the opposition could not be shaken. It witnessed the rise at Court of a more youthful, more Westernized group to which the Tsar was sympathetic. Prince Odoevskii, Prince L'vov, Morozov, and Romadonovskii were among those on the lay side. Vonifatiev, Neronov, and the circle of priests centered at the Blagoveshchenskii Cathedral represented the clerical side which was clearly in agreement with the secular group regard-ing Westernization and innovation. Together they shared belief in the principles of Moscow as the Third Rome.

To further these notions and raise the prestige of the Church at the nation's center, these groups summoned famous preachers from the countryside (Avakum, Lazar', Daniil, Login). But the theocratic ideology of one universal Orthodox

137

Tsar of all Christians was not necessarily conducive to the nation's people as a whole. They were being pushed to the center stage, to world horizons still foreign to them. And from the south-west came many scholars, some of suspect views. "It is with vexation that indigenous Muscovites felt that these south-western colleagues did not feel the deeply held ideal of Moscow the Third Rome in the same fashion as they did. The group of Stefan Vonifatiev singularly strove to attain the ideal by all possible means, realizing it would be pleasant to all. But not all understood the ideal in the same way, whether in its contents or the ways and means toward its attainment."[25]

Initially, Nikon's own ideas were more reflective of the provincial. But as his contacts and his work within Moscow circles increased, he came to hold grandiose notions of an universal Orthodox tsardom. He felt in the extreme that to serve such a notion Russians would have to equate themselves with the Greeks. Therefore, book corrections had to proceed principally by comparison with Greek texts. This by itself did not constitute any method, other than one of spurious condescension to suspect Greek models. As such, it proved costly for the negative perceptions of reform it engendered.

Kliuchevskii makes a keen observation here. He notes that the intransigence of a large group of priests and people is rooted in the conception of the Church that had come to prevail. Russia being the Third Rome, free from foreign oppression, had become, it was assumed, the protectress of Orthodoxy. Its faith, not marred by dominance by other people, remained purest of all the Orthodox and the accolade "Third Rome" sounded well in Russian ears. The burden of maintaining faith had become theirs and it had become the custom to view Russia as repository of the Orthodox truths. This, more local conception ran counter to traditional views of Orthodoxy as ecumenical in nature with the result of constricting Orthodoxy into a geographic frame-

---

25. Kartashev, op. cit., p. 122.

work. Having accepted this meant the immutability of the Russian texts and church books, of its faith, and its rituals. It also meant that correction could not really be countenanced without strong doses of fervent suspicion.[26] The large segment of the populace that felt this way was usually against Nikon. It is remarkable how the analysis supports Nikon's ecumenical leanings which constantly sought outlet.[26] (The modern Soviet view of the reform is conveniently summed up thusly: 'Of course, the Church reform would not have drawn forth any "schism" if there had not been in the Russian feudal serf government of that time sharp social and class contradictions".[27] It is a summary view in that the element of class struggle is stressed as the sole determining criterion).

Nikon, in delivering his sermon at his consecration as Patriarch, spoke of his desire that God spread the Orthodox kingdom from sea to sea, and that unity would finally be achieved. His ecumenical notions were struck by a phrase in the Acts of the Council of Constantinople (1593) which confirmed the establishment of the Patriarchy in Russia in 1589. Nikon had asked Epifanii Slavinetskii to translate the Acts for him. The phrase of interest to him dealt with the idea that the Russian Church should be in accord with Greek rituals and that the Third Rome could not be different from the Second (Constantinople). The effects of this became apparent in the initial manifestations of reform, as in the deletion made in the new Psalter of 1653. Realization of the entanglements that would follow might be at the basis of the various and constant oaths

---

26. Kliuchevskii, III, op. cit., pp. 294-96.

26. Perhaps at this juncture we should take historiographic heed of Kapterev's book, on Nikon and Aleksei (op. cit.) in which he curiously posits throughout that Nikon had nothing to do with any reforms, that Tsar Aleksei was the responsible party for pushing them through, that Nikon had no realization of his role, etc... The argumentation does not merit acceptance and the conclusions are tenuous. However, the existence of this view should be noted.

27. Vodovozov, op. cit., p. 343.

that Nikon forced the Tsar and boiars to take so as to insure compliance with the letter of his reforms.

Nikon's infatuation with the ecumenical mandated that he stay in touch with the Near Eastern Patriarchs. Sometimes, his own conceptualizations regarding this were excessive. Nikon had written to Paisius I, Patriarch of Constantinople, a letter containing 28 questions. This occurred after the tribulations of the Moscow Council of 1654, after which Nikon felt he needed additional support with the reforms and revisions undertaken. He expressed his willingness to submit the findings thereof.

The reply from Paisius I arrived in May, 1655. It was signed by Paisius, 24 metropolitans, one archbishop, and three bishops. The reply stressed: unity within the Church is not disrupted by different rituals, but by heresy and other major evils. Minor differences are of no consequence since the Church developed these piecemeal in various regions; only major points of faith were to demand such stringent attention. Paisius counseled Nikon to end the Church troubles and offered to send a compilation on the key points of the faith as eleborated by his synod.[28] But here Nikon did not feel to be the submissive Grecophile. He disregarded the judicious counsel he had sought.

The reform proceeded. It was not easy for many, too many, people had to be convinced of its rectitude and too many never became convinced. Opposition was steady and on many levels. By 1654, Neronov even had begun to use the antichrist notion in reference to Nikon and his aims[29] (a powerful weapon when presented to people whose intelectual underpinnings in matters of faith were few). If fireworks could scare the peasants[30] then the image of antichrist was far more fearful, a terrifying harbinger of impending apocalypse. It was an image more real than any fireworks could be. Add to these the very many tech-

---

28. Kartashev, op. cit., p. 157.

29. *Materialy*, I, pp. 51-69; and passim.

30. See an interesting example of this (The Dutchman Klenk in Ustiug in 1674) in Rovinskii, op. cit., Apdx., pp. 175ff.

nical and methodological problems, the political ramifications, the weight of the tribulations, and one wonders at Nikon's persistence.

Curiously, after 1656, Nikon's own interest ebbed in this whole, vast project. Nikon gave scant attention to textological corrections once it became clear to him that his grandiose ideas of Church supremacy stumbled in the path of a growing State. His innovations are exaggerated, for whatever purpose they served, the ulterior motive of ecclesiastical position was paramount. It would be clarifying to know what texts were actually used by the correctors, how many of them, how frequently. Unfortunately there are few hints at these answers. It is a mark of Nikon's fortitude, short lived though it was, and, in a sense, the enduring impetus of his work and efforts, even given his loss of interest, that the task of correcting and collating continued even after his departure from the Patriarchal seat in 1658.[31] If we look eight years later, at the 1666 Council which deposed him, and then at the 1667 Council which accepted the many measures and reforms he had propagated during his brief reign, we see a similar parallel. For though Nikon drew condemnation, his work gained acceptance. The degree to which obduracy and greatness intermingled, along with excessive grecophilism taken in the name of a broader ecumenical outlook is still debated when measuring Nikon.

---

31. A list of corrected texts which appeared in the early 1660's is to be had in Makarii, *Istoriia*, XII, pp. 638-39.

Chapter 8

Schism

Chronologically speaking the origin of the schism cannot be placed in any one year. It took many years for it to grow into a movement. The year 1653 might be construed as a starting point, for it was then that some opposition had mobilized against the initial incursions of Nikon's reforms. The years 1666-67 and the Church Councils thereof can legitimately be seen as closing out the opening period of consolidation, for the Council of 1667 formally anathemized the Old Believers and forbade the propagation of their faith.

It may be recalled that in 1653 Nikon issued his orders concerning troeperstie and some lesser changes. It may not have seemed that on the basis of first changes serious disjunctions would have occurred. But it did so happen. Avvakum, Neronov, Login, Daniil and others began to wage a campaign againt the innovations and Nikon. The campaign included petitions to the Tsar, outright agitation, refusal to adhere to the new strictures, refusal to use the new issue of the Psalter, and so forth, not to cite the vehemence of personal attacks.

The response of Nikon and the government, and it is to be understood that from the start the Patriarch knew that he could not act as churchman only, was to mete out immediate punishment to the principals.[1] At first it was relatively mild, being mostly in the form of exile to monasteries. Later it was to take on much cruder elements that did nothing to stop the growth of schism. In 1654, Bishop Paul of Kolomna, one of six churchmen out of thirty five present at the sobor called by Nikon to judge on the imperative need for correction of texts, was exiled. Having been the only one at the sobor who spoke out strongly against the "proposed" innovations, he was the target for more severe measures. He died in unknown circumstances in exile, having undergone beating.

Avvakum has already been discussed in his various roles. His co-believer Ivan Neronov was a similarly passionate defender of the old belief. From the very beginning of the reform he geared his many and talented energies on behalf of the cause. Like Avvakum he seemed instinctively able to understand at this early juncture the underlying motifs and the potential changes the reforms would engender. In 1653 he is already writing Tsar Aleksei, begging him: "... please, I pray, calm the storm that is disturbing the Church..."[2] But the letter is from the Spasso-kammenyi Monastery where he had been sent. Such restrictions did not really impede his activity and in 1656 the activity is prolonged and damaging enough to cause his anathemization. But he was pardoned in the following year and allowed to use the old books if he desisted from agitating. Though he agreed, it was only a temporary expediency on his part.

This early visceral reaction was compounded by the personal clashes already mentioned above. The degree of ardor

---

1. Makarii, *Istoriia*, XII, pp. 139-44. Here, again, is an example of Ecclesia and State working together. The old formula (frequently seen in the West) of the Church being forbidden to shed blood led to concert with the State. The Church judged, the State carried out the judgement and meted out punishment. The classic example, of course, is the Spanish Inquisition. In the Russian Church, inquisitorial methods advocated by visiting Greek prelates did not commence in any substantial scale until after the Council of 1682.

2. "Poslanie Protopopa Ivana Neronova k Tsariu A.M. iz Spassokamen-nago Mon. ot 6-go Noiabria 7162 (1653 g)", *Materialy*, I, p. 38.

was high (on both sides). The Old Believers began quickly to benefit from the halo of martyrdom, and those suffering for their faith commanded great respect. Avvakum, on the way to exile to Siberia, and while there, worked openly, and successful for the old faith. A mystique, so to speak, began to be built up, and it was greatly enhanced by the phenomena of "visions". Many Old Believers began, almost from the start, to claim that they had visions.[3] These visions generally portended evil and catastrophe to the audiences who heard the tales. They were especially effective when disasters, such as the cholera outbreak in Moscow in 1654, struck. Visions then took on the aura of truth and the Old Believers took on more adherents.

As we have seen above, this period saw a rise in relations with the Near East (and the Balkan areas) with a resultant flood of foreign churchmen and prelates. A large segment of the Russian population (including much of the lower clergy) was far from co-responsive to these incursions. Many felt that Nikon's infatuatuation with innovations stemmed from the excessive contacts and such ideas gained credence in their minds when visiting prelates commented very favorably on the correction of texts (as did, e.g. Patriarch Makarios of Antioch). The large number of foreign books, as those brought back from the Near East by Arsenii Sukhanov, did not always meet with approval. And anger was particularly real when visiting hierarchs indulged (be it at Nikon's or the Tsar's requests) in Russian Church affairs. Even many of the more progressive Russians could not be too happy with facts such as these: the first anathema pronounced on Old Believers was (in February of 1656) by foreigners; Makarios of Antioch, Metropolitan Gavriil of Serbia, and Gregorius, Metropolitan of Nicaea.[4]

In such actions it is not difficult to see how both the Church and the State which in Russia, as Fedotov notes, rarely

---

3. Makarii, *Istoriia*, XII, pp. 208-09.
4. Ibid., p. 190.

came into conflict and functioned more in terms of collaboration and encroachment,[5] engendered dissatisfaction among people. With individual exceptions, the Old Believers were not anathemized themselves until the Councils of 1666-67 and attempts at reconciliation were frequent. The Tsar was hurt at the rise of schism and, at first, reluctant to take final steps toward its eradication. To have Avvakum come back to the fold was an idea dear to him. But the point of collaboration was important, for no action, symbolic or otherwise, as that allowed to visiting churchmen, could have occurred without patriarchal or governmental consent. This may be one of the reasons why even some writers who are inimical to Nikon do not view him alone as the cause of schism;[6] circumstances were such that he was a cog in an unstoppable wheel. Nikon's granting of permission of the Greek language to be used (on occasion) in the service should be placed in the same framework.[7]

Nikon left the Patriarchy in 1658. It was becoming apparent, even to foreigners,[8] that his base of support was slipping, that Tsar Aleksei himself was not averse to heeding the continuous admonitions and protests of the nobility. One of the two "great sovereigns" was departing, willingly though it may have been.[9] His departure played a role in the schism.

---

5. Fedotov, op. cit., I, p. 401.

6. Andreev, op. cit., pp. 8-9.

7. Makarii, *Istoriia*, XII, p. 291.

8. "Puteshestvie v Moskoviiu Barona Avgustina Meierberga", *ChOIDR*, 1874, no. 1, sect. iv, p. 171.

9. There was then debate over usage of the term "great sovereign", normally reserved only for the Tsar. Nikon claimed this title was granted to him by the Tsar, and this is generally accepted. The only place I have seen where this is disputed is in Episkop Makarii's work where he feels that the usage sprung from churchmen who so called Nikon in the early 1650's. Makarii, *Istoriia*, XII, p. 343. This, however, does not rule out the standard (and Nikon's) version that the Tsar granted Nikon the title in the early 1650's (probably 1652 or 1653). If that seems the case, and it is plausible enough, then obviously churchmen would call Nikon in that fashion. Nikon himself talks about the things he had been subjected to (and touches on this point) in "Pis'mo Patriarkha Nikona k Tsar' gradskomu Patriarkhu Dionisiiu (1666 g.)," *ZORSA*, vol. 2, 1861, p. 515.

When Nikon decided to leave the Patriarchy on that fateful day (July 10, 1658) he gave a speech to those assembled in the cathedral. It was a speech redolent of animism and pathos. He spoke of the infirmity of the Patriarch in the face of increasing (governmental) opposition, of the changes in the Tsar, of his desire to leave his high post. He elicited great response from the people who, cryingly, did not wish him to leave.[10] It was a speech and a scene that prompted the Tsar to say when he was given word of it: "It seems that I am sleeping with open eyes and all this is a dream".[11] It was also a speech that led to controversy on the question whether Nikon had promised never to return as head of the Church. It is sometimes claimed that Nikon said he would accept ànathema were he ever to return to his former position as Patriarch. It is not difficult to surmise who put this forth. As Spinka wrote: "His opponents insisted that before he left, he had renounced his patriarchal office and had invoked an anathema upon himself if he ever returned".[12] Nikon, in contrast, always adamantly insisted that no such statement was ever made by him.

Wherever the truth lies, Nikon's departure had an enlivening effect on the progress of schism. Neronov and other old believer leaders now functioned openly and made their message more non-compromising than ever. There was one factor which was mitigating in nature. Since Nikon left he had, in old believer eyes, committed a compromising act. How seriously could the innovations and the reforms within the Church be taken if the figure most responsible for their promulgation, and one who had felt strongly enough about opposition to exile and punish detractors, had himself suddenly turned his

10. Gibbenet, *Izsledovanie*, I, pp. 22-36, and passim. Pavel F. Nikolaevskii, *Obstoiatel'stvo i Prichiny Udaleniia Patriarkha Nikona s Prestola* (SPB: 1883?), pp.20-21. Hereafter cited Nikolaevskii, *Udaleniia*.

11. *Nikolaevskii, Udaleniia*, p. 23.

12. Matthew Spinka, "Patriarch Nikon and the Subjection of the Russian Church to the State", *Church History*, vol. X, 1941 (no. 4., Dec.), p. 360.

back on the fruit of his activity? Secondly, many Old Believers correctly saw that Nikon's authority with the Tsar had fallen, that the Tsar's faith and trust in Nikon was perhaps irrevocably shaken.[13] Both circumstances favored a more direct, a more virulent effort on behalf of the harried older values. And it must have created at least an illusion of hope, for if the Tsar accepted Nikon's departure, then perhaps it portended better for the Old Believers.

As pointed out above (ch. 6) the period 1658-60 saw a substantial growth and development of raskol'nik literature.[14] It definitely reflected the mounting pressure exerted by the old belief and its protagonists. The pressure came in various forms. One was the effort to help elect a new Patriarch, one who would be partial to the old books and practices. Neronov is much in the forefront here, sending (at least) two petitions to Tsar Aeksei on the necessity of a rapid selection of a new Patriarch to replace Nikon.[15] Perhaps he thought to push the election through while the Old Believers had some breathing room. But Aleksei, who called a sobor in 1660 to consider the matter, realized the problems involved and the canonical restrictions. A wider council would have to be held with the presence of Nikon's peers.

Or so it was thought. The Acts of the Council of Constantinople (1593) confirming the establishment of the Patriarchy in Russia had also granted Muscovy the right to choose a Patriarch without the participation of, or consultation with, Near Eastern Patriarchs. This was clearly known to Tsar Aleksei and Moscow's officialdom. Explanations why it was so specifically ignored, even though Slavinetskii's translation had been available for about seven years, must range as follows: a) the Tsar wished additional support for the move since the circumstances of Nikon's departure did not fit easily into canonical strictures;

---

13. For both points see Zenkovsky, *Staroobriadchestvo*, p. 261.
14. Borozdin, op. cit., p. 104.
15. *Materialy*, I, pp. 167-92.

b) he was acting in accordance with his own broad ecumenical Greco oriented views; c) court politics of the time dictated such a move.

Another form can be seen in the writings themselves. Spiridon Potemkin (uncle of Rtishchev) wrote (ca. 1658) his "Words Against the Heretics" wherein he very seriously discussed many of the problems (ritual, the growing seculari- zation as a threat to Christian society, changes in the texts) inherent in the controversy. The hegumen Feoktist (a friend of Neronov) touched on the theme of antichrist (observing that the manifestation would be spiritual), and the Archimandrite Antonii of the Spasskii Monastery protested, in an extensive message to the Tsar, the correction of the texts. The Bishop Aleksandr of Kolomna (formerly of Viatka) wrote a treatise and addressed it to the Tsar (1662), analyzing the many Nikonian re- forms.[16] And there were many others. The tracts just listed were all by men who were reasonably educated, scholarly, and eloquent. These were not intellectual stabs from bleak depths, but reasoned treatises. They became ever harder to ignore. As Makarii has stated (in a slightly different, but applicable context): "... many old believer ideas were put into print not in the form of resolutions on ritual, but as dogmas..,"[17] i.e. tenets of old belief came to have (or already, to a large extent at this time, had) the force of dogma.

In practical terms the raskol was establishing itself firmly in the 1660's. There were already various groups settling in forests, or in other more desolate regions. Many of them boy- cotted the Church by not participating in any of its formal activities. Sometimes this was done irrespective of whether the

---

16. For an excellent discussion of these see Zenkovsky, *Staroobriadchestvo*, pp. 262-66. In general, a number of Old Believer writings of this early stage are to be had in *Materialy*, passim. In addition to the men writing listed in the text, others were the elder Efrem Potemkin) of the Biziukov Monastery), the elder Serapion (of the Simonov Monastery in Moscow), the elder Avraamii (of the Iosif Volokolamsk Monastery), the elder Epifanii, etc., See Makarii, *Istoriia*, XII, pp. 627-28, and Makarii, *Raskol*, pp. 170-71 for expanded lists.

17. Makarii, *Raskol*, p. 139.

church in question followed the old ritual or not. Radical groups, about the time of the Councils, began (sporadically though be it) the practice of self-immolation. Similarly, cases of open rebellion become more prominent. Preaching spread the schism quickly for though the written tracts laid many foundations they took far longer to seep through. We have seen some examples already. Others who traveled and spread the note of dissent were Dosifei and Kornilii who worked on Don River area, the monk Iosif Istomin, exiled to Siberia in 1660 and where he became the major planter of old belief, Kapiton (the infamous) in the Kostroma region, the elder Sergii Saltykov (whom Avvakum considered a good candidate for the hierarchy) and many more.[18] Their message was oral, direct, and not easy to contradict. Its effect was there to see. Though the government acted against this phenomenon, it did so without significant energy and it is to the post Great Council period that persecution in its true state can be attributed.

The famed case of the Solovetskii Monastery is instructive. This monastery, perched on an island in the White Sea, was one of the most prestigious in Russia not only for its inordinately rich spiritual heritage, but also for its economic pre-eminence. Barsov notes, in speaking of the northern littoral, that the Novgorodians had long been drawing profit from this region. "But, commercial exploitation could not bring cohesiveness to the varied population and could not have a salutory effect on the alien tribes. It was helpless in the task of bringing in people to work and in the creation of a civil community in the wild forest region. As is known, the Solovetskii Monastery became such an organizing force and structural center."[19] In view of its uniqueness and its prestige it became all the more tragic that the Solovetskii Monastery was the object of a governmental siege for eight years. The situation came about in the following way.

18. Ibid., pp. 169ff. Also Makarii, *Istoriia*, XII, pp. 629-31.

19. E.V. Barsov (ed.), "Akty Otnosiashchiesia k Istorii Solovetskago Bunta", *ChOIDR*, 1883, book 4, sect. v, part 1, p.i. Hereafter cited *Akty, Solovetskie.*

The Solovetskii Monastery had misunderstandings with the government from the time of the Ulozhenie (1649) which stopped a major land expansion program at the monastery. Other minor points caused discontent. But in 1657 everything took on new dimensions for it was in that year that the reformed service books were given it to use. The monastery, with Archimandrite Il'ia at its head, simply refused to use them. Attempts by authorities to install monastic heads favorable to the reforms ended in failure; and when Archimandrite Varfalomei agreed to accept the new texts, the brethren themselves deposed him.[20] The defiance was very real, even though at this juncture there were no specific instructions regarding the use of 'New" books issued to the monastery.

After the Councils of 1666-67 and formal anathema of the Old Believers the government, in a sense, was compelled to act in ultimate response to the intransigence of the Solovetskii Monastery. The noted petition of 1667, written by Gerontii, (the fifth, which became a key tract of the raskol) protested in vain (though claiming that irrespective of circumstances they would not bow to the newer dictums). As Robert Crummey comments: "Their response left the authorities no choice but to accept a humiliating setback or to use force".[21]

The following year (1668) another petition to ther Tsar again fell back on tradition in its argumentations. Our forefathers knew nothing of reforms. These led to "a new, unknown faith invented by his own (i.e. Nikon's — N.L.) knavish wisdom and did not follow apostolic tradition or that of the Fathers".[22] It was in the same year that government troops besieged the

---

20. Makarii, *Istoriia*, XII, pp. 631-37, 674-79; also Robert O. Crummey. op.cit., pp. 16-21.

21. Ibid., p. 19.

22. "Chelobitnaia Solovetskago Monastyria Krakova Poslana k Velikomu Gosudariu k Moskve, v 1668 Godu v Oktiabre Mesiatse", D.E. Kozhanchikov (ed.), *Tri Chelobitnyia Stavschika Savvatiia, Savvy Romanova i Monakhov Solovetskago Monastyria* (SBP: 1862), p. 148. Incidentally, the year as such does not appear in the title but is deduced by the athor from the text. Hereafter cited Chelobitnaia Colovetskago Monastyria 1668.

monastery. The siege was only partially effective for there was still some movement in and out. The surrounding countryside was on the monastery's side and helped when it could. Ten years of uninterrupted propagation of the old belief in the region by the monastery had done its task. The same applies to other religious houses like the Anzersk hermitage which, too, evidently, accepted the raskol,[23] and sympathized with the besieged.

Forced to act against the Solovetskii by the dictums of the Councils (and prodded strongly by the visiting Greek prelates), the State's siege turned the rebellion from a purely religious one into a total one. (My description in these paragraphs strongly follows Kartashev and Akty Solovetskie, cf. ftn. 19).

The surrounding votchinas belonging to the monastery were occupied. Leaders of the revolt within the monastery were Nikanor (a retired archimandrite of the Savvino Zvenigorodskii Monastery), Gerontii (the treasurer), Azarii (the cellarer), and Faddei (a layman in the monastery's service).

From the beginning, orders were given not to fire upon the monastery. The first commander of the besieging forces was Volokhov, replaced in 1672 by Ievlev. Instructions were given to apply some pressure but no firing was to be permitted, nor an attack attempted.

The Solovetskii Monastery had enormous reserves. Its barns and granaries were full, and in addition to its food supply it had 90 canons and 900 puds of gunpowder. (These were necessary since, as an outpost on the White Sea, the monastery had been attacked on numerous occasions in the past by forces of Western nations). In 1670, the monastery itself opened fire on the besiegers. Archimandrite Nikanor walked along the wall and towers with his thurible censing the canons and saying... "our dear ones — our hope lies in you." Government forces did not

---

23. "Otpiska Godudariu Kholmogorskago Voevody Naryshkina o Stroitele, Startsakh i Sluzhebnikakh Anzerskoi Pustini, Pribyvaiushchikh v Raskole", *Akty Solovetskie*, pp. 67-70.

return the fire. The use of weaponry created some discord within as Gerontii led a faction opposed to its use.

In 1673, a council of monks within the Solovetskii decided that no more prayers be said for the Tsar. Hieromonks and priests refused to accept this and were thrown into cells. Inner conflict had begun. More defectors from the monastery crossed the ice to leave. Hunger and scurvy raised their heads. Some died without last rites and were interred without proper burial services. The decisive moment was approaching. Tsar Aleksei gave orders to end the revolt. In the meantime, the elder Feoktist defected and showed the military a secret passage into the monastery. The army crossed the ice on January 22, 1676, and entered the cloister. The siege was over.

The revolt which, as Crummey observes, '... had begun as a protest against the ecclesiastical novelties and against the principle that the state and hierarchy could impose such changes on an independent monastery"[24] was now over too. When the besiegers had finally acted it made no difference that the besieged were monks. The ones that escaped spread the old belief, traveling where they could. The resistance of the Solovetskii Monastery was as long as it was heroic. As the monks themselves said eight years previously in their petition: "it would be better to die a temporal death than suffer eternal damnation; or the Tsar and the new teachers will cast us to the flames, torture us, or have us split in half. But we shall never betray the traditions of the apostles and our fathers!"[25] The temporal death they had vowed to accept was theirs.

By acts such as these the schism ingrained itself. It had now come the full circle, from its start on religious grounds to the inclusion of an anti-government stance. This, it must be stressed, was not always prevalent though the increasing frequency of its appearance was highly disturbing. As Vernadsky notes: "... the

---

24. Crummey, op. cit., p. 20.
25. *Chelobitnaia Solovetskago Monastyria 1668*, p. 181.

danger of the situation for the government's stability lay not as much in the theology of the Old Believers, as in the sympathy and support that the old believer movement was gaining from large sections of the population, whose motives were not merely religious but social and political as well. Though religious in its origin and its essence, the Old Believers' opposition to authority was potentially the nucleus of a widespread revolutionary movement."[26] Of course, there is the notion that in the political sense the schism never threatened the government,[27] though this may be discounted. Some old believer groups that had emigrated to neighboring countries actually participated in raids onto Russian soil.

Nikon's oponents did not believe that his reform measures were meant for the restoration of the original but were merely indiscriminately innovative.[28] They spoke of high handed method, of whimsical change, of travesty of the religious traditions of the land. They were not generally as open minded as Bishop Aleksandr (of Viatka, then Kolomna), himself a proponent of the old belief, who maintained that differences in the texts did not, per se, imply heresy.[29] It was a rather enlightened view for it was not based on the simplicities of the more fanatical preachers. Avvakum himself well understood that with the departure of Nikon all would not necessarily be well. The Councils of 1666-67 did, after all, accept most of Nikon's proposals. Tsar Aleksei and other government officials also understood that the more perceptive of the Old Believers did not fall into the trap of thinking all would change with the departure of Nikon. His evil notions themselves had to be eradicated.[30] Though the personal element was always strong in this struggle, it was obviously submerged in the greater task —

26. Vernadsky, op. cit., V, part 2, p. 696.
27. Andreev, op. cit., pp. 10-11.
28. Ibid., p. 73.
29. Makarii, *Istoriia*, XII, pp. 616-18.
30. Borozdin, op. cit., p. 125.

the restoration of the ancient verities. In this the schism did not ultimately succeed. The State and the Church remained committed to reform. But, in another sense it did succeed for thousands upon thousands chose to remain in the fold of the real Church as they understood it. The old books were kept and used, the old prayers chanted, and two fingers were still used for the sign of the cross. In this example of a dedication often linked to personal destruction the old belief can claim a victory. It may be said that it felt it had to live and die for a higher morality.

Chapter 9

The Great Councils of 1666-1667

The Councils of 1666-67 play a decisive part in our history and they can be considered a key to the seventeenth century for they break with the old and are portent of the new.[1] They are the outgrowth of practically all the major controversies of Aleksei's reign — the development of schism, the liturgical and book reforms, Nikonianism, and political discontent arising from religious dissent. Much of this has been already discussed. Before moving to the Great Councils themselves, some aspects of their antecedent must be mentioned.

The Council of 1660 had originally convened to settle the case of Nikon who had vacated the patriarchal seat in 1658. It had wished to depose him formally and elect a new Patriarch but the attempt was thwarted by circumstances. There was no precedent in a case of this sort where the Patriarch had himself

---

1. Billington considers them (though he specifically mentions the 1667 sessions) the decisive point of the XVII c. (in Russian, "perelom"). In fact, he feels this to be "as far reaching in its implications as the Bolshevik coup d'etat exactly 250 years later", Billington, op. cit., p. 121, for he views the raskol (like the Revolution) as "the culmination and climax of nearly a century of bitter ideological controversy which involved politics and aesthetics as well as personal metaphysical beliefs".

vacated his position though still maintaining his title. Canonically, also, as Nikon himself pointed out, the lesser churchmen could have no formal say regarding his deposition and in the election of a new Patriarch.[2] This contravened the Acts of the Council of 1593 (see chapt. 7) which Nikon himself had ordered Epifanii Slavinetskii to translate. But for the expediency of the moment, it was forgotten by all.

Nikon noted other irregularities of the Council. The Council was convened without the consent of the Patriarch. It did not act independently but with the prodding of the Tsar. Nikon himself was not called to the Council and his aide was not heard.[3] And, to add further to the confusion, the Greeks present at this council spoke highly of Nikon and considered that in leaving the Patriarchy he had sinned as a man but was not guilty in dogmatic terms.[4] Therefore, it was decided that the Near Eastern Patriarchs be invited to a great council for proper adjudication of the case. The makeup of the Council of 1660 was insufficiently strong to cope with the many facets of the situation as it then stood.[5] Historically, this begged the question. Yet, with the pro-Greek trend, solidarity on all matters with Near Eastern Patriarchs was sought.

Epifanii Slavinetskii was instrumental in the outcome, for he had protested the decision to oust Nikon that the Council was considering even though it was unclear regarding the canonical rules and implications. The acceptance at the opening session of the Council of depositions against Nikon by Metropolitan Pitirim and of Prince A.N. Trubetskoi was

---

2. Nikon said much the same again in 1662 in writing to the Tsar. And it was a position he maintained constantly. Gibbenet, *Izsledovanie*, II, p. 75.

3. These and other irregularities are discussed in Zykikin, op. cit., II, p. 199.

4. Gibbenet, *Patriarkh Nikon*, pp. 231-32.

5. It was not strong enough (and prepared enough) though among the churchmen present were Metropolitans Makarii of Novgorod, Lavrentii of Kazan', Pitirim of Sarsk, Michael of Greece, Iona of Rostov, and Archbishops Markel of Vologda and Filaret of Smolensk. Gibbenet, *Izsledovanie*, I, p. 76.

tenuous. "Both of them asserted categorically that Nikon had abdicated and had sworn to that effect."[6] The fact that these were written nineteen months after the incident did not seem to matter.

The decision to call the new council with the participation of the Near Eastern Patriarchs came in December, 1662, and it was tentatively to take place in 1663. However, considering the pace of contemporary time everything was not resolved and the Patriarchs did not arrive until November, 1666. In this long interim period of four years a number of things occurred. First was the development of the schism, an item that had finally to be treated at the Great Councils (even though originally this was not scheduled).[7] Secondly, all manner of attacks (following the example of the Council of 1660) descended on Nikon (see ch. 5) under presumption of safety, immunity and the wish for vindictiveness. It was as if "... the intrigues with which Nikon's enemies chained him had no bounds..."[8]

Thirdly, in preparation for the Councils, much correspondence took place between the principals. The Eastern Patriarchs were contacted, for example, with the series of "Questions" prepared by Ligarides and Streshnev. Much as the "Questions" were intended to incriminate Nikon, the Russian officials were somewhat dismayed to observe that two of the four Patriarchs were very careful in their statements. They did not wish to implicate Nikon. In fact, they recommended that leniency be the keynote in judging Nikon.[9] These two Patriarchs, Nektarios of Jerusalem and Dionisios of Constantinople were pro-Nikon and refused to come to Moscow for the trial (not being sure of the

6. Vernadsky, op.cit., V, part 2, p. 587.
7. The question of the schism and the trials of individual Old Believers were essentially to be handled by the Russian churchmen and government officials. It was in Nikon's case that the visiting prelates were to have most say. As we shall see, the Greeks had far more say than expected.
8. Gibbenet, *Izsledovanie*, II, p. 84.
9. Gibbenet, *Patriarkh Nikon*, p. 246.

necessity for such procedure). The question of confirming new Patriarchs was nothing new to the Near Eastern prelates, themselves frequently subject to depositions and installations. Nektarios even suggested reconciliation and that Nikon be reinstated to the Patriarchy. The other Patriarchs, Makarios of Antioch and Paisios of Alexandria consented to come to help judge Nikon (and perhaps to come away with some reward for their aid). Nikon himself attempted to contact Dionisios in 1665 but, as noted above (ch. 5), his letter was intercepted.[10]

To begin a solution of the problem of the Old Believers the Council of 1666 was convened (April). At its first session basic procedures were formulated. All those participating in the Council would be asked three questions: a) how do you view the Eastern Patriarchs (insofar as their legitimacy as hierarchs is concerned)? b) do you accept the Greek church books? and c) how do you view the Council of 1654 (at which Nikon mandated the revisions of church books)?[11] Affirmative answers were expected and obtained from all for the government wished to keep firm control of the direction of the Council.

The second session (April 29, 1666) was primarily taken up with the Tsar's speech on the reasons for the Council. Session three saw the appearance of Bishop Aleksandr of Viatka (then Kolomna). He was the only bishop (of those invited) who was sympathetic to old belief and he had, some years earlier, written a tract in its behalf. Now he renounced his former stance and accepted the innovations he had previously decried.[12] Vernadsky notes that "having signed the declaration he decided to discontinue any overt resistance to the established church, and signed a

_____

10. *ZORSA*, 1861, v. 2, pp. 51-30; Gorchakov, *Monastyrskii Prikaz*, op.cit., pp. 92-95.

11. *Materialy*, II, pp. 63-64; Makarii, *Raskol*, op.cit., p. 175; Vernadsky, op.cit., V, part 2, p. 605.

12. *Materialy* II, p. 78-79. In general, I have based my description of the Acts of the Council on this source, *Materialy*, II, esp. pp. 49-144. For a nice, condensed (but accurate) description see Makarii, *Raskol*, pp. 175-78.

special abnegation of all his previous protests against the Nikonian books".[13] It is interesting to note that Aleksandr was not forced to pronounce anathema on the old faith personally (a conciliatory gesture on the Council's part).[14] It is also noteworthy that no defenders of the old belief were to be allowed at the trials.

Avvakum made the fourth session a notable one (May 13?). He acted with his customary personal vigor and force and all else seemed supereragatory. He refused any idea of compromise and talked independly and haughtily to the judging members. "We are fools for Christ's sake. You are strong and we are weak."[15] In being brought to Moscow for judgement he had suffered the additional indignity of having his beard cut. "And God's enemies also cut off my beard. What can one do? Wolves have no pity for sheep! They tore it off like dogs and left only a tuft, [of hair] just like a Pole's, on my forehead."[16] The Council pronounced anathema on him, defrocked him, and sent him away, still the unbending recusant.[17] In leaving he cursed and damned the Council itself. The Acts of the Council refer to him as "slanderer and rebel", one with a "whore's tongue".[18]

At the fifth session Nikita Dobrynin (Pustosviat) was called. He had written a famous and well conceived petition on behalf of the Old Believers. This was now discussed and found wanting. Nikita himself maintained a firm position and defended his tenets. He also took the occasion (as had Avvakum) to revile Nikon and accuse him of countless heresies (including such disparate examples as those of the Judaizers and Nesto-

---

13. Vernardsky, op. cit., V, part 2, p. 605.

14. Zenkovsky, *Staroobriadchestvo*, pp. 286ff.

15. This, in its English version, from his autobiography; Zenkovsky, *Epics*, p. 364.

16. Borozdin, op. cit., p. 143.

17. It should be observed that these are not yet final sentencings of the Old Believers. Judgment of them continues in the following year, 1667. It is then that final decisions regarding the old belief and individual leaders are made.

18. *Materialy*, II, pp. 79-82.

rianism). Several months later he wrote the Council and asked forgiveness, humbly beseeching it to believe that he would now be a true son of the established Church. Still later, and here he parallels many Old Believers, he reverted to the old faith. The acceptance of the new books and the established Church at the Councils of 1666-67 by many of the Old Believers was just a ploy, an answer to the exigencies then extant.

The deacon Feodor was tried at session six. He did not renege and was sent to a monastery from which he wrote his acceptance of the reforms. The acceptance was again short-lived. Efrem Potemkin had his turn at session seven. The same general charges were presented and much in the same accusatory tone as had prevailed throughout. But he decided to repent and confess to error. He (Efrem) then "through the beneficence of the Holy Ghost, woke up as from a deep sleep and awakening and realizing his deviation from the path of salvation, and shuddering from the terror that now possessed him, began to berate the old belief and his own previous madness and to expose the evil teaching. In confessing his sin, many bitter tears rolled from his eyes."[19] The eighth and ninth sessions followed much the same pattern.

Judged at the tenth session were such luminaries of the schismatic movement as Ivan Neronov (now the monk Grigorii), Feoktist,[20] Gerasim Firsov (of the Solovetskii Monastery), the hieromonk Avraamii and others. All, for the moment, turned on the old belief and subscribed to the new. It is a point of wonder whether the members of the Council seriously believed these professions. Were they really expected? Could Neronov who had, since the 1630's, struggled so selflessly to

---

19. Ibid., p. 98-99.

20. There is an interesting sidelight here. At his trial Feoktist had submitted a prayerful disquisition to the Council. In it were many explanations and reasons why Feoktist (and others) had been motivated to take their stand for the old belief. This tract was, in the XVIII c., included in and old believer anthology, but omitted was the part where Feoktist expressed his readiness to accept the new books, corrected according to the old texts. *Materialy*, I, ftn. 2, pp. 344-45.

maintain purity in the Church and elevate its moral tone be legitimately believed when he condescended and said yes to the prosecutors? It would seem not but perhaps two factors might be cited in this speculation. First, returning to the example of Aleksandr of Viatka: some measure of compromise might be seen in the sense of willingness to accept retraction. Secondly, it is quite conceivable that the Council (and here Tsar Aleksei's influence is indisputably paramount) was satisfied to accept these retractions on the assumption that they meant a promise to refuse participation in future agitation and spread of schism. It is hard to believe that the members, knowing the power they held at the trial, could expect a complete turnabout in the hearts of the Old Believers. This was all made academic within one year.

The eleventh and final session (July 2) of this first phase of the Councils took the form of a general exhortation and admonition to the clergy on the foibles of the raskol.[21] Much was said about the Old Believers. They were pictured as ignorant, and this applied not just to common people but to the clergy as well. Their "violence" was cited. So was their gradual tendency to escape the dictates of the ecclesiastical hierarchy. Mixed in were general guidelines for the faithful; among these were more frequent confession and communion, the need never to be lazy in seeing those that were sick, attempts to curtail wandering monks, etc... Priests were also admonished to prevent the poor from walking inside churches during services to beg; they were to stand still like the rest of the populace during holy liturgy. And if spiritual exhortations were to meet with contempt, then those of a corporal variety might prove more persuasive.[22]

---

21. I view the Councils in four general phases: A) the first phase, initial trial of Old Believers, spring-summer 1666; B) second phase — deposition of Nikon, November-December, 1666; C) third phase, election of the new Patriarch, January 1667; and D) remaining business, final decrees and rulings on old belief, and so forth, spring-summer 1667.

22. *Materialy*, II, pp. 119-44.

Curiously, regarding Nikon whom the Council was to judge five months hence, the statements were mild. It was offered that it was not Nikon alone who introduced the correction of church books. In this project he had the advice of the most holy Greek Patriarchs, of the whole Russian government, the hierarchy of the Church, and the Council (sobor). Furthermore, the corrections, ostensibly, were made according to ancient Greek and Slavonic texts.[23] In ways this resembles a defense of the Patriarch and the tone is almost anomalous. It is to be remembered that the man, not his work, stood trial in December of 1666.

Patriarchs Makarios of Antioch and Paisios of Alexandria arrived in Moscow on November 2, 1666. Five days later the next phase of the Councils commenced. Nikon's trial was finally to take place. The first four sessions of this phase of the Council were essentially preparatory. They dealt with briefing the visiting prelates on Nikon's wrongdoings (a briefing charged to Ligarides!), discussed some questions of legitimacy (e.g. did the Tsar have the right to summon this Council?), and went over some correspondence. Nikon was present at session one and threee.[24]

Nikon was treated coldly at his trial. The charges put to him were: leaving the Patriarchy, disrespect to the Tsar (in the intercepted letter to Patriarch Dionisios), his persistence in calling himself Patriarch, the exiling of Bishop Paul of Kolomna, and so forth.[25] The first two charges were considered the most serious and Nikon denied them both. His denial regarding this was during the third session. (It was a session where Russians at their own Church Council read excerpts in

23. Ibid., p. 125.

24. The major sources for Nikon's trial are *PSZ*, I, no. 397, pp. 649-56; *Materialy*, II, pp. 166-81; and the superb discussion in Makarii, *Istoriia*, XII, pp. 683-752. For a brief exposition the general reader may see Vernardsky, op. cit., V, part 2, pp. 601-04.

25. Makarii, *Istoriia*, XII, pp. 629-723.

Greek from the "Kormchaia Kniga" — the "Pilot Book", thought to be relevant to the proceedings). It did little good, for the defense that he was allowed was perfunctory. The "Refutation" that Nikon wrote in reply to the "Questions and Answers" (submitted to him by Ligarides and Streshnev) was not permitted to be conveyed to the Council. The impression was generally one of a formality.

Nikon was not allowed to be present at the sixth session (December 3) where the charges against him were further discussed. But he was summoned to the seventh session (December 5). Here again the charges were repeated and emphasis laid on the main accusations. Nikon continued to maintain his previous position — that he had not sworn that he would never return to the Patriarchy, that he committed no disrespect against the Tsar and the government, that he was not guilty of labeling people heretics. He claimed that he had left the Patriarchy to escape the ire of the Tsar. The Tsar in turn swore that this was impossible.[26] Nikon even tried to negate the competency of the Council itself, a rather difficult task.[27] The Council read to him canonical rules of the right of a Council's judgment over him but Nikon even tried to reject the validity of these.[28]

On December 12, 1666, at the eighth and final session of this second phase of the Great Councils, sentence was pro-

26. *PSZ*, no. 397, p. 652; *Materialy*, II, p. 172.
27. The Council was quite legitimate and really a major gathering of prelates. To note how ecumenical it was I will list those present among the Metropolitans and Archbishops. To keep the list workable I will delete the bishops and the archimandrites present. The number of non-Russians present is highly indicative. Patriarchs present: Makarios of Antioch and Paisios of Alexandria. Metropolitans: Pitirim of Novgorod, Gregorius of Nicaea, Lavrentii of Kazan', Kozma (Cosimo?) of Amasya, Iosif of Astrakhan, Iona of Rostov, Filofei of Trabezond, Paul of Sarsk and Podonsk, Daniil of Varna, Paisios of Gaza, Epifanii of Georgia, Feodosii of Belogorod, Feofan of Chios, and Athanasius of Iconium. Archbishops: Simon of Vologda, Ananii of Astrakhan', Filaret of Smolensk, Stefan of Suzdal', Ilarion of Riazan', Iosaf of Tver', Arsenii of Pskov, Manasii of Pogoiansk. The list is taken from *PSZ*, I, no. 397, p. 650.
28. Makarii, *Istoriia*, XII, p. 729.

nounced. Nikon was guilty as charged. He would be formally deposed as Patriarch and also unfrocked. He was to again become a plain monk. Banishment to the Ferapontov Monastery was to occur the very following day. As it has been stated: "He was ordered to stay until his dying days in a monastery where unhampered and silent he could lament his sins..."[29] Simultaneously with the sentencing, orders were given to relieve Nikon of any formal ties to the three monasteries he had built.

In deference to the large number of foreign prelates the sentence was first read in Greek, then in Russian![30] It is curious that these men were generally less lenient in treating the case of Nikon than were the Russian bishops.[31] The reverse might have been thought. Patriarch Makarios, who had found it so proper (and profitable) to support Nikon's reform during his first sojourn to Russia now found it proper to do exactly the reverse. His participation was not muted and he personally removed Nikon's cowl in the process of unfrocking. The role of Ligarides, who had been entrusted with the review of the Acts of the Council of 1660 and numerous preparations for the Great Councils, was still extremely important and he helped the visiting Patriarchs form their opinion in patently negative fashion.

As we have seen above, (ch. 5) Makarios and Paisios were not averse to machinations. They had already been disavowed by the Patriarch of Constantinople and were, upon their return to the Near East, themselves formally deposed. Paisios was even jailed for illegal appropriation of gold. The Old Believers from the beginning maintained unblinkingly that the real motive for their presence was pecuniary.[32] This was certainly part of the truth and there is corroboration in the evidence. Makarios and

29. Gibbenet, *Izsledovanie*, II, p. 370.
30. *PSZ*, I, no. 397, p. 653. The text of the statement is to be seen on pp. 654-56.
31. Zenkovsky, *Staroobriadchestvo*, pp. 292-93.
32. Eleonskaia et. al., op. cit., pp. 166-67.

Paisios, knowing full well the displeasure of their peers (Patriarchs Parthenios of Constantinople and Nektarios of
Jerusalem), wrote a letter that seems hopeful of increased good
will. They write (to Parthenios): "We trust that the usual alms
granted from here to the Patriarch of Constantinople and other
Patriarchs will be renewed, and even hopefully in larger
quantity".[33] It does seem clear that they did very well while in
Moscow and returned with numerous riches. People in their
retinue, or those who had given help, were also rewarded. The
Tatar Mamai Kasimov, for example, who helped the two Patriarchs in their trek north, was given a ten year trade concession
in Moscow.[34]

Two further points should be mentioned concerning this
judgement. The fact of Ligarides' duplicity and the disavowal of
the two Patriarchs made the situation very uncomfortable for
the Russian government. Scandal could ensue. In view of the
significance of the Councils, the inordinate length it took to
organize them, and the urgent intent of the government to
finally settle a number of thorny issues, it was decided to
temporarily forget these compromising facts and keep them
secret. It was to have been a diplomatic secret with only a few
chosen figures privy to the disconcerting news. But Nikon's
sources in the capital were evidently still quite good for he
publicly brought up the question at his trial.

The second item deals with Nikon's actual deposition. All
four of the Eastern Patriarchs had sent two papers to Moscow
prior to the Councils: "Answers of the Patriarch" (in reply to a
series of questions submitted by Moscow) and "Principle
Concerning the Power of State and the Power of the Church".
These papers, containing canonical excerpts, comments, and
their own interpretations, clearly pointed to the power of the
State over the Church. Among other aspects they included
references to divine right, and to the Tsar's right to appoint Pa-

---

33. Makarii, *Istoriia*, XII, p. 752.
34. *PSZ*, I, no. 411, pp. 697-98.

triarchs.[35] As such they fit well into the direction that the Russian Church was heading. Certainly such preparatory steps greatly aided Peter. This also fit well into the general pattern of Church-State relationships, whether in Russia, The Near East, or Europe. Only State authority could be said to have gained.

The Council now recessed until January, 1667 at which time a new Patriarch was to be elected. Prior to that came a very quick manifestation of the Church-State struggle. "As soon as Nikon disappeared from the scene, Russian bishops began voicing their opposition to the Caesaro-Papist attempts to curb the authority of the church. As a matter of fact, they continued Nikon's line of argumentation. It was the locum tenens Metropolitan Paul of Krutitsy (prior to the ordination of Ioasaf as Patriarch) and Archbishop Ilarion of Riazan' who became spokesmen for those bishops whom the Old Believers had dubbed "Nikonian" because of their approval of changes introduced by Nikon in church manuals and rites and who were so called by the Greek members of the sobor because of their sharing Nikon's views on the relations between church and state."[36] The irony is already evident. Nikon, whose deposition was so ardently sought, had also been most successful in retaining the rights of the Church. Now, with his ouster, it was his position that was being defended.

Paul and Ilarion, for their strenuous efforts, were temporarily barred from holding services and given severe warnings. Paul was likewise barred from his position as locum tenens.[37] These penalties were of short duration for their attempt was not really to subvert. Furthermore, Paul and Ilarion agreed to accept whatever strictures and regulations were to emanate from the Council. In expressing the stand of the bishops, however, they had success for it became clear to the government that some concessions would have to be made.

---

35. Zenkovsky, *Staroobriadchestvo*, pp. 294-96.
36. Vernadsky, op. cit., V, part 2, p. 607.
37. Ably discussed in Makarii, *Istoriia*, XII, pp. 754-59.

168

Saddled by troubles with the Old Believers further alienation could not be allowed. The bishops had given great support in the moves against Nikon. Their reward was to come in the abolition of the Monastyrskii Prikaz. "Consequently, what he (the Tsar — N.L.) had refused to Nikon he now granted to Nikon's former foes, his new followers. The Monastyrskii Prikaz was closed, and the clergy was exempted from the jurisdiction of lay courts."[38]

The session held to elect the new Patriarch (January 31, 1667) though full of ceremony was essentially anticlimatic. None of the three candidates (Ioasaf, archimandrite of the Holy Trinity Monastery, Kornilii, archimandrite of the Bogoroditsa Tikhvinskii Monastery, and the monk Savva, cellarer of the Chudov Monastery) was of particular distinction.[39] The Council elected Ioasaf, certain, at least because of his age alone, to be pliable. He was, as the statement reads, tendered "... to be a good administrator of the Church and exterminator of the newly budding schisms".[40] The third phase of the Councils was now complete.

The fourth and final phase of the Great Councils commenced on February 26, 1667.[41] Sessions were held until late summer (probably ending in August).[42] They took on an importance of the first order and it is not too much to say than an irrevocable break was made with the history of the Church as it was known up to that time in Russia.

The Council again re-affirmed the new texts and Nikon's reforms. Since this phase of the Councils dealt with much de-

---

38. Vernadsky, op. cit., V, part 2, p. 608.

39. For the announcement of the election of the new Patriarch, see *PSZ*, I, no. 399, pp. 669-70.

40. Ibid., p. 670.

41. For this phase of the Councils see *PSZ*, I, no. 412, pp. 698-715. For the best secondary account see Makarii, *Istoriia*, XII, pp. 765-92.

42. The chronology of these sessions is less precise, hence the lack of specific dates of these sessions in the text.

tail, it did discard a few of Nikon's less significant changes.[43] But such did in no way impinge on the overall acceptance of his reforms. And it made final rulings on Nikon's monasteries and votchinas (held by him as Patriarch). The Tsar would adjudicate some and the rest would be taken care of by the local eparchies.

Insofar as the Old Believers were concerned the Councils took final decision, forever changing their status. Now, formally, the Old Believers were castigated and anathemized. While they were still recalcitrant the blessings of the Church would be forever removed. But the Councils' last phase went further. It made the Old Believers subject to civil law as well, thus making them liable to corporal punishment and trial by the government.[44]

Sadly, the heavy hand of the Greeks was evident in these decisions. In addition to the constant flow of Greek prelates, there were numerous Greeks of dubious distinction who resided in Moscow. Ligarides is the perfect example, sufficiently trusted in the highest matters of Church-State politics. His roles were many: adviser, organizer of anti-Nikonian measures, guide to visiting prelates, an active participant in the Great Councils. He was even asked to write refutations of Russian tracts, such as his work condemning the famous petition of Nikita Dobrynin.

Another Greek came to the foreground at this juncture. This was Dionisios, former archimandrite of the Iverskii Monastery on Mt. Athos. He had been living in Moscow for many years. Dionisios had prepared accusations against the old belief for the Councils. This text served as the basis for the judgement by the Eastern Patriarchs, and appears in the Acts of the Councils almost verbatim in some sections. Dionisios's ideas

---

43. For example, Nikon's ruling that criminals given the death penalty be disallowed the last rites was rejected.

44. The Council, in support of this ruling, cited, among other sources, the 2nd, 4th, and 7th Ecumenical Councils; *PSZ*, I, no. 412, pp. 705-06. Also, Makarii, *Istoriia*, XII, p. 776.

were curious: Russia had been acceptable in its religious practices until after the fall of Constantinople. Once it had lost its dependency on the Greeks, it took on new trappings incompatible with Greek practice (an amazing reversal of the historical positions! — N.L.). Now was Russia's chance to be back in good graces. To be so, it had to make heretical old Russian ritual and its practitioners anathemized. Coevally, the major underpinning of these positions, the Stoglav Sobor of 1551 (in itself a superb and distinct achievement) had to be totally abrogated and harshly rejected! "For this reason, Dionisios, the Patriarchs, and, alas, all the Russian fathers of the Council of 1667, placed on the defendant's bench all of Russian Muscovite Church history, condemned it, and rescinded it."[45]

The rationale used for rejecting a previous council of such magnitude fell back on the example of the seven original Ecumenical Councils. They had changed existing statutes of preceding councils. Another section of the Acts of the 1667 sessions states that no Eastern Patriarch had been present, hence the failure of the Stoglav — a colossal dismissal by the Greeks of Russian autocephaly from 1449-1667. This type of reasoning and haughty polemic had never appeared in any Russian tract or treatise, of any argument of the Church against the Old Believers, or by Nikon, brusque as he was. Only the foreign hand is evident here. For reasons such as this, Kartashev notes, the Greeks were hated by the Bulgars, Rumanians, and Arabs.

There were other indignities (which, lamentably, neither the Russian churchmen nor the Tsar were capable of forestalling, bowing as they did to "Greek authority."). Many lesser questions were constantly settled simply with references stating, "let it be according to the practice of the Eastern Church." The most final indignity that portended the greatest harm was the insistence by the Greek hierarchs present that the Old Believers,

---

45. Kartashev, op.cit., p. 180. My discussion of this topic closely follows Kartashev, esp. pp. 177-83, where it is so luminously presented.

171

in addition to being labeled heretics and anathemized, also be subjected to corporal and capital punishment meted out by the State, to "punish those of evil faith by civil law as well, and to execute them and torture them in assorted ways."

This gradually began to take hold in Russian practice and was cemented by the Council of 1682. The decision to bring the Greek Patriarchs was therefore an incalculably tragic mistake, a mistake multiplied by a Russian acquiescence that in itself was a product, and perhaps an admission of a misplaced trust, excessive idealism, and a feeling of helplessness in the face of Greek tradition. That this is no casual adducement is further evidenced in the Acts of the 1667 sessions wherein the process of book correction was terminated. Textual correction and reform were broken off and the stinging feeling was that over two generations of these procedures had produced no unifying principle, no indisputable agreements, no peace among the people. Only discord had been sewn on all sides and in the face of it, there was a helplessness that could stoop, in the end, to "Greek authority."

And the Greek prelates themselves? They exulted in their letters. Writing to the Patriarch of Constantinople, they noted that they had perforce devised "ad majorem graecorum gloriam," and that henceforth alms from the Tsar would be guaranteed to the great see.

This made the raskol real, for, in effect, the Old Believers could now be considered enemies of the State as well. It is this ruling which was the backbone of government measures taken against the old belief and implementation began soon after the Council's close. The time of disputation was, in effect, over. Repression would come to the forefront. The Old Believers did nothing to aid their own cause for they continued strenuously in their resistance.

Old Believer leaders such as Avvakum, Lazar', and Epifanii were brought before the Council anew. Now they were tried, again categorically refusing to admit error. They were exiled to Pustozersk in the north. The tongues of Lazar' and Epifanii

172

were cut for blasphemy. Avvakum, at one of the hearings stated: "...I wish that the Council held in the reign of Tsar Ivan Vasilievich be the true guide..."[46] He was referring to the Stoglav Sobor of 1551 but the Council abrogated it as a valid council of the Church (see above). It was a radical ruling in terms of Russian religious history and made much firmer the commitment to the new.

The Council, in re-arranging some of the Church customs and practices into channels deemed necessary, made many decisions and pronouncements that dealt precisely with church practices and with discipline. With most of these there was no quarrel for practical good and moral improvement was sought. A survey of a number of these rulings is instructive.

The last Council ruled, as has been observed, to abolish the Monastyrskii Prikaz.[47] This did not come to completion until December 1677, but the brunt of the decision had positive and immediate applications for the Church. The number of eparchies was increased to make more viable the administration of the Church. The eparchial (diocesan) bishop, by the greater consolidation of the eparchy's holdings, could now administer more efficiently. Also, it was suggested that the hierarchy convene (preferably at least once annually) more frequently than before. The possibility that this lack of communication among administrators of the Church had been conducive to the growth of schism was raised.[48]

Roman Catholics were forbidden to be re-baptized (thus invalidating a decree of the esteemed Patriarch Filaret). Those who begged entry into the monastic ranks as a means of escaping the bonds of marriage, were to be rebuffed. Marriage itself was treated. The customs of joking (ritualistic in nature) and nonsensical teasings by friends and bystanders as the marriage

---

46. *Materialy*, II, pp. 21-26.
47. *PSZ*, I, no. 412; Makarii, *Istoriia*, XII, p. 785; Gorchakov, *Monastyrskii Prikaz*, pp. 95-98.
48. Makarii, *Istoriia*, XII, pp. 779-81.

parties went to church (much of this was scatological in tone) were to be refrained from.[49] Simony, of which we hear almost nothing in the sources, was forbidden thus suggesting that it did show its head from time to time.

The general attempt to heighten discipline can also be seen in a number of other measures geared to the lower clergy and the people. Among these are admonitions to the priest to teach his calling to his own children, to not leave the orders of his own volition, to have the people stand in orderly fashion in church, to have "...each priest teach in his parish that meat not properly killed was not to be eaten, that swimming in the nude, shamelessly before men and women, be stopped" and so forth. These, as many other rulings, were not new. They had to be reinforced due to constant popular transgressions. Many of them were scarcely implemented for the vagaries of the human condition were not so simply governed and controlled. The more significant decisions, such as those regarding the new eparchial structures, the re-assigning to the Church of its traditional juridical prerogatives, of the permission to widowed priests to continue serving, had significant effect on Russian ecclesiastical practice. These can be said to have been beneficial and worthy of the Council's attention.

Taken in toto, the Great Councils are paramount in importance. The breadth of topics considered by them was impressive. Their rulings forever "...determined the basis of the future relationship of Church and State to the Old Believers. They also determined the inner structure and the way of life of the raskol'niks. From this time on the raskol'niks were formally excommunicated from the Orthodox Church..."[50] Tsar Aleksei had once lamented (at one of the 1667 sessions) with a note of genuine piety, the havoc being created in the pious body of Orthodoxy. "The Heavenly Father has sewn the fields of our

49. Ibid., p. 785; *PSZ*, I, no. 412, p. 699.
50. Plotnikov, op.cit., p. 58.

Orthodox realm with the fertile wheat of pious devotion, but when we, God's anointed, were placed guardians of it, we dozed and the covetous enemy sewed the bitter seed of discontent. This seed was the profusion of sprouting schisms whose pernicious tenets attempted to uproot the wheat of God's word, the true catholic faith. Already their blasphemous teachings have spread not only to town, region, and land given us by God, but even into this city, they have blown in and reached our very hands in writ and our ears in word."[51]

In condemning the adversaries the Councils confirmed the Nikonian reforms. This proved to be an irreversible step. The same might be said of the Russian decision to bring Near Eastern Patriarchs and other hierarchs to the Councils. For they, especially in view of the books corrected by Nikon along Greek lines, were generally emphatic in supporting the changes. This, too, predicated the impossibility of returning to the old ritual.[52] Nikon was at this time already in exile trying to clear himself with the Tsar. In writing to Aleksei he evidently hoped to have the full hearing he had been denied.[52] Whether he felt a chance for reconciliation is a moot point.

The inadequate hearing given to Nikon is one of a number of what we may call improprieties of the Councils. We have already observed the roles of the Patriarchs Makarios, Paisios and the Tsar's false aide, Ligarides, among others. The Tsar himself had final say in approving the protocols. Zyzikin writes that the Tsar ratified the protocols of the Councils and deleted whatever he wished. "Thus at the Council of 1667, all the debates concerning the respective powers of Church and State which occurred on the 14th, 15th, and 17th of January, 1667 were removed. For presented there was indisputable testimony against the Caesaro-Papist understanding of the unlimited

51. Shchapov, op.cit., p. 5.
52. Zenkovsky, *Staroobriadchestvo*, p. 259.
53. "Pis'mo Patriarkha Nikona k Tsariu Alekseiu Mikhailovichu (1667)", *Letopis'Zaniatii 1911* (Barskov, ed.), op.cit., pp. 93-104.

power of the Tsar."[54] Here the Tsar acted not as a member of the Council but supra to it.

There is also some difficulty in the notes of the Acts of the Council. Simeon Polotskii was in charge and exercised his privilege (given him by the Tsar) of changing some speeches or substituting them with those of his own composition. Some of the Tsar's own speeches were amended.[55] These irregularities, though unpleasant to countenance, had no significant effect on the outcome or the decisions of the Great Councils. Whether the Russian Church, and the State, were left better as a result can still be debated. Of the fact that major change had occurred and direction was changed forever there can be no debate.

54. Zyzikin, II, op.cit., p. 200.
55. Zenkovsky, *Staroobriadchestvo*, pp. 282-83.

Chapter 10

The Point Of No Return

The years immediately following the Great Councils were, as Zenkovsky calls them, "years of last hope".[1] The Councils deepened the cleavage between the government, the hierarchy, and the side of the old traditions. "Until the Council the struggle regarding ritual occurred within the Russian Church and irrespective of all the irreverancies exchanged by both sides, the defenders of the old faith remained a part of the body ecclesia. Now, the anathemas of the Council placed them outside the Church and removed them from the right to partake of the sacraments and the consolation of the Church. At the same time it deprived the Church itself of any canonical and moral power over them."[2]

This formalized, or made de facto, a condition that had been developing along these lines (i.e. outside the established order) for a number of years. It is as apparent in the growth of the popularity of elders and monastic hermits as it is in the whole thrust of the old believer movement. The official

---

1. Zenkovsky cuts these years at 1670 though such a classification could easily be extended, perhaps to 1682 when new, draconic measures were passed against the Old Believers.

2. Zenkovsky, *Staroobriadchestvo*, p. 305.

177

hierarchy was with increasing frequency simply skipped over and spiritual solace was sought elsewhere.[3] This is not to say that the Old Believers had from the start worked under that presumption. Part of their indomitable fervor can, in fact, be attributed to the desire to amend the innovative proceedings of the Church and align it along more amenable models. However, at this juncture (i.e. post-Council) the desire was no longer operative.

The old belief thus formally had no influence in the Church or in government. In Crummey's determination, "Old Belief, after 1667, was an indistinguishable blend of opposition to the liturgical reforms, foreign cultural influence, bureaucratic centralism, and social injustice".[4] The latter element is questionable. It has never been clear why opposition to social injustice is peculiarly that of Old Believers. But accepting the "blend" or diversity of strands in old beliefs overall, it is not surprising that the Old Believers had no specific platform. Government pressure had always elicited some measure of unified response, but never yet to a preponderant degree. The propensity for the individual response and for sectarianism was already evident.

It has been said that: "The open break-away of the raskol occurred afer Nikon had lost his importance..."[5] Now, not only his demise but the decrees of the Great Councils served to surface the schism as never before. It was a time when direction was urgently needed but not always had. The open animosity of the established order was now a rule of State to be followed. Those unrelenting in their activity against old belief could only expect commendation. Metropolitan Ilarion was so commended in 1667 for his unremitting efforts.[6]

---

3. See suggestions to this effect in Schmeman, op.cit., p. 370.

4. Crummey, op.cit., I have expressed a reservation, (however slight) of this formula in my review of Crummey's book. See N. Lupinin, *Church History*, Dec., 1971, pp. 496-97.

5. Gibbenet, *Patriarkh Nikon*, p. 254.

6. Dobroliubov, op.cit., I, p. 9.

In any discussion of the formal aspects of the schism the schism cannot simply be broken down into those who accepted and those who rejected Nikon's reforms. "The real schism was, rather, the basic split between the Muscovite ideal of an organic religious civilization shared by both Avvakum and Nikon and the post-1667 reality — equally offensive to both of them — of the church as a subordinate institution of a secular state."[7]

The diversity of response was considerable. Ideas regarding the end of the world that began to appear in Russia in the early XVII century gained great headway. These were uniquely a part of the idea of antichrist.[8] In his person was the imminent apocalypse and the point of differentiation was among those who either viewed antichrist as being already present and those who suspended the more negative side of their judgment and said merely that his precursor/s were plaguing the Russian land. It has been stated that it was not aspects of ritual but the idea of antichrist that was the moving force behind the raskol.[9] It is not a suggestion that can be lightly discarded.

Miliukov, in his study, observes what he terms the "maximalists" (those wishing to speed the coming of the Kingdom of God). He discusses the growing attempts by this faction, that of the "priestless," who began to refute the necessity of priests, to live by their own rather unrestricted convictions, and to create a new form of faith. Common here was the renunciation of all old belief because of the imminence of the end of the world. People did not stop to reason how they could live without the Church but how they could die with dignity.[10] In this pernicious time it often did not matter whether death came by immolation, starvation, and other esoteric forms. In the attempts at creating new faith some of the more radical old believer groups did not seem to realize that the forms being created by them had, in terms of

---

7. Billington, op.cit., p. 158.
8. The idea of antichrist is ably handled by Cherniavsky, op.cit.
9. Schmeman, op.cit., p. 377.
10. Miliukov, op.cit., p. 57.

actual rites and practices, gone far beyond the innovations of Nikon.[11] Radical proposals such as fleeing to the forests, forbidding marriage, and viewing the priesthood as unnecessary could never even have been dreamed of by Nikon. Yet, these were all inherent strands of radical Old Believers such as the "priestless". They could be led no further than to the gruesomeness of immolation.[12]

The "priestless" in later years came to use as one of their arguments against their opposite, the "priestists", a quotation from St. John Chrysostom. "The church does not exist in its walls, but in its rules. When attending church, do not go to the edifice but to the light; the church is not in the walls and roof, but in the faith and life."[13] It is not clear whether in its specific form this argument was used by the very first groups of "priestless." But, its tone is unmistakenly applicable, especially in the call to "the faith and life".

An overwhelming sense of despair and disillusionment characterized the Old Believers at this time. They were convinced that salvation could not be found in the circumstances of associating on a day to day basis with Nikonians. This greatly abetted the desire to run from the world much as the despair at finding salvation in this world led to the passionate desires for suicide.[14] This, as we have seen, was activated by means of fire and blatant appeals to self-imposed death appear even in Old Believer poetry. One poem reads:[15]

> "Do not give up my dear ones,
> To that seven-headed serpent[16]
> Run to the mountains, the caves,

---

11. Zenkovsky, *Staroobriadchestvo*, p. 341.
12. These manifestations, in terms of a truly mass effect commence in the 1670's and continue sporadically in the remaining decades.
13. As cited in Miliukov., op.cit., p. 76.
14. Rozhdestvenskii, op.cit., pp. xiv-xvii.
15. Ibid., pp. 2-21.
16. i.e.antichrist.

There build large fires
And burn yourselves in them,
Suffer for me, my dear ones,
For my Christian faith;
I will then, my beloved
Open the gates of paradise
Lead you into the Heavenly Kingdom
And will myself live with you eternally.''

Many who chose to run did by no means intend to martyr themselves to please the radical preachers or serve so destructive a notion. They were content merely to go far enough to escape the claws of persecution. They wished to live peacefully, to have some measure of security and non-interference in what they deemed the rectitude of their religious ritual. Their sense of brooding pessimism was far more subdued and not likely to reach the radical solution.

For a number of Old Believers the area of Starodub was, in the 1670's, far enough away. Here towns such as Trubchevsk and Briansk (among others) had, especially among the traders and merchants, substantial numbers of Old Believers. At the Council of 1681 the Tsar himself noted that the towns of Putivl' and Sevsk harbored many Old Believers. Lileev, who has studied this locality, feels that perhaps such considerations were instrumental in the establishment of new eparchies in this area at that time.[17] In the Ryl'skii uezd (district) there were, already in the 1670's two old believer monasteries (the L'govskii and the Monskii).[18] They were centers of the raskol in their areas.

For others even such areas as Starodub were uncomfortably close to the reaches of administrative control. These people went further south as, for example, to the Don regions. There Dosifei and Kornilii had long been propagating the old belief. This

17. M.I. Lileev, "Iz Nachal'noi Istorii Raskola v Starodub'e", *Kievskaia Starina*, vol. XXVI, 1889, Aug., p. 388.
18. Ibid.

area was a haven for run-away serfs and other dissidents of all kinds. The Old Believers, by taking advantage of the privileges of the Don, created new anxieties for the government. The government well knew that the flight of Old Believers to the Don was partly motivated by the practice of the people there not to extradite those sought by the central administration. These new refugees found welcome and were not rebuffed by their new hosts. The towns of the upper Don River were especially hospitable.

A decree of the regent Sophia in 1685 already complained of the large number of schismatics in this area. In 1686, Prince Golitsyn was ordered to send a gramota to hetman Frol Minaev specifying that he and his forces take pains to disperse the Old Believers, arrest them, and burn their houses. All this came to little fruition and in the following year, 1687, the government demanded the extradition from the Don of the old believer priest Samoila and five associates. This had no precedent and caused much worry. But, Minaev did not wish an open rupture with Moscow and talked his subordinates into complying with the demand. In May, 1688, the six were given up, to be executed in Moscow.[19] Moscow again proved its intention of carrying on the struggle against the Old Believers to all quarters. An area, traditionally safe, had been traduced and now lost some of its autonomy.

The north of Russia drew a great number of Old Believers. Old belief had grown there from the very start for the north proved amenable to the dissidents. Large areas previously uninhabited to any notable extent and huge stretches of deeply forested land provided adequate cover. A considerable degree of autonomy in local ecclesiastical practice also made a number of people reluctant to accept any impositions from the capital. And, old believer leaders such as Avvakum, Lazar', and others

---

19. My description of this case is based on Pushkarev, *Trans. Rus. — Amer. Scholars*, II, pp. 24-25. For the raskol in the Don area see V.G. Druzhinin, *Raskol na Donu v Kontse XVII Veka* (SPB: 1889).

had been greatly instrumental in sewing the fertile seed of schism. One of the most stunning examples of revolt for the cause of the raskol, that of the Solovetskii Monastery, is a phenomenon of the north.[20] The heroic case of its mass martyrdom and resistance to an eight year siege made conversion to old belief (if we may so phrase it) a much easier task, for the people in the immense area tied to the strings of the Solovetskii Monastery greatly approved this sacrifice which only added to its glory and fame. Some of the most successful examples of old believer communities are to be found in the north and Professor Crummey has ably traced perhaps the most famous of all, the Vyg.[21]

Areas of greatest dispersal in the north were the coastal regions and, closer, the Kerzhenskie forests of the Nizhegorod Domain. The Siberian steppes attracted others. Beyond Russian borders, Old Believers moved to Sweden (Lifliandiia district), Poland (esp. Vetka), Austria (in the Carpathian foothills and Belaia Krinitsa), Prussia, and Turkey (Danube, Crimea, and the Caucasus).

From 1682 a new and even stricter phase is determinable in the struggle against the Old Believers. It is then that the famous "Uvet Dukhovnyi" (Spiritual Decree) is published at the instigation of Patriarch Ioakim.[22] Ioakim (1674-90) had from the start of his church career been adamantly active against the schism. This Uvet was a successful polemical tract against the Old Believers.[23] In that same year the Council (commenced in 1681) completed its sessions. Aside from rulings of ecclesiastical

---

20. See chapter 8.

21. Crummey, op.cit.

22. It is sometimes stated that it was written by Patriarch Ioakim himself but, in fact, it was done so at his direction by Archimandrite Afanasii of Kholmogorsy. See on this tract Slukhovskii, op.cit., pp. 99, 117-18, 125; Ustiugov (Ustiugov ed.), op.cit., p. 324.

23. It also has the interesting quality of having a preface of an ideological nature stating the government's role in culture (and honoring the significance of the major book collections). Other volumes with similar prefaces were the Service Book of 1655, and especially the Gospel Commentaries (exegetical in nature) of Feofilakt (Theophylactes the Bulgarian XI-XII c.) issued in 1649 and again in 1698. See Slukhovskii, op.cit., p. 125.

nature that echo the Councils of 1666-67, it also passed stronger measures against the Old Believers. They were now forbidden to gather in their own houses for the purpose of prayer. The clergy was now compelled to inform the government of Old Believers so punitive measures might be taken. What the Council of 1682 actually did was to structure a system of repression against the Old Believers. It was the first time in Russian history, as Kartashev notes, that the spirit of the Western inquisition had been manifested. Over a half century of continuous foreign influences had helped to foment the notion of counteracting any opposition. This was further facilitated by the spectre of an opposition that had come to mix the religious with the political. The Councils of 1666-67 had given the State the right to use force and arms against the Old Believers. But not much was done. The thrust of the efforts by the Church and the monastic establishments was to convince by persuasion, to talk with the recalcitrants in an attempt to bring them back into the fold. Only extreme cases were turned over to the State. Now, with the political mix, the hierarchy turned over the fight to the State and the year 1682 became a pivotal year in the struggle against the Old Believers. A decree of this year also widened the powers of the bishoprics in fighting the old belief.[24]

All told, government activity against the Old Believers took on a force far greater than ever before. The 1680's is the period of terrible persecution and execution and the Council's order to burn Avvakum and his fellow leaders at their place of exile in Pustozersk at the stake served as a signal. The signal given by the Streltsy rebellion of 1682 when a number of Old Believers took active part in the attempt at coup d'etat was not ignored. The implication of their role in an actual armed movement aimed at overthrowing the government could not but draw the sternest responses of the State.

As government repression increased the number of cases of

24. Zenkovsky, *Staroobriadchestvo*, pp. 401ff. Plotnikov, op.cit., p. 151. Kartashev, op.cit., pp. 234-40.

immolation did likewise and literally thousands upon thousands died. The first year of mass sacrifice was 1672. From 1676-1687, some 1,929 people burned in the Poshekhonskii district of Iaroslavl'. In 1679, the priest Dometian in Tiumen' organized an immolation that took 1,700 lives. And in 1687, on Lake Onega, in the Paleostrovskii Monastery, 2,700 people met their end by fire. The figure by 1690 totaled ca. 20,000. Some Old Believer historians such as Ivan Filippov approved of these burnings.[25] It was not till Evfrosin's famous refutation of immolation (1691) "Otrazitel'noe Pisanie o Novoizobretennom Puti Samo-Ubiistvenykh Smertei" (Refutation of the Newly Invented Method of Suicide) that the craze abated though it did not stop immediately. In 1685 more regulations were issued to combat the Old Believers. Among them were: 1) constant abusers of the Church were to be burned, 2) the preachers of immolation were to be executed, 3) followers were to be subjected to corporal punishment and sent to monasteries where they were to be kept under strong guard, 4) those who sheltered Old Believers were to be punished, 5) Old Believers' property could be confiscated.[26]

Years of last hope were over. Sheer despair had replaced them. Confusion was rampant and irresponsible preachers had practically as much force as the true leaders. The psychosis of millenium, of apocalypse, was thin. How many successive years could the imminent end be preached? In their various places of hiding, in their homes, in distant forests the Old Believers all had to face very primal questions and they answered them as best they could. Perhaps as the flames began to consume their flesh panic said no, but panic went with the smoke to become, in its evanescence, nonexistent, a trace on the surface of human suffering. Others who answered these questions in more positive fashion faced a life of hardship in the face of a hostile world. Each, in such disparate ways, made their commitments. Truly these were years of no return.

---

25. Kartashev, op.cit., p. 241.
26. For these and others see Zenkovsky, Ibid., p. 413.

Chapter 11

Epilogue and Conclusion

In summation, perhaps most pertinent is the observation of considerable change taking place in Russian society, of a constant flux. It was far from the static society generally thought. This trend was in evidence long before Peter. It was a trend that was irreversible, hence all the more potent. We have seen throughout the human emotions and commitments involved, both in a degree that forbade the thought of compromise.

Tsar Aleksei was a rather strong figure. He found the innovations of Nikon worthy of support, ultimately not given to Nikon himself. For example, the Tsar himself presided over and took major part in the Great Councils of 1666-67 which were of paramount significance in making the break with the past complete. The Councils were long in planning and did not come unexpectedly. They were in response to the many perturbing religious events of the period.

The people were an extremely strong moving agent in the whole drama. Rich or poor, it was their response to the vast jumble of trends that forced action from the established Church and the State. Whether it was an increasing fascination with Westernism, and with it a rising secularism, or the reverse, xenophobic outbursts of indignation, it was the people who elicited so much response. This, like other facts of this period, (for example, the much more active role of Tsar Aleksei) is rarely noted. In so doing, the people were only acting in a custom familiar to all previous Russian history where people were heard and where they expressed themselves frequently and openly.

The Muscovite period of Russia history was ending rapidly. All the signs pointed to this fact. The living fact, Peter, was born in 1672. Russian people were to rejoice. Pitirim, Metropolitan of Novgorod, wrote to one area (the Lodomsk) under his jurisdiction imploring the people therein to "hold tranksgiving services and ring the bells for the universal joy of mankind at the birth of His Majesty the Tsarevitch".[1] The message was repeated countless times by countless officials, and countless clergymen. Nobody could guess that Peter's destiny entailed what it did. There were more immediate matters. And nowhere was their urgency more obvious than in the Church.

The Church was the repository of more that was Muscovy than any other Russian institution. Now it was torn asunder, never to be repaired. There was no longer unity in the religious and ecclesiastical spheres, a unity that had been so much at the heart of the Russian experience. The central question had been, in the turbulence of these years, how to keep religion at the center of Russia life.[2] The reign of Tsar Aleksei was a multidimensional attempt to deal with this question and all its immense ramifications. The problems posed by the question were not solved.

There were many reasons why solution was no simple matter. The Church was being subjected to a three way struggle for its control, the principals being Patriarch Nikon, the Old Believers, the State. Mutual interrelations often became inordinately entwined and rarely led to edification. Instead, confrontation seemed the order of the day.

---

1. "Zapis' o Sovershenii Molebstvie po Sluchaiu Rozhdeniia Tsarevicha Petra Alekseevicha", *RIB*, XXV, Apndx., col. 256-57.
2. Billington, op. cit., p. 127.

Confrontation began almost from the moment of Nikon's ascendancy to the Patriarchy in 1652. Nikon, a stern, energetic, and impressive figure of a man had as his goals: a) to maintain or increase the independence of the Russian Church, b) introduce (on a wide level) the reform of Church service books, manuals, etc.., and c) give the Russian Church a more ecumenical character. His own personality and often arbitrary methods in the furthering of his goals proved a hindrance and he was not able to make solid his claims for the independence of the Russian Church. The Councils of 1666-67 saw to that even though they made a concession to the Church by taking the first step in the dissolution of the Monastyrskii Prikaz. The reforms of liturgical books and church manuals (and other similar innovations) were generally accepted. On the third point the answer is open, though it should be said that at least temporarily, a more ecumenical character was evidenced in the Russian Church. On a personal level Nikon failed although it took the whole power of the State and the Tsar to depose him and make negligible his strength and influence.

In the Old Believers we have, on an increasingly mass level, the example of traditional Russia fighting for a hallowed past and purity of spirit. The Nikonian reforms were seen as travesties on both. They had to be fought and stopped. The Old Believers, at first victims of Nikon, became later the victims of the State, even though Nikon himself was cast out by the State. It ultimately did not matter to the Old Believers who their persecutor was. In both cases they saw the coming of antichrist, the closing of an era, the dying of true faith. They resisted with a fervor ultimately dogmatic, frequently fanatic, and often self-destructive in scope. Their elemental honesty and their message drew thousands of adherents, a situation dangerous enough to warrant the most draconian responses of the State. Religious dissent, some of it edging into political dissent, became an uncomfortable phenomenon in Russia. Though its eradication was sought, it turned out to be impossible. The intensity of their defense of the old faith, and conversely, their struggle against what they thought to be the new, made compromise impossible. With their formal anathemization the Old Believers were cast from the Church and its ministrations. It is sometimes suggested that this removed the best and purest strand within the Church, leaving it in the hands of those more likely to accept reform and innovation. There is merit in this suggestion. But it must be said that this strand was also a narrow one, great though it was. As Fedotov states: "With the schism, a great, though narrow, religious force left the Russian Church, bleeding it white a second time."[3]

Parallel to these developments was the inescapable thrust of growing Westernization and secularization. It too was strenuously opposed but with ever increasing desparation. Secularization and Westernization cannot be seen in narrow terms for they began to affect most aspects of Russian life. It is true, of course, that Western techniques were more acceptable than Western ideas and beliefs.[4] But on all three levels there was opposition for the ideals of old Muscovy were still strong.[5] The struggle of the Nikonians and the Old Believers broke the power of the Church. The steady growth of Westernism eroded the cultural base of traditional Muscovy. In both cases the past became irretrievable. As always, there were those who fought for the past, its good and bad features, with honor, glory, reason, and unreason. As it was gradually being lost we can ask two very basic questions: how many truly realized at the time the significance of the contemporary events they had committed themselves to, and hence the validity of their struggle, and secondly, how can we measure the loss or gain in terms of the hearts and minds given by men in often selfless struggles for what they termed the truth? It is such questions of the spirit that are hardest for history to answer but perhaps they are also the most important questions for history to ask.

---

3. Fedotov, op. cit., II, p. 392.

4. Billington, op. cit., pp. 123-24.

5. A number of these points are touched upon in Joseph T. Fuhrman, *Tsar Alexis: His Reign and His Russia* (Gulf Breeeze, Fla.: Academic International Press), 1981.

Selected Bibliography

PRIMARY SOURCES

Books

Aleksei Mikhailovich, Tsar. *Sobranie Pisem Tsaria Alekseia Mikhailovicha.* Moscow, 1856.

Dmytryshyn, Basil (ed.). *Medieval Russia, A Source Book, 900-1700.* New York: Holt, Rinehart, and Winston, Inc., 1967.

Dobroliubov, Ioann. *Istoriko-Statisticheskoe Opisanie Tserkvei i Monastyrei Riazanskoi Eparkhii.* 2 vol. Zaraisk: 1884-85.

Fedorova, M.E., and Sumnikova, T.A. (ed's.). *Khrestomatiia po Drevnerusskoi Literature.* Moscow: Vyshaia Shkola, 1969.

Fedotov, G.P. (ed.). *A Treasury of Russian Spirituality.* New York: Sheed and Ward, 1948.

Gibbenet, N. *Istoricheskoe Izsledovanie Dela Patriarkha Nikona.* 3 vol. SPB: 1882-84. (Note: this source is included here in that vol. 3 is a collection of documents).

Likhachev, D.S., and Dmitrieva, L.A. (ed's.). *Izbornik.* Moscow: 1969.

Kotoshikhin, Grigorii. *O Rossii v Tsarstvovanie Alekseia Mikhailovicha.* 4th ed. SPB: 1906.

Kozhanchikov, D.E. (ed.). *Tri Chelobitnyia Stavshchika Savvatiia, Savvy Romanova, i Monakhov Solovetskago Monastyria.* SPB: 1862.

Opisanie Nekotorykh Sochinenii Napisannykh Russkimi Raskol'nikami v Pol'zu Raskola. SPB: 1861.

Pamiatniki Izdannye Vremennoiu Kommissieiu dlia Razbora Drevnikh Aktov. 4 vol. 2nd ed. Kiev: 1846-59.

Paul of Aleppo. *The Travels of Macarius* (Extracts: selected by Lady Laura Ridding). London: Oxford University Press, 1936.

191

Polnoe Sobranie Zakonov Rossiiskoi Imperii. Sobranie Pervoe. 1649-1830. SPB: 1830.

Rybakov, A.S., Shvetsov, K.N., and Nosov, P.G. *Staraia Vera, Staroobriadcheskaia Khrestomatiia.* Moscow: 1914.

Stoglav (Kozhanchikov edition). SPB: 1863.

Stroev, P.N. *Spiski Ierarkhov i Nastoiatelei Monastyrei Rossiiskoi Tserkvi.* SPB: 1877.

Subbotin, N. (ed.). *Materialy dlia Istorii Raskola za Pervoe Vremia Ego Sushchestvovaniia.* 9 vol. Moscow: 1874-90.

Zhovtis, A.L. (ed.). *Drevne-Russkaia Literatura. Khrestomatiia.* 2nd rev. ed. Moscow: Vyshaia Shkola: 1966.

Periodicals and Learned Societies

Chtenie v Imperatorskom Obshchestve Istorii i Drevnostei Rossiiskikh. 1863, bk. 2, pp. 1-108; bk. 3, pp. 109-218; bk. 4, pp. 219-322. "Sbornik Tserkovno-istoricheskikh i Statisticheskikh Svedenii o Riazanskoi Eparkhii."

————. 1873, bk. 3, sect. IV, pp. 1-104; bk. 4, sec. IV, pp. 105-68; 1874, bk. 1, sect. IV, pp. 169-216. "Puteshestvie v Moskoviiu Barona Avgustina Meierberga."

————. 1883, bk. 3, sect. I, pp. 1-150. Dm. V. Tsvetaev (ed.). "Pamiatniki k Istorii Protestanstva v Rossii, Sobrannye Dm. V. Tsvetaevym."

————. 1883, bk. 4, sect. V, pp. i-iv, 1-92. "Akty Otnosiashcheisia k Istorii Solovetskago Bunta."

————. 1888, bk. 1, sect. III, pp. 1-12. Bezobrazov, P.V. (ed.). "Gramota Konstantinopol'skago Patriarkha Ioannikiia k Tsariu Alekseiu Mikhailovichu ot 1 Marta 1652 Goda."

————. 1896, bk. 3, sect. I, pp. i-iv, 1-235. "Saraiskaia i Krutitskaia Eparkhiia. Dokumenty Izvlechennye iz Arkhiva Moskovskoi Dukhovnoi Konsistorii Chlenom-Sorevnovatelem Sviaschennikom Solov'evym."

————. 1896, bk. 3, sect. V, docum.No. 9.April 28, 1658), "Gramota Tsaria Alekseia Mikhailovicha A.L. Ordinu-Nashchokinu o Pozhalovanii Ego v Dumnye Dvoriane." docum. No. 10 (August 3, 1658), "Ukaz Tsaria Alekseia

Mikhailovicha o Dache Vdove Okol'nichago Kniazia N.I. Lobanova-Rostovskago..."
————. 1896, bk. 4, sect. I, pp. i-vi, 1-94. Kholmogorov, V. and G. (ed's.). "Istoricheskie Materialy o Tserkvakh i Selakh XVI—XVIII st." sect. IV, see docum. No's. 2, 3. 4.
————. 1906, bk. 3, sect. III, pp. 129-228. "Iakov Reitenfels. Skazaniia Svetleishemu Gertsogu Toskanskomu Koz'me Tret'emu o Moskovii (Padua 1680 g.). sect. V, docum. No. 2 (February 1651), "Chelobitnaia Goroda Moskvy Tserkvi Zhivonachal'nyia Troitsy..."
————. 1906, bk. 4, sect. I, pp. i-vi, 1-120. Rozhdestvenskii, N.V. (ed.), "Makarii Patriarkh Antiokhiiskii v Rossii v 1654-1656 gg. Dokumenty Posol'skago Prikaza," sect. III, pp. 1-24, Pirling, Pavel (ed.), "Novye Materialy o Zhizni i deiatel'nosti Iakova Reitenfelsa."
————. 1909, bk. 3, sect. IV, pp. 9-13. "O Dome Sviashchennika Tserkvi Vozneseniia Gospodnia, za Nikitskimi Vorotamy, v Moskve, 1670-1676 gg."
Letopis' Zaniatii Imperatorskoi Arkheograficheskoi Kommissii za 1911 god. 1912, No. 24, pp. 1-424. Barskov, Ia.L. (ed.), "Pamiatniki Pervykh Let Russkago Staroobriadchestva."
Letopisi Russkoi Literatury i Drevnosti. 1861, pp. 117-73. Avvakum, "Avtobiografiia Protopopa Avvakuma."
Pamiatniki Drevnei Pis'mennosti i Iskusstva. 1885, no. 54, pp. 1-59. Arkhimandrit Leonid, "Diakon Lugovskoi po Tatishchevu Pisatel' XVII Veka i Ego Sochinenie o Sude Nad Patriarkhom Nikonom."
————. 1906, no. 161, pp. 169-216. Simon, Pavel (ed.), "K Istorii Obikhoda Knigopistsa, Perepletchika i Ikonnago Pistsa pri Knizhnom i Ikonnom Stroenii."
————. 1916, no. 188. Nikol'skii, N. (ed.), "Sochineniia Solovetskago Inoka Gerasima Firsova po Neizdannym Tekstam."
Russkaia Istoricheskaia Biblioteka, Arkheograficheskaia Kommissiia. vol. XII, XIV, XXV, "Akty Kholmogorskoi i Ustiuzhskoi Eparkhii." vol. XXXIX, "Pamiatniki Istorii Staroobriadchestva XVII v."
Russkii Arkhiv. vol. 42, part 2, pp. 603-14. Titov, A. "Cherty

Monastyrskago Byta v XVII Veke. Kelar' Dionisii Omachkin."

Starina i Novizna. bk. 15, 1911, pp. 34-179. "Iz Arkhiva Tainykh Del. Sobytiia Pridvornoi Zhizni Tsaria Alekseia Mikhailovicha."

Vremennik Imperatorskogo Moskovskago Obshchestva Istorii i Drevnostei Rossiiskikh. bk. 15, 1852, part 2, pp. 1-134. "Perepisnaia Kniga Domovoi Kazny Patriarkha Nikona, Sostavlennaia v 7166 godu, po Poveleniiu Tsaria Alekseia Mikhailovicha."

Zapiski Moskovskago Arkheologicheskago Istituta. vol. VI, 1910, part 2, pp. 1-192. Rozhdestvenskii, T.S. (ed.), "Pamiatniki Staroobriadcheskoi Poezii."

Zapiski Otdeleniia Russkoi i Slavianskoi Arkheologii Imperaskago Russkago Arkheologicheskago Obshchestva. vol. II, 1861, pp. 423-590.

SECONDARY SOURCES

Books

Akademiia Khudozhestv SSSR. Nauchno-Issledovatel'skii Institut Teorii i Iskusstva. *Istoriia Russkago Iskusstva.* 2 vol. Moscow: 1957-60.

Andreev, V.V. *Raskol i Ego Znachenie v Narodnoi Russkoi Istorii.* SPB: 1870.

Billington, James H. *The Icon and the Axe.* New York: Random House, Vintage, 1970.

Bolshakoff, Serge. *Russian Nonconformity.* Philadelphia: The Westminster Press, 1950.

Conybeare, Frederick C. *Russian Dissenters.* (Harvard Theological Studies, X) Cambridge: Harvard University Press, 1921.

Cracraft, James. *The Church Reform of Peter the Great.* Stanford: Stanford University Press, 1971.

Crummey, Robert O. *The Old Believers & the World of Antichrist: the Vyg Community & the Russian State 1694-*

1855. Madison, Milwaukee, London: The University of Wisconsin Press, 1970.

Denisov, L.G. *Pravoslavnye Monastyri Rossiiskoi Imperii.* M: 1908.

Drevnie Ikony Staroobriadcheskogo Kafedral'nogo Pokrovskogo Sobora pri Rogozhskom Kladbishchem v Moskve. Moscow: Staroobriadcheskaia Arkhiepiskopiia Moskovskaia i Vseia Rusi, 1956.

Druzhinin, V.G. *Raskol na Donu v Kontse XVII Veka.* SPB: 1889.

Eleonskaia, A.S. et.al. *Istoriia Russkoi Literatury XVII-XVIII Vekov.* Moscow: 1969.

Entsiklopedicheskii Slovar': Brockhaus-Efron. (82 vol.). SPB & Leipzig: 1890-1904.

Fedotov, G.P. *The Russian Religious Mind.* vol. 1, New York: Harper Torchbooks, 1960, vol. 2. Cambridge, Mass.: Harvard University Press, 1966.

Filimonov, Georgii (ed.). *Opisanie Pamiatnikov Drevnosti Tserkovnago i Grazhdanskago Byta Russkago Muzeia P. Korobanova.* Moscow: 1849.

Florovsky, George. *Puti Russkago Bogosloviia.* Paris: 1937.

Frere, W.H. *Some Links in the Chain of Russian Church History.* London: Faith Press, 1918.

Fuhrmann, Joseph T. *Tsar Alexis: His Reign and his Russia.* Gulf Breeze, Florida: Academic International Press, 1981.

Gehring, Johannes. *Raskol i Sekty Russkoi Tserkvi 1003-1897 g.* SPB: 1903.

Georgievskii, V.T. *Freski Ferapontova Monastyria.* SPB: 1911.

Golosov, Prot. Aleksandr. *Tserkovnaia Zhizn'na Rusi v Polovine XVII Veka i Izobrazhenie eia v Zapiskakh Pavla Alleppskago.* Zhitomir: 1916.

Golubinskii, E. *Istoriia Russkoi Tserkvi.* 2 vol. M; 1904-1911.

Gorchakov, M. *Monastyrskii Prikaz (1649-1725 g.)* SPB: 1868.

Gorchakov, M. *O Zemel'nykh Vladeniiakh Vserossiiskikh Mitropolitov, Patriarkhov, i Sv. Sinoda (988-1738 gg.).* SPB: 1871.

Grigorii, Arkh. Kazanskii. *Istinno Drevniia i Istinno Pravoslavnaia Khristova Tserkov.* 3rd ed. SPB: 1856.

Gudzii, N.K. *Istoriia Drevnei Russkoi Literatury*. 6th ed. Moscow: 1956.

Kapterev, N.A. *Patriarkh Nikon i Tsar Aleksei Mikhailovich*. 2 vol. Sviato Troitskaia Sergievskaia Lavra: 1919-12.

Kartashev, A.V. *Ocherki Po Istorii Russkoi Tserkvi*. 2 vol. Paris: 1959.

Kliuchevskii, V.O., *Kurs Russkoi Istorii*. 8 vol. Moscow: 1956-59.

Kniazkov, S. *Kak Nachalsia Raskol Russkoi Tserkvi*. 2nd ed. Rostov-na-Donu: 1906.

Lazarev, V.N., Podobedova, O.I. and Kostochkin, V.V. (ed's.). *Drevne Russkoe Iskusstvo — XVII Vek*. Moscow: 1964.

Likhachev, D.S. *Chelovek v Literature Drevnei Rusi*. Moscow: 1958.

Makarii, Episkop. *Istoriia Russkago Raskola, Izvestnago pod Imenem Staroobriadstva*. SPB: 1855.

Makarii, Mitropolit. *Istoriia Russkoi Tserkvi*. 12 vol. SPB: 1877-91.

Makarii, Archim. *Pamiatniki Tserkovnykh Drevnostei. Nizhegorodskaia Guberniia*. SPB: 1857.

Maksimov, S. *Razskazy iz Istorii Staroobriadstva po Raskol'nich'im Rukopisiam*. SPB: 1861.

Malyshev, V.I. *Ust'-Tsilemskie Rukopisnye Sborniki XVI-XX vv*. Moscow and Komi: 1960.

Massie, Suzanne. *Land of the Firebird: The Beauty of Old Russia*. N.Y.: Simon & Schuster, 1980.

Mel'gunov, S.P. *Staroobriadtsy i Svoboda Sovesti*. 2nd ed. Moscow: 1917.

Meierberg, A. von. *Al'bom Meierberga — Vidy i Bytovyia Kartiny Rossii XVII Veka*. SPB: 1903.

Miliukov, Paul. *Outlines of Russian Culture*. (Part I, Religion and the Church). New York: A.S. Barnes & Co., Perpetua Book edtn., 1960.

Modern Encyclopedia of Russian and Soviet History. (General editor: Joseph L. Wieczynski). Ongoing & projected at 50 vol. Entries on XVII c. figures, and specifically entries by Nickolas Lupinin:
Donskoi Monastery. vol. IX

Epifanii Slavinetskii. vol. X.
Ferapontov Monastery. vol. XI.
Hermogen. vol. XIV.
Job (Iov). vol. XV.
Kirillo-Belozerskii Monastery. vol. XVII.
Novodevich'e Monastery. vol. XXV.
Novoierusalimskii Monastery. vol. XXV.
Patriarchate in Russia. vol. XXVII.

Nasonov, A.N. *Istoriia Russkago Letopisaniia XI — Nachala XVIII Veka*. Moscow: 1969.

Nazarevskii, A.A. *O Literaturnoi Storone Gramot i Drugikh Dokumentov Moskovskoi Rusi Nachala XVII Veka*. Kiev: 1961.

Nichols, Robert L. and Theofanis George Stavrou (ed's.). *Russian Orthodoxy under the Old Regime*. Minneapolis: University of Minnesota Press, 1978.

Nikolaevskii, Pavel F. *Iz Istorii Snoshenii Rossii s Vostokom v Polovine XVII Veka*. SPB: 1882.

Nikolaevskii, Pavel F. *Obstoiatel'stvo i Prichiny Udaleniia Patriarkha Nikona s Prestola*. SPB: 1883?

Nikolaevskii, Pavel F. *Iushka Mikliaev (Epizod iz Tserkovnobytovykh Otnoshenii Kontsa XVII Veka)*. Moscow: 1888?

Nikol'skii, P.V. *Monashestvo na Donu*. Voronezh: 1909.

Nil'skii, *Chteniia po Istorii Russkago Staroobriadcheskago Raskola*. SPB: 1889-90.

Ovchinnikova, E.S. *Portret v Russkom Iskusstve XVII Veka: Materialy i Issledovaniia. Moscow: 1955*.

Pascal, Pierre. *The Religion of the Russian People*. Crestwood, N.Y.: St. Vladimir's Seminary Press, 1976.

Perov, Ivan. *Eparkhial'nyia Uchrezhdeniia v Russkoi Tserkvi v XVI i XVII Vekakh*. Riazan': 1882.

Plotnikov, K. *Istoriia Russkago Raskola Staroobriadchestva*. 7th ed. SPB: 1914.

Poltoratzky, N.P. and Sorokin, P.A. *Na Temy Russkie i Obshchie* New York: Izdatel'stvo Obshchestva Druzei Russkoi Kul'tury, 1965.

Pshenichnikov, o. Aleksandr. *Kratkoe Istoricheskoe Opisanie*

Pervoklassnogo Voznesenskago Devichiago Monastyria v Moskve. Moscow: 1894.

Pushkarev, Sergei G., Vernadsky, George, and Fischer, Ralph T., Jr. *Dictionary of Russian Historical Terms from the Eleventh Century to 1917.* New Haven and London: Yale University Press, 1970.

Riabushinskii, V.P. *Staroobriadchestvo i Russkoe Religioznoe Chuvstvo.* Joinville le Pon: France, 1936.

Rice, Tamara Talbot. *Russian Icons.* New York: Marboro, n.d.

Robinson, A.N. (ed.). *Issledovaniia po Slavianskomu Literaturovedeniiu i Fol'kloristike.* Moscow: 1960.

Rovinskii, D.A. *Obozrenie Ikonopisaniia v Rossii do Kontsa XVII Veka.* SPB: 1903.

Rozenkampf, Baron. *Obozrenie Kormchei Knigi v Istoricheskom Vide.* Moscow: 1829.

Runciman, Steven. *The Great Church in Captivity.* Cambridge: Cambridge University Press, 1968.

Russkii Biograficheskii Slovar'. 25 vol. SPB: 1896-1913.

Sakharov, A.M. *Obrazovanie i Razvitie Rossiiskogo Gosudarstva v XIV-XVII vv.* Moscow: 1969.

Savich, A.A. *Vklady i Vkladchiki v Severno-Russkikh Monastyriakh XV—XVII v.* Perm: 1929.

Schaeffer, Natalia. *Russkaia Pravoslavnaia Ikona.* Washington: 1967.

Shchapov, A. *Russkii Raskol Staroobriadstva.* Kazan': 1859.

Schmeman, Prot. A. *Istoricheskii Put'Pravoslaviia.* New York: Chekhov Publishing House, 1954.

Slukhovskii, M.I. *Bibliotechnoe Delo v Rossii do XVII Veka.* Moscow: 1968.

Smirnov, P.S. *Istoriia Russkago Raskola Staroobriadstva.* SPB: 1895.

Smirnov, P.S. *Vnutrennie Voprosy v Raskole v XVII Veke.* SPB: 1898.

Smolitsch, Igor. *Russisches Mònchtum: Entstehung, Entwicklung und Wesen 988-1917.* Wùrzburg: 1953.

Sobolev, N.N. *Russkii Ornament.* Moscow: 1948.

Soloviev, S.M. *Istoriia Rossii s Drevneishikh Vremen.* 29 vols. in 15 books. Moscow: 1959-66.

Tiumins, Valerie A. (with George Vernadsky). *Patriarch Nikon on Church and State: Nikon's "Refutation".* The Hague: Mouton, 1982.

Trenev, D. *Ikonostas Smolenskago Sobora Moskovskago Novodevich'iago Monastyria. Obraztsovyi Russkii Ikonostas XVI-XVII Vekov. S Pribavleniem Kratkoi Istorii Ikonostasa s Drevneishikh Vremen.* M: 1902.

Ustiugov, N.V. (ed.). *Russkoe Gosudarstvo v XVII Veke.* Moscow: 1961.

Varlaam, Archimandrit. *O Prebyvanii Patriarkha Nikona v Zatochenii v Ferapontove i Kirillove Monastyriakh.* Moscow: 1858.

Vernadsky, George. *A History of Russia.* 5 vol. New Haven and London: Yale University Press, 1948-69.

Vodovozov, N.V. *Istoriia Drevnei Russkoi Literatury.* Moscow: 1962.

Ware, Timothy. *The Orthodox Church.* Baltimore, Md.: Penguin Books, 1963.

Yuzova (Iuszova), I. *Starovery i Dukhovnye Khristiane.* SPB: 1881.

Zenkovsky, Serge (ed.). *Medieval Russia's Epics, Chronicles, and Tales.* New York: Dutton & Co., 1963.

Zenkovsky, Serge. *Russkoe Staroobriadchestvo.* (Forum Slavicum, band 21). München: Wilhelm Fink Verlag, 1970.

Zernov, Nicolas. *Moscow the Third Rome.* London: Society for the Promotion of Christian Knowledge; New York: Macmillan, 1937.

Zverinskii, V. *Material dlia Istoriko — Topograficheskago Izsledovaniia o Pravoslavnykh Monastyriakh v Rossiiskoi Imperii.* 3 vol. SPB: 1890-97.

Zyzikin, M.V. *Patriarkh Nikon. Ego Gosudarstvennyia i Kanonicheskiia Idei.* 3 vols. Warsaw: 1931-39.

Periodicals and Learned Societies

Chteniia v Imperatorskom Obshchestve Istorii i Drevnostei Rossiiskikh pri Moskovskom Universitete. 1865, bk. 1, sect. I, pp. 1-101. I.S. "O Tserkovnom Sudoustroistve v Drevnei Rossii."

————. 1871, bk. 4, sect. I, pp. 39-44. Aleksandra Dimitrieva, "Po Povodu Stat'i G-na. Kostomarova: Tserkovno-istoricheskaia Kritika v XVII Veke." pp. 45-62, "Moskovskii Sobor o Zhitii Blagovernyia Kniagini Anny Kashinskiia."

————. 1888, bk. 1, sect. I, part 1, pp. 1-137. Arkhangel'skii, A.S., "Bor'ba s Katolichestvom i Zapadno—Russkaia Literatura Kontsa XVI — Pervoi Poloviny XVII Veka." part 3, pp. 1-132. Dobroklonskii, A.P., "Solotchinskii Monastyr' — Ego Slugi i Krestiane v XVII Veke."

————. 1896, bk. 3, sect. II, pp. 1-18. Kirpichnikov, A.I. (ed.). "Russkoe Skazanie o Loretskoi Bogomateri."

————. 1909, bk. 3, sect. IV, pp. 13-22. Savva, V.I. (ed.), "Ob Odnom iz Spiskov Zhitiia Patriarkha Nikona." pp. 22-24, "Prigovor po Delu Kvirina Kul'mana i Kondratiia Nordermana."

Church History. vol. X, 1941, Dec., pp. 347-66. Spinka, Matthew, "Patriarch Nikon and the Subjection of the Russian Church to the State."

————. vol. XXX, 1971, Dec., pp. 496-97. Review by N. Lupinin.

Drevnosti. Trudy Moskovskago Arkheologicheskago Obshchestva. vol. VIII, 1880, sect. I, pp. 1-95. Zhiznevskii, A.K., "Drevnii Arkhiv Krasno-Kholmskago Antonieva Monastyria."

————. vol. XX, 1904, pp. 81-98. Redin, E.K., "Litsevyia Rukopisi Sobraniia Grafa A.S. Uvarova."

Etnograficheskoe Obozrenie. 1906, no. 3 & 4, pp. 242-301. Mozharovskii, A.F., "Dukhovnye Stikhi Staroobriadtsev Povolzh'ia."

Kievskaia Starina. vol. XXVI, 1889, pp. 377-401, 597-614. Lileev. M.I., "Iz Nachal'noi Istorii Raskola v Starodub'e."

Letopisi Russkoi Literatury i Drevnosti. vol. V, 1863, part 2, pp. 153-78. "Oblichenie na Nikona Patriarkha, Napisannoe dlia Tsaria Alekseia Mikhailovicha."

Russkaia Mysl'. no. 2, 1882, sect. II, pp. 332-57. Prugavin, A.S.,
"Raskol i Ego Izsledovateli."
————. May 1911, sect. II, pp. 62-71. Filosofov, D., "Staro-
obriadchestvo i Pravoslavie." pp. 72-81, Mel'nikov, A.,
"Samobytnost' Staroobriadchestva."
Russkaia Starina. vol. 43, 1884, Aug., pp. 223-54. Gibbenet,
N.A., "Patriarkh Nikon po Vnov Otkrytym Materialam."
Russkii Arkhiv. vol. 43, 1905, bk. 3, pp. 592-99. Aleksandr Moz-
harovskii, "Cherty iz Istorii Staroobriadchestva."
Sbornik Filologicky. Trida Ceske Akademie ved a Umeni, Sva-
zek XII, 1940-46, pp. 153-259. Florovskii, A.V., "Chesh-
skaia Bibliia v Istorii Russkoi Kul'tury i Pis'mennosti."
Slavic Review. vol. XXV, no. 1, March 1966, pp. 1-39. Cherniav-
sky, Michael, "The Old Believers and the New Religion."
Zapiski Istoriko-Filologicheskago Fakul'teta Imperatorskago S.
Peterburgskago Universiteta. XLVII, 1898, pp. 1-348.
Borozdin, A.K., "Protopop Avvakum."
Zapiski Russkoi Akademicheskoi Gruppy v S.Sh.A. (Transactions of the Association of Russian-American Scholars in
the U.S.A.). vol. II, 1968, pp. 5-26. Pushkarev, S.G.,
"Donskoe Kazachestvo i Moskovskoe Gosudarstvo v XVII
Veke."
————. vol. II, 1968, pp. 31-59. Arseniev, N.S., "O Dukhovnoi
i Kul'turnoi Traditsii Russkoi Sem'i."
————. vol. V, 1971, pp. 184-87. Lupinin, N., "A Letter from
Tsar Aleksei to Nikon; Commentary and Translation."
————. vol. VI, 1972, pp. 300-05. Lupinin, N., "The Project
of Jacobus Reutenfels."

Appendices

Prefatory Note to the Appendices

The appendices which follow are meant to shed further light to the text. Thus, the Chronology, for example, avoids excessive detail on political and military events and concentrates more on points of reference for the subject of this book. The same applies to the glossary. Any person wishing complete treatment of these should consult any of a number of standard references works and texts.

CHRONOLOGY (Selected)

1624-38	Series of Cossack and peasant rebellions.
1630's	Extreme instability of the southern frontier.
1630's	Activity of The Zealots of Piety commences.
1632	Petr Mogila establishes his school in Kiev. It is based on the Jesuit model.
1640	Mogila and Kozlovskii publish the "Pravoslavnoe Ispovedanie."
1642-44	The iconography of the Uspenskii Cathedral in Moscow is completed.
1645	Mogila's "Short Catechism" (Sobranie Kratkiia Nauki ob Artikulakh Very) is published in Kiev; re-issued in Moscow in 1649.
1645, 1646, 1649, etc..,	Decrees issued to limit excessive unregulated travel to and from the Near East.
1648	Rebellion in Moscow triggered by rise in price of salt.

203

1648	Rebellion in the Ukraine begins; led by Bogdan Khmel'nitskii.
1648	Publication of The Book of Faith. Predicts end of the world.
1648-49	Feodor Rtishchev rebuilds a monastery and establishes a school there. Monks to teach there were brought from Kiev.
1649	Patriarch Paisios of Jerusalem arrives in Moscow.
1649	Promulgation of the Ulozhenie (Code of Laws). The Monastyrskii Prikaz (Monastery Department) comes into effect.
1649	Death of Petr Mogila.
1649	Arsenii Sukhanov's first trip to the Near East mences.
1649	Nikon made Metropolitan of Novgorod.
1650-1700	114 books translated into Russian and published.
1650	The Kormchaia Kniga (a Russian Nomaconon) is published.
1650	Church of the Savvinskii Starozhevskii Monastery in Zvenigorod is built and the iconography completed.
1651	Edinoglasie is instituted (see glossary).
1652	Death of Patriarch Iosif. Nikon is made Patriarch.
1652	The Arkhangel'skii Cathedral in Moscow is iconographically painted.
1652	Moscow's foreign quarter, the Nemetskaia Sloboda, is established.
1652	Relics of St. Filipp are brought to Moscow (July).
1653	Statute on Court Duties is issued.
1653	Church Council held. Institution of reforms commences.
1653	Avvakum and Ivan Neronov are exiled.
1653	Revised edition of the Kormchaia Kniga appears.

1653	Publication of the Psalter (in February).
1653	Tsar Aleksei places Patriarch Nikon in charge of the Printing Office (December).
1654	Start of war with Poland; continues sporadically until 1667.
1654	Church Council (March). Correction of texts and revision of Church manuals taken up.
1654	Bishop Paul of Kolomna is exiled by Nikon.
1654	Book collections of Russia combed for guidance in textual revisions.
1654	Cholera outbreak in Moscow and surroundings regions.
1654	The Pereiaslavl' Union (Russia & the Ukraine) is signed.
1655	Church Council held. Reforms again the topic, particularly the question of book corrections.
1655	Patriarch Makarios of Antioch arrives in Moscow.
1656	Start of war with Sweden.
1656	Church Council held (May). Support given to Nikon. Trial and condemnation of Neronov.
1656	Period of inflation begins.
1657	Death of Bogdan Khmel'nitskii.
1658	Dmitrii Firsov writes his tract, "Poslanie k Bratiu o Slozhenii Perstov." Became a key work in Old Believer polemical literature.
1658	Nikon leaves the Patriarchy in dispute (July 10).
1658	Spiridon Potemkin's book, "Words Against the Heretics," appears; another key Old Believer tract.
1658-1660	Considerable rise of Old Believer literature.
1660	Church Council attempts to formally depose Nikon.
1660	Avvakum is recalled from initial exile.
1661	War with Sweden ends.
1662	Rebellion in Moscow because of debasement of currency; the "copper coin riot."
1664	Avvakum returns to Moscow.

205

1664	Postal service is commissioned.
1664	Message of Patriarch Nektarios of Jerusalem to Tsar Aleksei regarding Nikon.
1664	Nikon writes his Refutation to the "Quetions-Answers" of Boiar Streshnev and Paisios Ligarides.
1665-66	Vladimirov writes his treatise on art.
1666	The Zaikonospasskii School opens in Moscow with Simeon Polotskii at its head.
1666-67	The famed Church Councils are held (see the chapter in the text). Nikon is deposed Dec. 12, 1666.
1667	The famous 5th petition of the Solovetskii Monastery appears. A pivotal tract of the old belief.
1667	Publication of Deacon Feodor's treatise "Reply of the Orthodox Defenders of Religion Concerning the Creed and Other Dogmas."
1667	Ushakov publishes his treatise on art. Like Vladimirov's, it states the desirability of more naturalistic depiction.
1667	New Statute of Trade is issued.
1667	Treaty of Andrussovo, ending war with Poland, is signed.
1668	Ushakov's painting, "The Tree of the State of Muscovy," is unveiled.
1668	The rebellion of the Solovetskii Monastery, occasioned by opposition to new reforms, begins. It ends in 1676 after an 8 year siege by government troops.
1669	Death of Mariia Miloslavskaia, Tsar Aleksei's first wife.
1670	Repression commences in the North against the Old Believers. Leaders like Avvakum, Lazar', and Feodor are punished. The same occurs in Moscow where Prince Khovanskii is publicly flogged.
1670-71	The Sten'ka Razin rebellion occurs.

1670-71	Two famous portraits of Tsar Aleksei are drawn.
1671	The imprisonment of Feodosiia Morozova, Evdokiia Urusova, and Mariia Danilova for old belief.
1672	The Court theater is established. It is directed by Johann Gregory, a German pastor.
1672 ff.	Immolations begin on a larger scale.
1674	Ioakim (Joachim) accedes to the Patriarchy.
1677	The Monastyrskii Prikaz is abolished.
1677-78	A census of taxable homesteads is taken; in 1679 the homestead ("dvor") is made the unit of taxation.
1680	Simeon Polotskii dies. His school is administered by Medvedev.
1681	Patriarch Nikon dies.
1681-82	Church Council is held to discuss schismatic incursions.
1682	The institution of "mestnichestvo" is abolished.
1682	The "Uvet Dukhovnyi" (Spiritual Decree) issued.
1682	The Streltsy Rebellion takes place in Moscow.
1683	A separate school of secular painting is in operation by this year in the Oruzheinaia Palata.
1685	Still more regulations issued against the Old Believers.
16 86	Treaty of 1686; permanent possession of Kiev and Smolensk to Russia.
1687	Slavo-Greek-Latin Academy inaugurated in Moscow. Two brothers, Ioannikii and Sofronii Likhudi, from Greece, were placed in charge. The Moscow Divinity Academy developed from this school.
1691	Publication of Evfrosin's tract, "Otrazitel'noe Pisanie o Novoizbrannom Puti Samo-Ubiistvennykh Smertei" (Refutation of the Newly Invented Method of Suicide).
1694-95	Completion of the frescoes in the Church of St.

	John the Baptist in Iaroslavl' (by Dmitrii Grigoriev and his school).
1697	Patriarch Adrian's "Instruction to the Priestly Elders" is issued.
1700	A school of music with substantial Western influence is functioning by this time.
1700	Patriarch Adrian dies. Peter does not fill the post.

GLOSSARY

altyn' — a monetary unit equal to three kopeks.

archimandrite — a clerical rank; head of a monastery.

boiarskie deti — sons of boiars; eventually came to denote a gentry class.

chelobitnaia — a petition of any kind sent to a government or clerical official.

desiatina — a land measure; through the centuries its equivalent size changed. Normally it was 2.7 acres though it went as high as 4 acres.

diak — a state (government) secretary.

dvoeperstie — a method of making the sign of the cross with two fingers (the forefinger and second finger).

dvor — court, homestead, servitors, retinue, yard.

dvorianin — a courtier; also, a member of the gentry, a noble. Usually held landed estates and accepted posts in both the military and the civil service.

dyarchy — notion regarding government taken from Byzantine times (e.g. from the Epanagoge of the IX c.) wherein the heads of the temporal and the clerical spheres would be supreme in their own spheres.

edinoglasie — the system, wherein the participants in the liturgical service (i.e. priest, choir, deacon) are chanting or singing at any single moment (not several at once as had accrued through incorrect practice). This produced greater order and clarity in the liturgy.

eparchy — the Orthodox term for diocese.

gost' — one belonging to the wealthiest class of merchants. The title "gost'" was honorary and conferred by the Tsar.

gramota — a document, deed, charter, or instruction.

hegumen (igumen) — the head of a monastery (equal to an abbot in the West).

iurodivyi — a "holy fool;" characterized by extreme religious fervor and self-abasement. Excessive humiliation was sought.

kopek (kopeck, copeck, kopeika) — a small silver coin which began to be minted in the XVI c.

Kormchaia Kniga — a digest of Church canons and laws; generally translated as "The Pilot Book."

mestnichestvo — the system wherein a person's administrative rank in government service corresponded to his seniority within the geneological structure.

mir — a local peasant community that was in charge of its own affairs. In the XVII c. the voevoda and the bureaucracy made incursions on its independence.

obrok — an annual fixed sum paid by the peasant for services, the use of property, and taxes.

okladchik — a service man assigned duties such as the distribution of money and materials to the various household units and homesteads (dvors).

okol'nichii — a court rank below that of boiar.

otpusknaia gramota — manumission papers for the serf. This was also used in reference to a monk; such a document permitted him to "wander" freely, rather than be tied to a monastery. An equivalent term which was also used is "blagoslovennaia gramota."

Oruzheinaia Palata — the Arms Hall.

Pechatnyi Dvor — the printing office or house.

ponomar' — a minor clerical official; a sextant, or reader in Church.

posad — a city; an urban settlement generally built around the inner walls.

posadskie liudi — dwellers of an urban settlement.

prikaz — a government department; among these were such as:

a) Posol'skii Prikaz — Office of Foreign Affairs
b) Pushkarskii Prikaz — Artillery Department
c) Monastyrskii Prikaz — Monastery Department
d) Prikaz Bol'shogo Dvortsa — Central Financial Office
e) Prikaz Tainykh Del—Department of Secret Affairs
f) Prikaz Kammenykh Del—Department of Stone Works

pustyn' — a hermitage.

Raskol — the Schism. (Raskol = schism, split, break).

skit — a monastery or hermitage of a very small size.

sobor — a council or an assembly; a cathedral.

stavlennaia gramota — the legal paper without which a priest could not officiate.

stol'nik — a high official at Court (or Palace). Only members of the boiar council (Boiar Duma) ranked higher.

troeperstie — a method of making the sign of the cross with the thumb and the first two fingers.

uezd — a district.

ukaz — a decree.

ulozhenie — a code of laws, statutes; the Code of Laws promulgated in 1649 is known as the Sobornoe Ulozhenie.

versta — a measue of distance; it equals 2/3 of a mile.

vkladchik — a donor or depositor; one who donated or made financial deposits into a monastery in return for the right to live there when old age came.

voevoda — a military governor.

votchina — a patrimonial estate.

zemstvo — (zemstva-pl.) — local self-government.

BIOGRAPHICAL SKETCHES OF LEADING FIGURES

ALEKSANDR, Bishop of Viatka and Veliko-Permsk. Born ca. 1608 in the Sol'vychegodskii posad; d. 16 Oct., 1679. Tonsured a monk in the Nikol'skii Koriazhemskii Monastery. Became a hegumen there in 1643. In 1651 he was transferred to the Spassokamenskii Monastery as an archimandrite. In June of 1655 he became the Bishop of Kolomensk and Kashirsk. In the same year he participated in the Church Council called to correct service books. He supported the reform effort at this stage. On December 5, 1657 he was assigned to the new eparchy of Viatka (in which he arrived in April of 1658). Here he came to oppose the new books. On December 30, 1662, he wrote a letter to Tsar Aleksei in which he expressed his opposition to Nikon, Streshnev, and Ligarides. He was tried at the Council of 1666; he proved penitent and was restored to his eparchy in 1669. In 1674 he gave up his position voluntarily and ended his days in the Nikol'skii Koriazhemskii Monastery in which he had begun his monastic and clerical career.

AVVAKUM, (for more on AVVAKUM see chapter 6). born 1615 or 1616; died April 1, 1681. Became a deacon at age 22. At age 24 was ordained a priest (ca. 1640). Was made archpriest and went to the town of Iurievets Povolzhskii in 1648. As before, the parishioners rose up against him and he went to Moscow. There he met Neronov and Stefan Vonifat'ev (the Tsar's confessor). Avvakum knew no Greek or any other language. He did not allow for the possibility of error: "In Church, it is Christ who rules and who stops it from sinning (making error — N.L.) in faith and in the questions of dogma..." "A small word this be it, but it contains the seed of great heresy." These statements express his feelings. Comes out openly against Nikon and (together with Daniil) begins labeling him an heretic and the forerunner of antichrist. In 1653 he is exiled to Siberia (first to Tobol'sk, then to the Daurian Tundra on the Lena River). In 1660 he is recalled to Moscow to which he arrives only in 1664. He meets frequently with the Tsar but is ultimately tried at the Council of 1666 and is again exiled. Many of his writings remain. Vol. V of *Materialy* (see bibliography) contains 35 of his works, vol. I has 2 others. In addition there are extant 4 letters to the Tsar, 1 message to Archimandrite Nikanor, 2 letters to diak Feodor, his "Life" (autobiography), seven theological tracts, three discussions of Holy Scriptures, and others.

BOBARYKIN, Nikita Mikhailovich, boiar with the rank of okol'nichii, then stol'nik (see glossary). From 1639-1640 was already involved in service to the Court. From 1643 - 1644 was a voevoda in Belgorod. In 1646 he was involved in the compilation of the Vladimirsk books. Was involved in the marriage arrangements of Tsar Aleksei to Mariia Miloslavskaia. In 1649 he accompanied the Tsar to Mozhaisk and received Polish ambassadors in Moscow. He was one of the voevodas assigned to the defense of Polotsk (against the Poles). In 1660 he became the voevoda of Vitebsk. Some difficulties with the Tsar in 1661 were overcome and in 1667 he was placed in charge of the collection and distribution of monies to soldiers. In 1663 he had already been placed on one of the seats of the State's central financial organ (Prikaz Bol'shogo Prikhoda). In 1668 he was named voevoda of Kazan' and in 1672 he was placed in charge of the Prikaz Bol'shogo Prikhoda. He liked to do good, was open, and was totally lacking in the self-serving mentality. This was the opinion of his contemporaries. Bobarykin was related to the Romanov and the Sheremetev families. Nikon opposed him, and he Nikon. His feud with Nikon was constant and he was a key figure in Nikon's loss of influence.

DOSIFEI, b. ?, d. before Oct. 1691. Was a hegumen of the Besednyi Nikol'skii Monastery near Tikhvin. He left his post to go to a hermitage. Monks from the Solovetskii Monastery began to come to him as one who was a prophet of the old belief. He had disseminated the old belief in the White Sea littoral. He commenced the peripatetic life, traveling around the White Sea, Moscow, the Black Sea. About 1685, he settled in the Don River area in the cloister of Iov (Job) one of the leaders of the Schism. Searches for the schismatics of the Don began in 1688. Dosifei settled on the river Agrakhani and died there. He commanded great authority in the schismatic movement. Avvakum asked him to pray for him and to give blessing. He was not an extremist in pursuit of schismatic tenets. He condemned the immolators: "They have killed themselves and have undergone unlawful suffering."

GERASIM FIRSOV, little known about his life prior to his arrival in the Solovetskii Monastery toward the end of the 1640's. Soon after, no earlier than late 1652, he left to go to Moscow. There he presented a petition to Nikon, already Patriarch, against Archimandrite Il'ia (Elijah) of the Solovetskii Monastery. Nikon ordered him to be beaten. Soon after he was returned to the Solovetskii. He was made an elder and became an adviser to Il'ia. In 1659, Il'ia passed away and Varfolomei became the archimandrite. Gerasim did not get along with him either. This came about because Varfolomei judged Gerasim Firsov guilty in the theft of a watch. (In general, he was already known among the brethren as being light of finger). He came to head a group of monks dissatisfied with Varfolomei as well as a group that strongly supported the old belief. When Varfolomei left for Moscow, Firsov began strong agitation against him. His role was well known in Moscow whereto he was soon summoned. He repented readily, enough to draw suspicion (at the Councils of 1666-67) and was sent under guard to the Iosif Volokolamsk Monastery. He died there in 1667. This man, who was not averse to drink and debauchery, wrote a treatise in 1658 that was instrumental in the history of the Schism. It was titled "Poslanie k Bratu o Slozhenii Perstov." It was the initial written effort in discussing the teachings regarding dvoeperstie (see glossary). Almost all later schismatic writers used his arguments without much reworking. The work is not particularly independent and utilizes many excerpts from other sources.

IOAKIM, Patriarch (Ivan Savelov), b. 1620, d. 1690. In 1655, Ivan Savelov lost his wife and children and entered the Mezhigorskii Monastery in Kiev. In 1657, he was taken by Nikon to aid in the construction of the Iverskii Monastery. After assignments in Novgorod and Moscow, he was made cellarer of the Novospasskii Monastery. In 1664 he became archimandrite of the Chudov Monastery. While serving here, he gained the friendship of the Tsar and courtiers. In 1673 he became the Metropolitan of Novgorod and rose to the Patriarchy in 1674. In general he opposed the influence coming from the West via Poland and hence was opposed to **Polotskii**, Medvedev, and **Golitsyn**. He headed the opposing party and in 1685 brought the Likhud brothers to Moscow to head the Greco-Latin-Slavic Academy. Jesuits, who had a school in Moscow, were expelled. Ioakim's rigidity extended to his frequent refusal to even sit at the same table with non-Orthodox. In his reign, the Kievan Metropolitanate was brought under Moscow's control. He was famed for his severity in dealing with the Old Believers. The deacon Feodor said that while still archimandrite of the Chudov Monastery, Ioakim, "more than anyone of the hierarchs boasted of our blood." But he also persecuted Nikon and did not attend his burial. He played a political role particularly after the death of Tsar Aleksei in 1676. He aided in the abolition of the mestnichestvo system and opposed Sophia in her regency. In his Church policy, he attempted to make the clergy financially independent relating to the Church. Many instructions were published during his reign. The "Uvet Dukhovnyi," "Slovo Pouchitel'noe," and "Shchit Very" are the most famous.

IOSIF, Patriarch, d. 15 April, 1652, He was born in the town of Vladimir on the Kliazma and became Patriarch on March 20, 1642. During his reign, he made an effort to make

Church practices more orderly. The most important event of his reign was the publication of Church service books in previously unprecedented numbers. Other books appeared: lives of Saints Savva, Sergii, and Nikon: works of the Church Fathers such as Basil the Great, St. John of Damascus, Chrysostom, Gregory, et. al;, apologetic and polemical works; canonical collections, and so forth. The books were copied from old Slavic codices and sometimes additions and changes were made. The group of book correctors then working was not inconsiderable. Among these were Ioann Nasedka, Mikhail Rogov, Archimandrite Sil'vestr, the elder Savvatii, Evfimii, and Matfei, laymen Shestoi Martemianov, Zakharii Afanas'ev, Zakharii Novikov. Many of the Church related arguments such as those regarding edinoglasie and book corrections commenced during his reign. Iosif himself supported mnogoglasie (or multi-chanting). The establishment of the Monastyrskii Prikaz did not draw a protest from him. He seemed to have a proclivity for enhancing his own riches. His reign as Patriarch is not distinguished for leadership. Rather, he was passive mentally and enfeebled physically. Many of the key events of this period occurred without his participation. When there was participation on his part, it was mainly that of an observer, or within the framework of his formal functions.

LAZAR', a priest from the town of Romanov on the Volga. Under Patriarch Iosif he participated in textological corrections. When Nikon became Patriarch, Lazar' was removed from his duties and for his opposition to Nikonian reforms was, along with Avvakum, exiled to Tobol'sk. Always active in the schismatic movement, he was brought to trial at the Councils of 1666-1667 where he spoke in more measured terms than Avvakum, but asked to be cast into the fires as proof of the rectitude of his position. In July of 1667 he was exiled to Pustozersk along with Avvakum, Feodor, and Epifanii. His tongue was cut, but with his friends, he waged a broad campaign by word and by epistle. He wrote of miracles and visions. His message to Tsar Aleksei is considerably more moderate than that of Avvakum, though he was closest of all to the raskol's leader. Punishment was meted out again in severe form and Lazar's tongue was cut again. The tone of his message became more passionate. In a letter to Tsar Feodor he wrote of Tsar Aleksei: "I have heard from the Lord that he sits in suffering; and this is for the sake of truth." Patriarch Ioakim began demanding the death sentence and Lazar' was executed on April 1, 1681: "For great calumny against the royal house, be they burned."

MOGILA, Metropolitan Petr, b. 1596, d. 1649. Mogila was the son of a Moldavian nobleman who fled his land in a dispute with Prince Kantemir. He studied at one of the L'vov brotherhoods and completed his education in Paris. He served in the Polish army, then took monastic vows in 1625. In 1627 he was already elected archimandrite of the Kievo Pecherskaia Lavra (the Kievan Crypt Monastery). Like the rest of the Kievan eparchy, it was subordinate to the Patriarchy of Constantinople. In November of 1631 he founded his own school in Kiev. This came to be the Kievan Theological Academy. It was modeled on Jesuit schools and Latin was the language of instruction. In 1640 (together with Isaia Kozlovskii) he wrote "Pravoslavnoe Ispovedanie" ("Confession of the Orthodox Faith"). In general it may be said that he successfully used Roman Catholic scholarship and educational methods to aid the Orthodox in their continuous struggle against Latin-Roman incursions in the Western border lands. He opposed the Uniates. In 1633 he was elected Metropolitan of Kiev, and held the position until his death.

NERONOV, b. 1591, d. 1670. Named Gavriil at birth; took the

name Ioann (Ivan) upon being ordained as a priest, and the name Grigorii upon taking monastic vows. Had considerable influence in Church affairs (and at Court) and was one of the key figures in the Schism. In 1649 he was assigned the post of cellarer in the Cathedral of the Dormition in Moscow; then, in 1649, was made archpriest at the Cathedral of Our Lady of Kazan'. He participated in the correction of service books, though Nikon was to remove him from this duty. A leading figure in the Zealots of Piety since the mid 1630's, he soon came to oppose the reformist movement as promulgated by Nikon. He underscored his opposition by coming to the public defense of men like Login and the Bishop Paul of Kolomna whom Nikon had exiled. For this he himself was sent to a monastery to do penance. He left and wandered from place to place, finally taking monastic vows in Pereiaslavl' in December, 1655. The Council of 1656 (May) condemned him and he was actively sought by the authorities. In January of 1657 he came to Nikon himself, saying: "I am the one you are looking for; the archpriest Ioann of the Kazan' cathedral, called Grigorii as a monk." He explained his positionn to Nikon and they met frequently thereafter. However, prior to again leaving Moscow he told the Tsar: "How long, sovereign, are you going to keep such an enemy of God? He has spread discord throughout the whole Russian land and has flouted your honor. One does not hear of your rule any more. All fear such an enemy." From 1658-1664 he lived in the Ignatiev hermitage. He wrote much and continued to give the oral sermons for which he was famous. He was judged for his adherence to the old belief by the Council of 1666 and, upon recantation, he was forgiven. In 1668 he was even made the archimandrite of the Danilov Monastery in Pereiaslavl'.

NIKON, Patriarch — see chapter 5.

ORDIN-NASHCHOKIN, Afanasii Lavrent'evich. From Pskov and an excellent diplomat, he began his diplomatic career under Tsar **Mikhail**. Involved much from the start in affairs dealing with Sweden, Poland, Lithuania. The Treaty of Andrussovo (1667) is largely his work. He knew Latin, German and Polish and was quite open minded toward innovations from the West; he thought the Western example was necessary for Russia. He also turned his attention to Persia, Central Asia, Khiva and Bukhara. He thought trade with all of these would be beneficial. He demanded certain autonomy in political and military matters and felt government men should not always wait for a word from the capital to commence action. He felt that the chief fault of Russian administration was that it was directed at misapplication of labor, not at the development of the nation's productivity; thus, he always aimed at the expansion of trade and industry. He supported Nikon, worked to strengthen the left bank of the Ukraine, was the author of the New Statute of Trade (Novotorgovyi Ustav) of 1667, and headed the Foreign Office among many other accomplishments. His independence led to a cooling of relations with Tsar Aleksei for he refused to go on a mission to Poland in 1671 that he thought would undermine the Treaty of Andrussovo. He entered a monastery in 1672 and died in 1680.

RTISHCHEV, Feodor Mikhailovich (1625-1673). He came from a noble family known for its piety and charity. He was in a daily contact with the Tsar and discharged various religious and educational duties. He was a man of extraordinary character who preferred the background over the limelight. He was loyal, even to old believer friends. In 1648-1649 he opened a school where Latin, Greek, Slavic, rhetoric, philosophy etc... were taught. He was the man at Court who mended arguments and who always worked for the most amicable solution to problems. He established hostels for the sick and indigent and paid for the upkeep with his own money. He helped foreigners in prison, paid ransom to Tatars for Russian prisoners, and covered the debts of those in debtors prison. All of this was done with his own money. He was given many duties on a formal basis but refused recognition; thus, he refused the rank of boiar when it was offered to him. His humility was matched only by his great humanitarianism. Always interested in religious affairs, he also founded a monastery and toward the end of his life, he continued his work for the poor by lending his efforts and money to fight the famine in Vologda in 1671.

SLAVINETSKII, Epifanii (b. ?, d. Nov. 19, 1675). A learned monk who was schooled in south-west Russia (in the brotherhood schools and the Kievan Academy) he was summoned to Moscow in 1649 (along with Arsenii Satanovskii and Damaskin Ptitskii). His function was to help with the formation of a school at the Chudov Monastery and to teach. His career, with the ascendancy of Patriarch Nikon, came to focus on textological corrections, translating, and writing. In this, his scholarship and competency came to the fore. Nikon had asked to have him translate the Acts of the Council of 1593 (which confirmed the Patriarchy in Russia) and several titles of the Epanagogue. The importance of his translating work can be underlined by citing some of his key translations, e.g. the Sluzhebnik (service book) of 1655, St. John Chrysostom (including his famous liturgy), Athanasius the Great, the Pentateuch, and many others. He was in charge of a group of monks (appointed 1674) in a project to translate the Bible into Slavonic. He wrote a number of his own works as well, including ca. 50 sermons, ca. 40 songs of epic type, and some hymns. He also compiled two lexicons: "Leksikon Greko-Slaviano-Latinskii," and "Leksikon Filologicheskii." His own work is stylistically clear and use of Church Slavonic is excellent. A supporter of Nikon, Epifanii's scholarship and cultural contribution are of the very first order.

SUKHANOV, Arsenii (1600-1668). Sukhanov was born in the village of Brusnitsyna in the Tula Province. His education was likely in one of the Western Russian brotherhoods and he was very well versed in Greek, Latin, Polish, rhetoric, grammar, and dialectics. When Patriarch Paisios of Jerusalem came to Moscow in 1649, Sukhanov went back to the Near East with him to observe Greek ritual in practice. Upon returning in 1650 he submitted a report to the Bol'shoi Prikaz which described his trip and delineated his theological disputations with the Greeks. In February of 1651 he left again for the Near East, visiting Chios, Rhodes, Egypt, Alexandaria and Constantinople, among other places. Upon returning he submitted a report to the Tsar. This composition is called the "Proskinitarii" (or sometimes the "Poklonnik") and is divided into three parts: a) description of his mission; b) discussion of the city of Jerusalem.; and c) the last section, titled "How the Greeks uphold Church ritual and chanting." In 1654, he made his final trip to the Near East. This time, he was given large sums of money to bring back to Russia many books. This he did, bringing some 505 rare editions from Mount Athos and 200 from other places. These were to be ostensibly used as references in the process of textual corrections undertaken by Nikon. Eventually they became central to the Synodal Library. From Jerusalem he brought back the plans of the Church of the Resurrection. These were used by Nikon to build the Novo Ierusalimskii Monastery. Sukhanov also wrote "Preniia a Vere" (Disputations on the Faith). As in most of his works, he treats the question of whether Greek practice was an acceptable model for Russia through analysis of books, services, rituals. In general he was very negative in his attitude toward Greek practice, though his answers interested both sides in the dispute. Nikon did not allow the "Preniia o Vere" to appear without emendations. The work came out in edited form and was widely used. Sukhanov did much work in the Pechatnyi Dvor (the Printing Office) for the remainder of his career. In 1665 he returned to the Holy Trinity Monastery where

he had been a monk and was buried there upon his death
in 1668.

Index

226